Contents

Religion and Morality

Introduction

This book has been written specifically to teach the subject content of the AQA Specification B Unit 2 (40552) and Unit 3 (40553) courses. It follows the unit outlines, moving through the topics in the order set out in the specification.

When sitting AQA GCSE RS each unit is examined through one exam paper of 1 hour and 30 minutes. All six topics within each unit are represented on its paper, though candidates are required to answer questions on only four topics. Each question is worth 18 marks, with quality of written response marked out of an additional 4 marks, so the total for the paper is 76 marks. In this book, a mock paper is provided at the end of each of the two units (see pages 83–88 and 173–78). Both are annotated to help demystify exam language and paper style.

The topics sections within this book cover each unit's content from a variety of angles, as well as providing the necessary information required by those studying for the exam. Each topic asks students to think about what they are being told, and about the implications of the issues. There are many opportunities for evaluation work, which forms 50 per cent of the total mark in the exam. Knowledge and understanding of the topics are important, but ability to apply that knowledge is vital to achieve the highest grades. The style of text is designed to encourage and develop exactly that.

The specification allows centres to prepare candidates to answer from one or more religious traditions on any question. This book allows study of a single religious tradition, or of several – all religious traditions are commented on for each element within each topic.

As this is an issues course, students should be encouraged to collect their own examples of the issues as met in the news. They can collect, add comments, give their own opinion, and even try to say what they think religion(s) would say. This will help with their recall and provide real examples to call on in the exam.

A revision outline is provided at the end of each unit. This is designed to support revision, but can also act as a checklist for students as they move through the course.

About this course

This course gets you to think about twelve key modern-day issues. Some of them will have directly affected you, or you will have direct experience of them. Some you will know of through other people's experience. Some you may only know of through the media. Keep in mind that you already have a whole load of knowledge about these issues, and you can use that in your exam. Your knowledge on the topics of this exam is probably greater than in any other GCSE you are studying because it is such a topical exam, with ideas close to the experience of young people. Be confident, and use what you know.

It's a Religious Studies exam, so you have to know the attitude of at least one religion. Some schools study just one because this stops the students confusing the ideas of several religions. Others study two because it makes it easier to get to the higher marks in the exam, because there is more to say. Whatever your school does, make sure you learn the religious bits – they are as exam-friendly as possible in this book. You can't get beyond about a D grade without knowing any religious stuff.

For the exam, you have to answer questions on four of the topics in each unit. All six topics will always be on the exam paper – you just answer four. Actually, you could answer more, because they'll still get marked, and the four best answered questions get taken forward as your marks. *But* people who do this, often don't get great marks. It is only ever a good idea if you have finished answering – at *your* right speed (not having rushed) – and still have loads of time left. If you are one of those people who has lots of time left in an exam, then why not do another question? You have nothing to lose, and potentially something to gain.

As you go through the issues, you will have opinions on and attitudes to them. That is good! You will be asked about your own opinion on many of the issues as part of the exam. So do take the chances to discuss and explain your own opinions – it helps you present them better in the exam when you have to.

Keep your eye on the news – there will be lots of stories that link to these issues in the time it takes to do this course. Those stories will certainly give you a wide range of examples to use in your answers when you are trying to explain or back up a point you make. Taking notice of them actually helps you understand the issues in more detail and from different points of view, so helps you express your own ideas better. Could it be the time to start a scrapbook?

What do I think?

Religion and animal rights

Religion and planet earth

Religion and prejudice

Religion and early life

Religion, war and peace

Religion and young people

Religious attitudes to matters of life (medical ethics)

Religious attitudes to the elderly and death

Religious attitudes to drug abuse

Religious attitudes to crime and punishment

Religious attitudes to rich and poor in British society

Religious attitudes to world poverty

The religious bit

Religion also has opinions on all the issues that come up in the course. This is an RS course after all, so you are going to see the attitudes of some religions. You will have to write about them in the exam if you want to get good grades. This means trying to understand what those attitudes are and where they come from – in other words, the beliefs and teachings of the religions. In this book, you'll be given a small number of beliefs and teachings for each religion on each topic. Quite often you can use these teachings in a few different topics (which always helps!). If a teaching will apply to more than one topic – use it.

This section gives you some general teachings, which you can apply to all the different topics. It cuts down the number of teachings you have to learn, and means you can understand these thoroughly. However, the best answers in exams always use beliefs and teachings that are specific to the topics, as well as the general ones. Don't forget to learn some of these when you meet them later, as well. Mark these two pages, or copy these teachings into the front of your book or file. Then use them as the basis for your work. When you study a topic, refer back to these to help you work out what the attitude will be to that topic.

 ## Buddhism

1 Reincarnation and **karma** – our words, thoughts and deeds create energies that shape our future rebirths. We need to make sure these are positive.
2 The Five Precepts (guidelines for living). These are: not harming others (**ahimsa**); using language kindly; not taking what is not freely given; not clouding our minds; no sexual misconduct.
3 Compassion (loving kindness).

 ## Christianity

1 **Jesus'** two key teachings: love God; love your neighbour.
2 Equality of all, because in Genesis we are told that God made each of us.
3 Justice (fairness) – since everyone is equal, everyone deserves fairness.
4 Forgiveness and love are ideas taught by Jesus, and shown in his actions.

ॐ Hinduism

Hindu holy books list many virtues. These include:

1 ahimsa (non-violence)
2 self-discipline
3 tolerance
4 service to others
5 compassion
6 providing shelter/support to others
7 respect for all life
8 wisdom
9 honesty with others and oneself
10 cleanliness.

 ## Islam

1 The **Ummah** – brotherhood of all Muslims. This means that all Muslims are equal, and deserve equal respect and treatment.
2 That everyone has to follow duties set by **Allah** (God), for example, the Five Pillars.
3 **Shari'ah Law**, which is Muslim law stemming from the **Qur'an** and Hadith, and applied to modern life by Islamic scholars.

Judaism

The Ten Commandments are found in the Book of Genesis in the Torah.

1 Love only G-d.
2 Make no idols of G-d.
3 Do not take G-d's name in vain.
4 Keep the Sabbath holy.
5 Respect your parents.
6 Do not kill.
7 Do not steal.
8 Do not commit adultery.
9 Do not tell lies.
10 Do not be jealous of what others have.

 ## Sikhism

The **Khalsa** vows:

1 Meditation and service to the One God, including worship, following the teachings, and wearing the 5Ks as a mark of the faith and devotion to it.
2 Do not use intoxicants.
3 Do not eat meat that has been ritually slaughtered (most Sikhs are **vegetarians**).
4 Equality of all people, leading to respect for all and a desire to fight injustice, and including not hurting others by theft or deed.

Sikh ethical virtues – sharing with others, including tithing (sewa); dutifulness; prudence; justice; tolerance; temperance; chastity; patience; contentment; detachment and humility.

Task

Choose a religion (or two) and, using the teachings from the religion(s) on pages ix and x, try to work out what a believer's attitude might be to the following:

a abortion (the deliberate termination of a pregnancy)
b dog fighting
c declaring war on a neighbouring country because your country wants their goldmines/reserves
d how you should treat people who are different from you
e whether it is right to use fertility treatment
f what we should do about drug addicts
g whether the death penalty should be reintroduced into UK law
h whether helping others should be a priority for religious people.

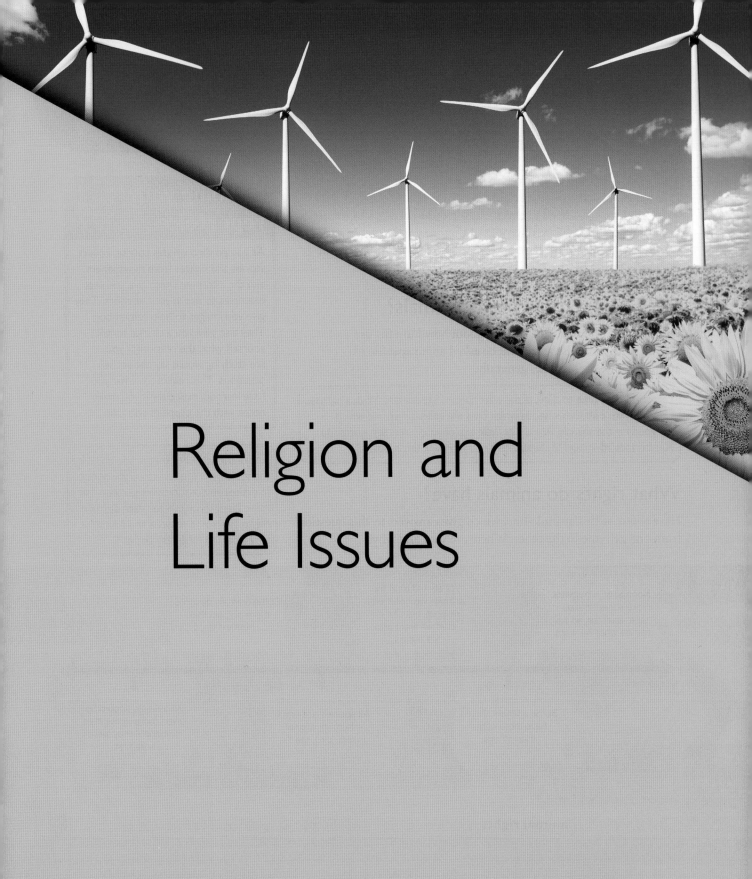

Religion and Life Issues

Religion and animal rights

This topic starts the course, and will start the exam paper. It has always been a popular exam choice on other courses, so let's enjoy it. We need to check out the different ways humans use animals; the rights and wrongs of that usage; the status and **rights** animals (should) have and what the religions think about the use of animals.

How do we make use of animals?

On this page, there are lots of ideas about how humans use and interact with animals. You could be asked about specific uses of animals as well as attitudes generally.

Let's take some time to think of the ways humans use animals. With a partner, come up with a list. Now decide which ones are good for us, and which are good for the animals. Are any of them exploitation? In other words, do humans take advantage of animals? Why do you think this happens?

What rights do animals have?

Have a look at this attitude-line, which gives answers to this question from one extreme to the other. Where are you, and why?

Building your repertoire

As you go through this course, collect stories and images from newspapers and the internet. These give you real examples to use in your answers. They give you images to help remember. They also give you a chance to ask yourself what the religion(s) you are studying would say about the situations. This reinforces what you have learned, especially if you make notes with the clippings you take.

Any of the attitudes on the line could be the statement you have to argue about in evaluative questions in the exam. Let's think them through – for each attitude, try to give some reasons and examples why a person might say them.

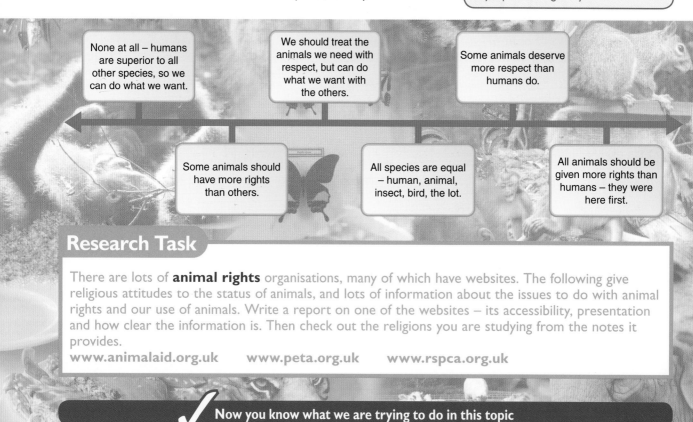

None at all – humans are superior to all other species, so we can do what we want.

We should treat the animals we need with respect, but can do what we want with the others.

Some animals deserve more respect than humans do.

Some animals should have more rights than others.

All species are equal – human, animal, insect, bird, the lot.

All animals should be given more rights than humans – they were here first.

Research Task

There are lots of **animal rights** organisations, many of which have websites. The following give religious attitudes to the status of animals, and lots of information about the issues to do with animal rights and our use of animals. Write a report on one of the websites – its accessibility, presentation and how clear the information is. Then check out the religions you are studying from the notes it provides.

www.animalaid.org.uk   www.peta.org.uk   www.rspca.org.uk

✓ Now you know what we are trying to do in this topic

Humans and animals

Can you imagine a world without animals? Even those we ignore can do vital jobs – wild bees pollinate plants and trees making sure that they continue to produce foods for us to eat.

Animals help us – pulling carts, for example. They give us companionship – have you got pets? They are part of our diet – when we eat them. Parts of animals are used in clothing and other types of manufacturing. We use them as entertainment – in **zoos** and circuses. We learn from them – from how they live and behave, as well as by experimenting on them. Birdsong and whale song can both soothe us when we feel tense. Many films and cartoons have animals as their focus and we take pleasure in that.

We also overwork animals – causing their death. We experiment on them, taking them away from their natural environments and killing them during or after those experiments. We buy them as pets, then mistreat them. We hunt them in cruel ways, sometimes just for our own enjoyment, not because we need anything. If an animal is in the way of a human project, it has to move, or die. We eat animals, usually produced on farms that are more like factories and that treat the animals like products not as living beings.

Every so often, we hear of animals that have killed humans or hurt them – a shark attack, or a dog biting someone. Some species are dying out, so plans to build are sometimes affected by where those species live. If you have ever had a kitten, it's not so easy to litter-train at first! Not all of them like us – they bite and sting. And why on earth are there wasps?

> What is the relationship between humans and animals – which side gets the best deal?

Are we different?

Well, most humans think they are superior to animals. The fact that we eat animals, but kill an animal that even bites a person, suggests that we think we are superior. We also make animals do things we'd never ask of a human – for example, the US marines now have dolphins that have been trained to seek and lay underwater mines. This suggests that we think they are less valuable than us because they are expendable.

Humans use reason and logic to work things out; animals seem to behave more out of instinct. Our technology is more advanced than any used by animals. Our ways of communicating are more complicated. Some religions also believe that God gave humans dominion (power) over animals, which has been interpreted to mean 'do as you like', at times.

> So, what does make us different?

Religions call animals '**sentient beings**' – creatures that have senses and can feel pain. They are either created by God deliberately (Christianity, Islam, Judaism and Sikhism), or are beings in the cycle of rebirth (Buddhism and Hinduism). In all cases, they have value. No religion says we can't use animals, but they all say we should treat them with respect.

The Basics

1 List some ways in which we use animals.
2 How are animals and humans different?
3 Explain why religious people should 'care for' animals.
4 **People should show animals more respect.**
   What do you think? Explain your reasons.

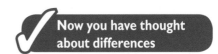
Now you have thought about differences

Introducing the elements of this topic

This topic isn't just about how we use and treat animals. You should know about specific ways we use and treat animals. You should be able to describe or compare those ways, and to explain the issues caused by each. You should be able to write about a range of ways, and bring ideas from all of those into your debates and then into your exam answers – especially the evaluative answers. So, the next few pages are going to take each way that is listed in the course information, and make you think about it.

The bits to learn
- A definition/description of each, including an example
- Why some people might see them as good
- Why some people might see them as bad
- What the religions might say

Have a look at the uses of animals that the course mentions. Do you understand what each is about? Go through them and write down, or discuss with your partner/group, what you know. See if you can already say something for each of those 'bits to learn' about each of the elements listed below.

- Saving animals from **extinction**
- **Hunting**
- Animals as companions
- Bull fighting
- Animals in sport
- The fur and ivory trades
- Transport and work animals
- **Genetic modification** of animals
- Farming of animals
- Cloning animals
- Zoos
- Treatment of wildlife

What the religions say

You already know that the religions think animals were either specially made, or are part of the same cycle of rebirth that humans are in. This gives animals a special status. Even if we believe humans are better or superior, animals still have value. From that we can guess that if we abuse animals in how we use them or treat them, there might be a consequence.

Let's look more closely at what the religions say. You can then apply their attitudes each time you meet an element. This is a really good way to reinforce the knowledge in your head, and so have a clear idea about their attitudes to animals overall.

From the next few pages, choose the religion(s) you have studied, and make notes on their attitudes to animals. You need to note:

- an overview of each religion's attitude to animals (Christians think animals were …)
- three to five teachings to use in exams (The **Bible** says 'God created everything'.)
- an explanation of how each teaching applies to the issue of animals. (When the Bible says 'God created everything', that includes animals, so they must be special.)

✓ **Now you know what this topic is about**

Religious attitudes to animal use

 ## Buddhism

Buddhism teaches compassion and non-violence. The intention behind any act is very important; if it is not compassionate, bad karma will result. Animals are part of the whole cycle of rebirth, and have a future as a human. It is important to show respect to all life.

Buddhism teaches:

- So long as sentient beings suffer, I will be there to help as much as I can. (Bodhisattva's Vow)
- To not hurt other sentient beings. (First Precept)
- Right livelihood includes not having a job that exploits animals.
- All living things fear being put to death. Putting oneself in the place of another, let no one kill nor cause another to kill. (**Dhammapada**)
- In some of his many lifetimes, the **Buddha** gave up his life to help animals.

Buddhist attitudes often come down to intention – why you are doing something. Do it for a positive reason, compassion, for example, and it is good, so long as the good outweighs any **suffering**. Do it for a negative reason, greed, for example, and it is bad. All this generates good or bad karma and that is what shapes our future lifetime(s).

Buddhists should try not to harm other beings. They should not have jobs or roles that cause suffering. They should also show respect to animals (as sentient beings) in any situation.

This doesn't mean they can't kill or eat animals; many Buddhists around the world do. Some monks will only eat meat if it is offered to them as alms. A Buddhist would accept the killing of an animal in pain or suffering where there was no other option. For sport, it is always wrong.

 ## Christianity

Christians believe that God gave humans dominion over the world and all in it. This gives them licence to use it as they wish, bearing in mind that God wants them to look after the world (**stewardship**), and will expect it back in good condition on **Judgement Day**.

Christianity teaches:

- God made the world and gave humans dominion over it. (Genesis)
- 'Scientists must abandon laboratories and factories of death.' (Pope John Paul II)
- Animals are a part of God's **creation** and as such deserve respect and protection. (St Francis of Assisi)
- Jesus said that God cares about even the sparrows.
- The earth and everything in it is the Lord's. (Bible)

Christians believe that because all life was created by God, it should be protected and looked after. The developed world, which is mainly Christian, is the biggest consumer of meat, has many factory farms, sees hunting as a sport and leads the world in using animals in medical research. At the same time, its zoos commonly protect endangered species, most families have pets, and animals are used as support for humans – police horses, guide dogs for the blind and so on. Many Christians today choose to eat organic and free range meat, if they are not vegetarian. Many actively campaign against hunting as sport. Many agree only with the use of animals in medical experiments, and encourage research in methods that do not use animals. There is a dilemma. For many Christians, use of animals is acceptable if they have been looked after well – humane treatment is the key.

On the Day of Judgement, Christians believe they will be called to account for their actions, including how they treated animals, and if they fought or supported the systems that cause animals to suffer.

Let's debate! There are statements at the bottom of the next few pages for you to discuss in groups. Write each statement on a big sheet of paper. Each group should then add the points they think of. Swap the sheets until everyone has seen each point. If you agree with someone else's point, tick it. If you disagree, put a cross and a reason why.

Hinduism

Respect for all life is central to Hinduism. All forms of life have the spark of the divine within them – the Ultimate Reality, **Brahman**. Most Hindus are vegetarians, and certain animals are considered very sacred in India, for example, cows and monkeys. The law of karma guides people's behaviour, so hurting animals would go against that.

Hinduism teaches:

- Avoid harming other sentient beings or forms of life. (ahimsa)
- Hindu worship includes respect for all of nature, and many deities are linked to specific animals, for example, Shiva and the cobra.
- By avoiding any harm to animals or to nature, humans will come to be ready for **eternal life**. (Laws of Manu)
- 'On a Brahmin … cow … elephant … dog … person of low caste, wise men look with equal eye.' (Bhagavad Gita)
- It is a duty of the grihasta (householder) stage of life to feed animals.

Respect for animals is key to Hindu life. At times animals are almost worshipped, for example, cows, the temple elephants and monkeys. Animals are part of the cycle of reincarnation.

Factory farming is seen as cruel and disrespectful. In the West, we send animals no longer good for farming to slaughterhouses. In contrast, there are retirement homes for cows in India.

Causing suffering to other beings can never be justified, even for medicine, so any kind of **animal experimentation** is wrong. This also means that any sport, like bull fighting, which causes suffering, is wrong.

In the Ramayana, Rama goes hunting. This may be taken to say that hunting for food is acceptable. Since every action gains us good or bad karma, Hindus have to weigh up what they do in terms of whether it helps or hinders them in future. The way they treat animals is part of this.

People who mistreat pets should be jailed.

Zoos should all be closed down, and the animals released.

☪ Islam

Allah created the world and all in it. Each human is a **khalifah** (steward) – and has a duty to look after Allah's creation. People's success in carrying out that duty will be assessed on Judgement Day, when everyone has to account for all their life's deeds before Allah. Using animals is fine, but you have to be able to show you treated them fairly.

Islam teaches:

- Humans are khalifah – trustees of the world, and its guardians. (Qur'an)
- Nature has been made inferior to humans, and can be used to improve the well-being of people and society.
- **Muhammad** (peace be upon him) insisted animals be well treated, given adequate food and rest, and if any are to be slaughtered, it is to be done in the most humane way possible. (**Sunnah**)
- Showing kindness to an animal is an act that is rewarded by Allah. (Sunnah)
- If a man unjustly kills any animal, he will be accused by the animal in front of Allah on Judgement Day. (Sunnah)

For Muslims, humans are superior to animals. However, animals must be looked after properly, not exploited or abused. Prophet Muhammad (pbuh) was very clear about this, and there are many stories in which he criticises people for their treatment of animals, or praises others. One story tells how he cut a piece out of his cloak, which was being used by a cat and her kittens, rather than disturb them.

Farming is important as it helps to feed people. However, in factory farms, animals do not get proper care or rest, which makes them haram. These farms usually send their animals to slaughterhouses, making the meat haram, because the killing isn't done following Shari'ah Law.

Experimentation has been very important in medical advances, but duplicate trials and non-medical testing are an abuse of our power as khalifah. It is better to experiment without animals.

Hunting is a sport in many Muslim countries, though the meat caught is usually eaten. Many sports involving animals are frowned upon, because of cruelty – like bull fighting.

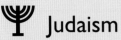 Judaism

G-d created the world and all in it, giving dominion over everything to man. Stewardship (the duty to look after G-d's creation in its entirety) is important in Judaism. Animals are inferior to humans, and can be used by them, but must always be treated well.

Judaism teaches:

- G-d made the world and all in it. He gave humans dominion over all. (Genesis)
- A righteous man looks after his animals. (Proverbs – Ketuvim)
- On the Sabbath Day, do no work, nor your animals. (Torah)
- Animals must be treated with respect because they are G-d's creation, but human life will always have more value than animal life.
- Do not be cruel to animals. (**Noachide Laws**)

Judaism has a duty to help and improve the well-being of others. This will involve the use and death of animals. However, any form of cruelty is wrong, and there are many laws within the 613 Mitzvot about looking after animals. These include giving them time to rest, adequate food and shelter, not causing them unnecessary suffering and not making them work too hard.

As part of G-d's creation, and for our use, we can use them as we wish, to help us, for example, guide dogs, police horses, animals of burden – all are acceptable, as long as they are treated well.

Farming is about providing food for people, and we need food to live.

Hunting is forbidden by Jewish law. It is seen as unnecessary to people's needs, and a cause of cruelty. Any meat from an animal that has been hunted is treyfah (unfit).

Animal experiments are only acceptable as long as they are for the advancement of medical science, because they help to improve the well-being of humans. However, replica trials and those tests that involve cruelty are forbidden.

Sikhism

All is the creation of God, and all life has within it the light of God. Sikhs should respect God's creation as a way of worshipping God. There are no clear teachings on certain things, and Sikhs are expected to act according to their own conscience so, for example, while many Sikhs are vegetarian, some choose not to be.

Sikhism teaches:

- If you say that there is God in every being, then why kill a chicken? (**Guru Granth Sahib**)
- God's light pervades every creature, and every creature is contained within his light. (Guru Granth Sahib)
- In the **langar**, only vegetarian food is served. Many Sikhs are vegetarian out of respect for God's creation.
- All food is pure, for God has given it for our sustenance. (Adi Granth)
- I enjoyed myself on the banks of the River Jumna … I hunted many tigers, deer and bears. (Guru Gobind Singh)

For Sikhs, the facts that God created everything, and that they have a duty to worship God through sewa (service to others), should mean they treat everything in the world around them with respect. So, any exploitation of, or cruelty to, animals would be wrong. Indeed, they are forbidden to eat halal meat because the slaughter method is considered cruel.

Farms are important to produce the quantities of food people need to eat. Those farms where the treatment of animals is poor are unacceptable.

The Gurus enjoyed hunting, so it is not forbidden. However, a distinction is made between the hunting the Gurus did, and hunting like bear-baiting, which is just cruel. The use of traps would also be wrong, as it is undoubtedly cruel.

Experiments for medical purposes help to improve the life of others, and so can be justified. Replica experiments, and those for testing products such as make-up are seen as wrong. Many Sikhs work in the medical system as a form of sewa.

We've learned most of our medicine from animal research, so it must continue.

Animal sports are fine because they entertain people.

This topic, your notes

Companions and helpers

Surveys tell us that 45 per cent of households in the UK have at least one pet. As societies get richer, more people keep animals as pets rather than working animals. Our pets seem to get a different status to other animals – we think of them differently. I bet you'd never have a pig sleep on the end of your bed, but you let your cat or dog! These animals are our 'friends' and companions – many people regard their pet with love.

There are many animals that help us, as well as being companions – guide dogs for the blind and hearing dogs for the deaf, for example. These specially trained animals help blind or deaf people be independent. Without them, their lives would be difficult.

Task

For each topic on pages 8–9, design a slide show. It must include:
- an explanation of what the topic is, including images
- information about a linked organisation (check the internet)
- a list of the benefits/pros
- a list of the problems/cons
- what you think the religion(s) you have studied would say about it, using teachings to back up your ideas.

Have you got a pet? How do you look after it? Does it help you? Is it your friend? Would you eat it, or experiment on it, or lock it up all its life with no exercise?

Transport and work

Humans have always used animals to help them work. We also use them to find drugs and explosives, to catch fish (cormorant fishing in Japan) and as vehicles. These animals are well looked after, even after they have been 'retired'. Many families own animals that provide them with food, and help them work their land. However, many animals are 'beasts of burden', spending their lives carrying huge loads, and eventually being left to die because they can no longer work.

Some of the issues:
- This is not their natural life – the necessary training is often harsh.
- Many beasts of burden are not fed or rested properly, and suffer all their lives.

Farming

Farming is the business of agriculture. Nearly all the food we eat has come from farms.

Most people in developing countries have very small farms with few animals. They are farming for their own family, selling any extra at a market. In the UK, we see factory, organic and free-range farms. Supermarkets sell meat from all these types of farms.

Some of the issues:
- Animals are not cared for properly because they are just products.
- Animals are forced to breed at unnatural rates.
- Nature versus profit – farming is a business.

✓ **Now you know about some work uses of animals**

In sport

horse racing … greyhound racing …
dog fighting … badger baiting

In many sports, animals are highly trained and well looked after. Mistreatment leads to punishments. However, many sports involve animals fighting against each other – like dog fighting and cricket fighting. These are considered cruel in many societies and can be illegal (such as dog fighting in the UK). None of these sports is how the animal would naturally live.

Some of the issues:
- It is cruel to make two animals fight.
- Even well-kept animals can just be slaughtered when they are no longer 'good enough'.
- The animals get injured.

Bullfighting

Bullfighting is the national sport of Spain. It is also found in Portugal, parts of France and in some South American countries. The matador uses set moves during the different parts of a fight with the bull(s) to distract, annoy and hurt it. Finally, it should be killed by one well-aimed sword stab through the heart.

Some of the issues:
- It is obviously cruel.
- The bull dies in great pain over a long time.
- Even when a bull is spared, few survive their journey back to their ranch because of the poor treatment of fight injuries.

Hunting

Hunting is when we chase and kill an animal. It could be for food, for fur or for sport. In the UK, many enjoy it as a blood sport.

Some of the issues:

Phil
Hunting for meat for your family is okay, I think. I don't agree with shooting a load of birds or animals when you don't need the food. What's the point, making them suffer like that?

I have seen some of the traps they use for hunting – horrible. The animals die slowly in agony. Some even try to bite their own limbs off to escape. My dog died in one of those traps – they don't just catch wild animals, see.
Ann

Jim
In hunting we chase an animal just for the thrill of the chase, and then, when it is too tired to escape, we let hunting animals tear it apart. That is wrong.

Tigers are nearly extinct, but are still hunted for medicine. They'll have to find other medicines when they've killed them all, so why not find them now?
Brad

What other sports use animals? Do the animals have training? Are there any sports that you think are worse than others for the animals? Can you name any 'blood sports'?

✓ Now you know about some sports uses of animals

Task

For each topic on pages 10–11, design a poster. It must include:
- an explanation of what the topic is, including images
- information about a linked organisation (check the internet)
- a list of the benefits/pros
- a list of the problems/cons
- what you think the religion(s) you have studied would say about it, using teachings to back up your ideas.

Experimentation

Animal experiments further our medical knowledge, test new drugs or test new products for harmfulness (toxicity). Medical science has always used animals. For example, many surgical procedures were perfected on animals. Some experiments just mean a change in the animal's diet, others do cause injury and even death. At the end of the experimentation any live animals are humanely destroyed. Since 1986, there have been specific laws to control experimentation.

The animals – mainly guinea pigs, mice, rats, rabbits, dogs and monkeys – are specially bred in farms.

Some of the issues:
- It is cruel. Even scientists accept the animals suffer – though for the greater good.
- There are alternatives, such as using tissue cultures.
- Animal genetics and human genetics are different, and often reactions are not the same.

Zoos

Zoos are places where animals are kept for people to look at. Most animals in zoos are from countries and climates other than the country the zoo is in. Zoos in rich countries do try to recreate conditions for the animals – they have specially shaped and built compounds, and their food is similar to their natural diet. Zoos in developing countries are not usually like this.

Many zoos are involved in programmes such as helping to re-establish endangered species.

Some of the issues:
- The animals are not in their natural environment.
- Animals in all zoos are caged over night every night (often their most active time in the wild).
- Breeding programmes are very expensive and, often, the animals bred cannot be released into the wild.

Genetic modification and cloning

This is about taking the DNA of an animal, changing it and creating new forms of the species. Scientists have been able to change the DNA of one species of pig, for example, so that its heart can be used in human transplants.

Cloning is when scientists make an exact replica of something by inserting its DNA into an embryo. The embryo is then replanted into an animal's womb to develop. Most famous is Dolly the Sheep (scientists needed 277 attempts; she lived for six years). This could be a way to save some endangered species.

Some of the issues:

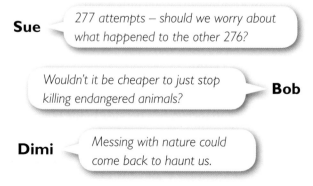

Sue — *277 attempts – should we worry about what happened to the other 276?*

Wouldn't it be cheaper to just stop killing endangered animals? — **Bob**

Dimi — *Messing with nature could come back to haunt us.*

The fur and ivory trades

Fur usually comes from farms that use battery methods to breed thousands of animals, and then electrocute them so as to not damage the pelt/fur. Most of the animals are wild animals, so keeping them in small cages all their lives is very cruel.

Ivory comes from elephants, which are killed for their tusks. It is an illegal trade across the world, though many people still like to own ivory objects. It is still very fashionable in the Far East today.

Some of the issues:
- We don't *need* fur or ivory.
- Fur farms are very cruel.
- Ivory poaching has endangered whole species of elephant.

Treatment of animals in the wild

Do you get birds in your garden? Do you feed them? What other wild animals do you see? How do you react when you see wild animals – with fear, curiosity, awe?

We see wild animals every day, and mainly ignore them. When they come near we often chase them away or kill them – think of foxes or rats.

Many of these species are now endangered. They all have an important role in the ecosystem, and many provide obvious beauty to our environment.

Some of the issues:
- Whose space is the world – ours or theirs or both?
- Are we endangering too many species?
- Should we support wildlife more through feeding, etc?

Preventing extinction of animals

Extinction of a species is when surveys and investigations and other counts all fail to find any example of a species over a fixed period of time. Humans have already made many species extinct. Scientists reckon over 16,500 species are currently known to be endangered (we don't know every species that exists). Once a species is extinct it is gone forever.

Some of the issues:
- All species have a key role in the ecosystem.
- The species we lose could have been helpful to medicine or research.
- Do we have a right to do this, for example hunting tigers to extinction for fun?
- Our children won't see these creatures – they will inherit a depleted world.

Polar bears are facing extinction

Research Task

Find out more about animal rights. Check out the work of these groups – RSPCA, IFAW, PETA, National Anti-Vivisection Society. You can learn more about the issues as these groups see them, and the ways in which these groups campaign for change. Check out **www.beep. ac.uk** – the Bio-Ethics Education Project. It provides really good information for the whole of this topic, and the next (Religion and planet earth), and also Topic 1 (Medical ethics) on Paper 3 (40553).

Vegetarianism

There are many reasons why people are vegetarian. These are usually to do with health, upbringing, religion and concerns about farming methods. Some people eat no meat or fish or dairy products at all (vegans); some choose to eat no meat or fish or meat products (vegetarian).

The Christian, Muslim and Jewish faiths all allow meat in their diets. Some Christians fast at certain times of year. Muslims and Jews may not eat certain meats, and must only eat ritually slaughtered meat (called halal for Muslims, kosher for Jews). This reflects the idea that God/Allah/G-d gave humans dominion over animals, and so they could be used by humans, including as food. Hindus and Buddhists, on the whole, are vegetarian, reflecting two important beliefs – ahimsa (non-violence) and respect for all life. However, it is also true that many Buddhists in Asia do eat meat, and certainly monks eat meat when gifted to them as alms. Many Sikhs are vegetarian to show respect for God's creation, and the Sikh langar always serves a vegetarian meal. The Jewish faith has very strict rules about food – its processing, cooking and storage (**kashrut**).

The Basics

1 Check back to pages 5–7 to find the one or two religions you have studied. For each, write the important teachings to do with animals. Add any other ideas you have come across in your studies (for example, that God created all life).
2 Use what you have written to write a paragraph on the attitude of each of your one or two religions to animals.
3 Re-use those teachings to try to explain the attitude of each to eating meat.
4 Why do people choose to be vegetarian?
5 Eating meat is disrespectful to God's creation. Do you agree? Give reasons and explain your answer, showing you have thought about more than one point of view.

Research Task

1 Find out about the dietary requirements of followers of the religion(s) you have studied.
2 Find out about the Vegetarian Society – **www.vegsoc.org**

✓ **Now you have thought about eating meat, and attitudes to it**

Topic 2 — Religion and planet earth

World Summit agrees targets for reduction of emissions

More medicine finds in rainforest

Big increase in environmentally friendly holidays

'Green' schemes appearing all over globe

ENVIRONMENTAL FILM WATCHED BY MILLIONS

SCHOOLS TEACH ENVIRONMENTAL VALUES

This topic is about the environment and, from the religions' point of view, humanity's duty to look after the environment. It considers the situation the modern world is in, and how governments are trying to tackle issues.

> How do we treat our world? Well or badly? Can you give some examples? Should we treat it better? Why?

Some key ideas include:
- Life is special or sacred. This means all life, not just human life. Humans have a duty or responsibility to look after it.
- Humans have a responsibility to look after the world – for God, for themselves, for other people now and in the future.
- Everybody has a role to play in looking after the natural world – not just some people.

The Basics

1 List some of the ways we damage our world.
2 Split your list into the ways individuals damage the world, and how companies might damage the world.
3 What responsibility do individuals have for looking after the environment? What about governments?
4 What makes it difficult to look after the environment? Give examples to show what you mean more clearly (think on different scales – at school, in your home street, in the country, across the world).

> Check out **www.beep.ac.uk** for elements of this topic – it will really develop your understanding.

✓ **Now you have thought about how we use the planet**

The origins of life

This course is interested in how life began. We can take the scientific route, which is a set of theories based on bits of evidence. Or we can take the religious route, which is stories based on what people say God told them. Whichever you choose to accept as your truth is fine, but you still need to know both for the exam.

How the world began

The Big Bang Theory says:

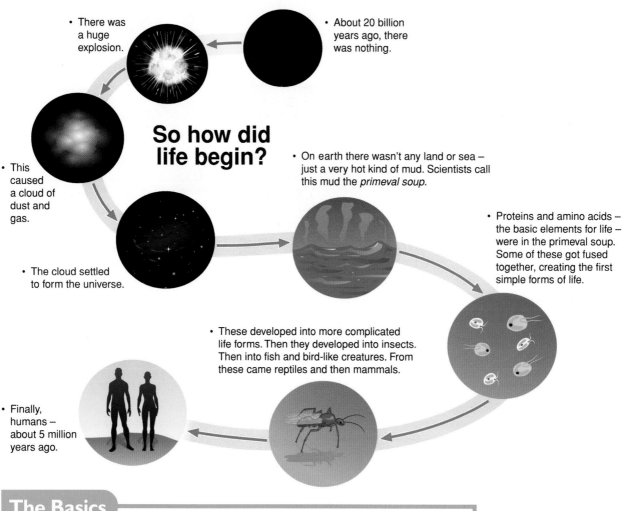

- There was a huge explosion.
- About 20 billion years ago, there was nothing.

So how did life begin?

- This caused a cloud of dust and gas.
- The cloud settled to form the universe.
- On earth there wasn't any land or sea – just a very hot kind of mud. Scientists call this mud the *primeval soup*.
- Proteins and amino acids – the basic elements for life – were in the primeval soup. Some of these got fused together, creating the first simple forms of life.
- These developed into more complicated life forms. Then they developed into insects. Then into fish and bird-like creatures. From these came reptiles and then mammals.
- Finally, humans – about 5 million years ago.

The Basics

1 Explain in your own words how science says the universe began.
2 Explain in your own words how science says life began.
3 Think about these ideas – why do some people disagree with them?
4 **Science explains everything we need to know.** Do you agree? Give reasons and explain your answer.

 Now you know the scientific beliefs about how life began

What the religions say

Religions each have their own ideas about how the world and life began. They are almost always linked to a God, and this gives religions a special attitude to the world around them. They feel responsible for the world because of their beliefs.

Creation

Christianity ✝, Islam ☾ and Judaism ✡ share the same story of how the world began. At the beginning of time, God created the world from nothing. It took six 'days', and after its completion God was pleased with it. The creation included the world (land, sea, vegetation, sun, moon, stars) and all life on it (fish, birds and animals). Humans were the final creation.

Hindus ॐ believe that Brahman is responsible for the universe. There are many creation stories in Hinduism. In one, Vishnu is said to sleep on a cobra in the middle of a vast ocean of nothingness. Vishnu wakes, and from his navel grows a lotus flower. Inside the lotus is Brahma, who creates the world. Shiva is also there, and he is responsible for the cycle of life and death in all of the creation.

Sikhism ☬ also believes that God created the world – everything comes from God, and without God nothing exists. God is the one who maintains life, so that it continues to exist.

Stewardship

This means 'looking after'. All religions believe we have to look after the world. It belongs to God, not us. By looking after the world, we show respect to God. In fact, in Islam ☾, Judaism ✡, Hinduism ॐ and Sikhism ☬ it is almost an act of worship to look after the world. In all the religions, stewardship is a duty that God has set for humans. A 'duty' is a responsibility, a job – so looking after the world is one of the jobs humans have to undertake.

Futures thinking

What does this mean?

You can probably work it out – it is thinking about the future. We all do that, so let's work out why it is key for religious people.

♦ Firstly, if I trash my house, I have to live in the mess. So, in terms of the world, whatever I do to it, I still have to live there.
♦ Secondly, others live there too, so they suffer. It's the same with the world – the damage I do affects others. In the future the things we do will affect our own children. And it's no good to say it wasn't us, it was our parents and grandparents, because the crisis point has been reached. Everybody has to help, whether or not they did anything to cause the problems.
♦ Thirdly, if I believe God made the world, and that I have a duty to look after it, then there must be a reward for doing my duty (or a punishment for not), so it is in my interests to look after the world for God as God will reward me (heaven).
♦ Alternatively, I might be Buddhist, Hindu or Sikh. In these cases, I believe I will live on earth again after dying in this lifetime. So stewardship is still in my interests, as I need to come back!

The Basics

1 Match these words and phrases:
   Creation   Duty to look after the world
   Stewardship   Impact of problems in the future
   Futures thinking   Idea that God created the world from nothing
2 Find a creation story from a religion and rewrite it. You could use images to retell it.
3 **Religious people have a bigger duty to look after the world than anyone else.** What do you think? Explain your opinion.

✓ Now you know some religious attitudes to the world

15

The earth and God – seeing God in nature

Have you ever seen something in nature that has amazed you – maybe left you thinking 'wow'? Or something that made you go silent in awe?

We really have to wonder why all these religions came up with the idea that God created the world.

Can you imagine the scene, many thousands of years ago, where a child asks his grandfather how all the world came to exist? Perhaps they are sitting around the fire, late in the evening, with a vast, star-filled sky above them. Imagine it – all is quiet except for the sounds of insects and animals, the fire crackles, the grandfather is telling stories from their people's history. The boy gazes at the world around him and the deep, inky blackness of the sky which is peppered with twinkling lights. It isn't difficult to imagine his grandfather telling him the story of how the world was made by a great being – the greatest of all, because only such a being could create the world. The beauty and sense of peace can't all just be an accident – it must have deliberately been done. How did this being make it? Well, there wasn't anything to start with, because beginnings are always empty. Then you need a place, then the right conditions before you put life on it, from simple to complex. So, the boy is satisfied – and even more awe-struck by the world around him that he now sees in a different way.

People see beautiful landscapes, sunsets, sunrises, waterfalls – these can make you feel privileged to have seen them, as if it were a special moment. That feeling is what we call 'awe'. The exam might ask you about 'awe and wonderment' – in other words, things that make you feel amazed in the way just described.

So, it isn't hard to see why nature can inspire people to think of God. Also to see that nature provides a proof of God's existence for many people. We, as simple humans, must wonder at this power which is shown in the created world. If we wonder at it, we must respect the God who made it, and even worship that God by looking after the world.

The Basics

1 What is 'awe and wonderment'?
2 Why do you think some people see God in nature? Use some examples from nature to show what you mean.
3 Find some pictures of nature that help to show this sense of awe.

Research Task

The Alliance of Religions and Conservation (**www.arcworld.org**) has loads of information on this topic, both the issues and what all the religions are saying and doing. Do some research online, and put together a project or presentation for the religion(s) you are studying. It will give you a better and clearer understanding of their attitudes and actions, which you can use in the exam.

Now you know how people are inspired by the world around them

World problems

1 Climate change and global warming

Climate change is what it says – the climate is changing. Scientists tell us that their records show the earth is getting hotter. So temperatures everywhere will get higher – this is *global warming*.

Why is it happening?

It could be that the earth's cycle is to get hotter and cooler over time – you've heard of the ice ages, when the earth froze over, well, this is the opposite. So, climate change and global warming could be part and parcel of the earth's life. However, scientists know that the activities of humans over the last 250 years, and especially the last 100, have speeded up temperature change. They estimate that the surface temperature of the earth will increase by between 1 and 4.9°C before 2100. This is mainly because of the gases released by burning fossil fuels for energy or transport. Scientists are telling us we need to act now because if we are the problem, then we should be able to solve it.

What are the consequences?

Imagine British summers being so hot that you don't need to go to Greece to get a tan! Sounds good? Well, hotter usually means drier, so plants and animals have to adapt or die. Hotter means more frequent extreme weather. Hotter also means some places become too hot to live in. The ice caps melt, so seas rise, so lands flood (and Britain isn't much above current sea-level). If it gets too hot, diseases like malaria and dengue fever will come to Britain. Still sound great?

Solutions?

Scientists say the key solution is to change our energy use. We need to find alternatives to fossil fuels (coal, oil and gas) so that the fuels we use either don't add to the problem, or are renewable. This is called *sustainable energy* – energy we can keep using without doing more harm.

The Basics

1 What is meant by 'climate change' and 'global warming'?
2 Why do scientists think the earth is getting hotter?
3 What is the main change we can make to try to slow this effect?
4 List as many forms of renewable energy as you can.
5 Imagine what school would be like if climate change happened. What problems would there be? What solutions can you come up with?
6 **A hotter world is a better world.** What do you think? Explain your opinion.

 Now you know about climate change/global warming

☸ Buddhist attitudes to the environment

Buddhists believe that all life, in all forms, should be respected – that means the natural world. Since everyone must live many, many lifetimes, it is important to protect the world for our own future, as well as our children's. Two key beliefs for Buddhists are *respect* and *compassion*.

The Dalai Lama has said:

- **Destruction** of nature and **natural resources** results from ignorance, greed and lack of respect for the earth's living things … This lack of respect extends to future generations who will inherit a vastly degraded planet.
- The earth is not only the common heritage of all humankind but also the ultimate source of life.
- Conservation is not merely a question of morality, but a question of our own survival.

Buddhism also teaches:

- Help not harm other sentient beings. (First Precept)
- Compassion for all life
- There are karmic consequences to all of our actions.

Looking after the environment isn't just about us – it's about the people of the future, it's about the other forms of life now and in the future. Ignorance and greed are two of the three poisons that keep people from enlightenment, and much environmental damage is because of people and companies wanting more (money, space, whatever else) for themselves.

See **www.earthsangha.org**

✝ Christian attitudes to the environment

Christians believe that God created the world and gave humankind stewardship – the responsibility to look after the world. Christians in modern times especially have seen the need to work to *heal the world*, and look after the environment.

Christianity teaches:

- God made the world, and gave the duty of stewardship to humans. (Genesis)
- The earth is the Lord's, and everything in it. (Psalms)
- Respect for life extends to the rest of creation. (Pope John Paul II)
- More than ever, individually and collectively, people are responsible for the future of the planet. (Pope John Paul II)
- I want to awake in you a deep admiration for creation, until anywhere thinking of plants and flowers, you are overcome by thoughts of the Creator. (St Basil)

Clearly, Christians believe that humans have a special role on earth, which is to look after the earth and animals. Since humans must face God on the Day of Judgement, all must carry out their given duties. If humans did not look after the world, or did nothing to stop its destruction, they should expect to be punished by God. Many Christians are motivated to do environmental work because of this belief.

See **www.greenchristian. org.uk**

2 Pollution

Pollution basically means there is too much of something, which has caused an imbalance and damage to the environment. Pollution can be of the air, water or land. We even now talk about light and noise pollution. Usually, it is a result of what humans have done.

> Can you think of some examples of pollution?

> Go back through your list – what are the potential problems caused by each kind of pollution?

Busy roads cause air pollution. This affects our health and drives some wildlife away. It also makes *acid rain*, so that when rain falls, it poisons the land and water, and damages buildings and structures.

Factories can cause water pollution by emptying waste into rivers, which poisons the fish. Fertiliser running off farmers' fields can kill all the fish, as it makes the algae grow too fast, taking the oxygen from the water. This is just one form of *toxic chemical* – chemicals that can kill in big doses. Too much *pesticide* does more damage to the ecosystem than intended, and can change its whole balance.

You have probably added to land pollution by dropping litter. It doesn't just look bad, it also kills wild animals who eat it, or get trapped in it.

In towns and cities, you see fewer stars than when you are in the countryside. The lights at ground level block out the stars – light pollution is affecting our appreciation of the beauty around us.

People who live near airport runways suffer from noise pollution, because of the sound of planes taking off. Even if the noise doesn't affect the people's hearing, it makes life unpleasant, and affects the value of their homes.

Pollution is a big part of the reason for the increasing temperature. Our waste produces the greenhouse gases that heat the earth.

The Basics

1. What do we mean by 'pollution'?
2. Give three types of pollution.
3. How does our pollution help to cause global warming?
4. **Pollution can't be stopped.** Do you agree? Give reasons for your answer, showing you have thought about more than one point of view.

 Now you know about pollution

3 Destruction of natural habitats

You have just read about pollution – pollution is one reason why **natural habitats** are being destroyed. For example, if a tanker spills oil into the sea, it wipes out life in that area, and degrades the land for many years. Check out the *Torrey Canyon* spill to get a better idea of this.

Another reason for the destruction of natural habits is deforestation, where huge areas of forest are cut down, for example, to create grazing land for cattle, or to create areas for building, mining and roads. The trees, of course, are the habitat for many species – so these species are affected, even dying out. Also, the trees convert carbon dioxide into the oxygen we breathe, so they help in the fight against global warming. Shame we are cutting so many down!

Land is cleared in Borneo for palm oil plantations. Orangutans lose their habitat, and are now an endangered species.

The rainforests also contain many plants that can be used as medicines, which are lost with deforestation. There are thought to be many species of animals and plants in the rainforests that we haven't recorded yet – they could become extinct before we have even studied them.

Clearing land to build factories, for farming, and for people to live on also causes the destruction of natural habitats. When we clear the vegetation, we take away the home of some animals. We also destroy plants, sometimes putting the species into danger of extinction.

> How could we make up for destroying these habitats?

The Basics

1 What is 'destruction of natural habitat'? What does this lead to?
2 Give some reasons why this happens.
3 How could we avoid this destruction?
4 **God gave humans dominion over the world. This means we can do what we like.** What do you think? Explain your opinion.

 Now you know about destruction of habitats

ॐ Hindu attitudes to the environment

Traditionally, Hindu life was very simple and relied on the environment. This was linked with beliefs about the **sanctity of life** and non-violence to form a religion that is peaceful towards the environment. Brahman (the Ultimate Reality) is in all life.

Hinduism teaches:

- Respect for all life
- Ahimsa – non-violence
- Hindus should focus on environmental values. *(Artharva Veda)*
- Trees have five sorts of kindness which are their daily sacrifice: to families they give fuel; to passers-by they give shade and a resting place; to birds they give shelter; with their leaves, roots and bark they give medicines. (Varaha Purana)
- Everything rests on me as pearls are strung on a thread. I am the original fragrance of the earth … the taste in water … the heat in fire and the sound in space … the light of the sun and moon and the life of all that lives. (Bhagavad Gita 7:7)

All life is seen as interdependent, including animal and plant life. All life depends on the environment, so everyone needs to protect and look after it. Hindus believe all souls will be reborn into more lifetimes on earth, so we have to look after it for our own future sakes. God is seen as part of nature, so protection and worship are important.

See **www.fov.org.uk**

☾★ Muslim attitudes to the environment

Islam sees the universe as the work of Allah. Humans are khalifah – stewards. Looking after the world shows respect to Allah.

Islam teaches:

- The world is green and beautiful, and Allah has appointed you his stewards over it. (Qur'an)
- The whole earth has been created as a place of worship. (Qur'an)
- When Doomsday comes, if someone has a palm shoot in his hand, he should still plant it. (Hadith)
- The earth has been created for me as a mosque and a means of purification. (Hadith)
- Prophet Muhammad (pbuh) gave the example of not wasting – he only washed in water from a container, not running water.

So, humans are the trustees of Allah's creation. Trustees look after things, not destroy them.

The creation reflects Allah. Allah knows who damages and who looks after his creation. Those who do not follow their duty to look after the world will be punished on Judgement Day by Allah.

The Muslim community is *Ummah* (brotherhood), including those in the past and future. Everyone has a duty to make sure they pass onto them a world fit to live in, not one damaged beyond repair because humans were selfish.

See **www.ifees.org**

4 Use and abuse of natural resources

Natural resources include vegetation, minerals and fossil fuels. Humans are using these in greater quantities and at a faster rate now than at any other time in our history. This is because of how technologically advanced we are. We can cut materials out of the ground faster and in greater quantities than ever before. We use more fossil fuels at a faster and greater rate than ever before. Our technology, cars and all forms of transport, for example, need more of them. More and more people in the world are getting more and more technology. We are also richer, so we use more resources. For example, more people go on holiday by plane, which uses much fuel.

Some of the fossil fuels, such as coal, are already running out. These fuels are limited in quantity and take millions of years to be formed. We either have to stop using them, or find a different source of energy, which is renewable. If we don't stop using them, and they run out, we will have to find a new source anyway.

What will be the problems caused if, for example, oil runs out?

It isn't just that these fuels are limited. They give off lots of the greenhouse gases, and cause the pollution that we have already mentioned. The more we use, the more the problems stack up. So, finding an alternative helps us with those problems too – it isn't something we can hide from.

The Basics

1. What do we mean by 'use and abuse of natural resources'?
2. Give some examples of how we use natural resources.
3. Give some examples of our overuse, or abuse, of natural resources.
4. Why do we need to find new ways to get energy?
5. What new energy forms could there be?
6. **Ban the use of fossil fuels now.** What do you think? Explain your opinion.

 Now you know about use/abuse of natural resources

5 Modern living

> Think about your life. What do you do to contribute to the problems we've read about in the last few pages?

It's really easy to think that global warming, pollution and so on are someone else's fault, and someone else's problem. It's also easy to think the problems are too big for us as individuals to do anything about. In our everyday lives, we put huge demands on the planet.

> Can you give examples of some of the demands of everyday life?

What are your answers to these questions? Do those answers matter?

1. Does your family have a car/cars?
2. Does your family ever throw food away?
3. Do you only eat organic and free-range food?
4. Do you eat 'fast foods'?

Cars use up fossil fuels, and are a major polluter. The gases they put out (**emissions**) add to the greenhouse effect. If you buy more than you eat, there is **waste** in all kinds of ways – the food, its wrappings, for a start. Most food has been grown using pesticides, which will have polluted its local environment. Rain on the crops runs off, taking the pesticides with it into the soil or nearby water as a poison. Waste goes into landfill sites, which emit greenhouse gases as their contents decompose. The meat for fast-food burgers often comes from herds that graze areas of cleared rainforest land, leading to the destruction of natural habitats.

So, you see, you are contributing to the problems we've read about. The question is – *what can you do about it?*

We could each take responsibility for our own contribution, and show respect to ourselves and the rest of the planet (now and in the future) by trying to solve the current problems. This is the message of governments and religions.

The Basics

1. Give two examples each of: emissions and waste.
2. How do the *demands* of modern living make the problems we have read about worse?
3. **People today only think of themselves, not the planet.** Think of reasons to agree and disagree.

 Now you have thought about the demands of modern living

♆ Jewish attitudes to the environment

Jewish sacred writings begin with G-d's creation of the world, and go on to state that G-d gave humans the duty of stewardship. There are many mitzvot (rules) about looking after the environment.

Judaism teaches:

- All is made by G-d and is good. Humans are given stewardship over the creation. (Genesis)
- The *Bal tashchit* (do not waste) precept can be interpreted as an instruction to conserve resources. (Torah)
- The earth and everything that is in it is the Lord's. (Ketuvim)
- All that I created for you … do not corrupt or desolate my world … there will be no one to repair it after you. (Midrash Ecclesiastes Rabbah 7:13)
- Love your neighbour as yourself. (Leviticus)

Clearly Jews have a duty to look after the world, and should do this by treating it with respect. For example, land is to be left fallow on a regular cycle. Increasingly, Jews are becoming more active in environmental work, and are linking existing Jewish values to the issue. For example, tikkun olam (repairing the world) could be interpreted as tackling environmental problems; tzedek (justice) is extended to mean justice for all of creation, including animals and the world itself. It isn't possible to 'love your neighbour' if you are wrecking the environment!

See **www.coejl.org**

Looking after the world

International efforts

Every ten years since 1972, there has been an Earth Summit. The first was held in Stockholm. Governments of countries from around the world attend these summits, and discuss issues affecting the world. These issues are directly or indirectly about the environment. In 1972, the meeting discussed the global environment and development needs of the world. These two things conflicted. Immediately, the governments began to seek solutions. The Stockholm Declaration and Action Plan set out principles for helping the natural environment, and the need to support nations through this process.

In the 1980s, 'Our Common Future' recognised that humans needed to find ways to meet the needs of all people and countries today, while not messing things up for people in the future.

In 1992, at Rio de Janeiro, agreements were reached on biodiversity and climate change. These led to the formation of the Commission for Sustainable Development. This said that we had to look for ways in which we could develop technologies that would keep going, for example, replacing fossil fuels with renewable energies.

Overall, these summits try to build agreements between nations. They try to help nations face the problems they have, while not heaping up problems for others or for the future. They try to stop the biggest nations from just doing their own thing at the expense of the smaller nations. They recognise that developing countries can't do the things that developed countries can – because they simply aren't rich enough. They try to encourage the sharing of the problems, and of the solutions. Most of all, they are designed to put these issues on to the highest, most powerful agenda of the world leaders.

Kyoto agreements (2002 Summit)

In 2002, 83 governments plus the European Union signed up to these agreements. Countries signing up *agreed to set targets* for the future.

1 Cleaner fuels – use of gas, rather than fossil fuels; using fuel-cell technology; using renewable fuels, such as solar, wind and wave energies; and use of nuclear technologies
2 Reducing the amount of carbon dioxide emissions

The USA and Australia later withdrew from these agreements, feeling they were not in the interests of their nations. They have set up their own targets.

If countries can stick to these targets, then the results will have a positive impact on reducing global warming. If we can do that, the ice caps will melt less quickly, the life forms in those areas will be less endangered and perhaps even saved, the increasingly freak weather we have seen will be reduced, the deserts may stay where they are, and so on, and so on. It really is a big deal for the world to solve.

Sikh attitudes to the environment

For Sikhs the natural environment is a gift from God and we have to take care of it. It only exists because God wants it to. Sikhs believe the world is now in a 300-year cycle (Cycle of Creation), which gives a greater need to look after the world.

Sikhism teaches:

- The universe comes into being by God's will. (**Guru Nanak**)
- In nature we see God, and in nature, we hear God speak. (Adi Granth)
- Respect for all life
- God created everything. (Guru Nanak)
- The Sikh ideal is a simple life free from conspicuous waste.

Sikhs believe they must perform sewa (service) for others, which should include the natural world. Looking after the world safeguards it for future generations – sewa for people in the future. They believe that you can't care for the environment without thinking about society's needs, because often environmental damage is a result of **poverty**.

The Sikh gurus said God is within everything, so in some ways damaging the world is like damaging God.

See **www.ecosikh.org**

Learn about the problems in more detail Recycle household waste Campaign to make government change

Encourage others to do the same

Be vegetarian

Eat organic

Walk don't drive

Sustainable development

This is at the heart of the Earth Summits and all the agreements. It is the idea that new technological developments should all be infinite, or very long lasting, as well as within the reach of nations. There would be no advantage in swapping coal as a fuel for something else that will quickly run out. Similarly, it would be no good finding a new technology that was simply too expensive for anyone to use.

The Earth Summit 2012 focused on sustainability. It gave two key challenges – how to build a green economy to achieve **sustainable development** and lift people put of poverty; and to improve the co-ordination of international efforts for sustainable development.

Conservation

You must have heard the term **conservation** (trying to protect an area or species). Sometimes it involves doing a whole load of repair and rebuild jobs somewhere, for example, to maintain the environment for an endangered species. It might include planting trees to protect an area from landslides. It might be declaring an area a nature reserve in order to protect wildlife and the environment there – this has happened in Borneo to protect orangutans.

It is becoming more common for people to take holidays that are based around conservation – either of animals, like working on a lion reserve for a few weeks in Kenya, or environmental, like rebuilding dry stone walls in Scotland to protect vegetation in fields beyond the pathways.

What about you – what can you do?

Check out the tape round the edge of this page – there are some ideas. Are there any you do already? Are there any you could do? Every little helps!

The Basics

1 What do we mean by 'international efforts' to save the planet?
2 Why do countries need to work together?
3 What are the Earth Summits, and what do they do?
4 Explain what we mean by 'sustainable development'.
5 Why are the Kyoto agreements important?
6 Explain, using examples, what we mean by 'conservation'.
7 List some of the things anyone can do to help the planet.

Building your repertoire

In order to show good understanding, you need to be able to write about how all people, whether religious or not, can help the environment. Also, if you know about international efforts – what governments and big organisations are doing, this will give you a greater breadth of knowledge to refer to.

Pray

Join an organisation, like Greenpeace

Go on an environmental action holiday

Pay for a tree to be planted

Grow a butterfly and bee garden **Don't waste stuff – buy only what you need** Use renewable energy

Now you know about solving the problems

Topic 3 — Religion and prejudice

Definitions

The two key words for this topic are **prejudice** and **discrimination**. If you can learn what they mean, it will help with this whole topic. The two words are linked but their meaning is slightly different.

Prejudice means to pre-judge something or someone, usually without any real evidence to base that judgement on. In most cases it is negative. We use the word to describe a person's dislike of certain other people, when they have no good reason. We talk about prejudice against colour, religion, age, nationality, sexuality or appearance. Prejudice is about what we *think*.

Discrimination is when we put these prejudiced ideas into action. We treat people differently or say things because they are not the same as us or what we know – we make known to them our dislike and it can have a great effect on a person's life. In Britain it is against the law to discriminate against someone. However, discrimination can be used *positively*, especially for minority groups, and we will see some examples later on. Can you pick out the example of positive discrimination in the pictures opposite?

What do you need to know?

You need to learn the words above, and then investigate how it all happens. It's important to know: what causes people to act in this way or even think ideas like this in the first place; what effect these actions can have; different types of discrimination; what religion(s) think about these actions and how they respond when discrimination happens; what the law says about discrimination; and finally, what some famous individuals have done to prevent and fight discrimination.

In order to bring all the areas of discrimination together, it will be useful for you to keep four key ideas in your mind.

Tolerance – to accept that people have different opinions and beliefs from your own

Justice – everyone has the same rights and deserves the same treatment

Community – a collection of people who live and work together to help each other so that everyone benefits

Harmony – when the community accepts each member – including their differences

I'm not being funny, love, but I'm not having a woman doctor.

No point giving him a job – too old.

Let's look a little deeper

What makes someone prejudiced and want to discriminate against others?

It is true to say that everyone can be prejudiced at times, even by accident. Not everyone will discriminate against others though because of their prejudice. Which is the more serious – the thought or the action? It is an interesting question to think about (and one that is often examined!).

The barrier wall around Palestinian areas in Israel

Prejudice can be like a brick wall – a barrier that stops people living, working and learning together as a community. It is very unfair and it only takes someone to be 'different' to be singled out for discrimination. The victims are almost always in the minority and find discrimination very hard to deal with.

There are five main reasons for prejudice:

1 Experience – Having a bad experience with someone might make you think everybody is like that. For example, maybe when you were young you were frightened by a grumpy old man and now you think all old men are grumpy.
2 Upbringing – Having been told bad things about a certain group of people by your parents, you might be prejudiced without even getting a

chance to know any differently. Our upbringing has a big influence on us, and our parents' words have a huge effect.

3 The media – Having seen something on television or read it in a newspaper (or other forms of media) that was very biased (it focused on only one fact or idea, taking it out of context), you might have believed it and so now are prejudiced.
4 Ignorance – When you've gone ahead and judged someone when you actually know nothing about them. For example, having a negative opinion about a group of people, whom you have never met or actually learned anything about – you don't know them, but you insult them anyway.
5 Scapegoating – When you blame or use others as an excuse for a problem. For example, Hitler blamed the Jews for the economic problems in Germany. He used the media and speeches to influence the German people so much that they also blamed the Jews, which cleared the way for the Holocaust. In actual fact, the Jewish people in Germany had done nothing wrong.

The Basics

1 What is meant by 'prejudice' and 'discrimination'?
2 Explain how the three pictures at the bottom of page 24 are examples of discrimination.
3 Give an example of prejudice in action (i.e. discrimination).
4 Why is 'tolerance' important in helping to prevent prejudice?
5 Explain some reasons why some people might be prejudiced.
6 Choose three of these reasons and give an example to demonstrate each one. Choose different examples to the ones shown on page 24.
7 **You need to change the way people think to prevent discrimination.** What do you think? Explain your opinion.

✓ Now you know why prejudice might happen

Can we challenge these ideas?

Let's look at some commonly used discriminative statements from the variety of people below:

> I think women should stay at home, so when I get married I won't let my wife work.

Adam

> I think young people these days are all layabouts, so I won't have them working in my firm.

George

> I saw two men holding hands. It's unnatural, so I thumped one of them when they walked past.

Andrea

> Me and my mate nicked this guy's prayer hat 'cos religion is a joke.

Richie

> I think fashions like Goths are horrible and I tell them that when I see them all dressed in black.

Reeta

> I was in McDonald's the other day and this fat woman sat at my table so I got up and walked out.

Suki

Task 1

In pairs, for each of the examples shown in the illustrations, work out:
a   What type of prejudice is being shown.
b   What was done to show discrimination.
c   What you could say to challenge each of these people.

Task 2: Snowballing exercise

Students should be in groups of four or five. Each group needs a large sheet of paper or a writing board.

In your life you have probably experienced or seen discrimination happen or watched examples of it on television. In your group, choose an example of discrimination to focus on and write it in the centre of your sheet/board. The sheet/board should now be passed in turn to each group to add a statement to challenge the example or what it describes, such as saying why the action is wrong and what could be done to deal with the situation.

Each group is given a few minutes to add to the new sheet/board in front of them. It is often the case that we can learn from others and sometimes what someone else says/writes can spark ideas of our own.

Try it for another task and see for yourself!

Positive discrimination

After looking at all this negative stuff you must remember that discrimination can also be positive. In some cases, benefits can be given to people in minority groups to give them greater chances. For example, over the last ten years the police and fire services have actually advertised for people in minority groups to apply for jobs. This would give an advantage to people from ethnic minorities, women or gay/lesbian groups – people who are often the victims of discrimination. The reason behind this was to try and make these services more representative of British society as it is today. Of course, positive discrimination can help in challenging prejudice.

> Can you think of any other ways in which we can discriminate positively?

✓ **Now you know how discrimination can be challenged**

Types of prejudice

On the following pages you will see that the religious teachings in this area are general and can be applied to all forms of prejudice. *Only focus on the religion(s) that you are studying.* Think about how each teaching/religious idea can be applied to each of the forms of prejudice. Remember – *tolerance, justice, community* and *harmony*. As soon as someone acts on their prejudice, it becomes discrimination.

Ageism

Ageism is prejudice against someone because of their age. Remember it can apply to anyone in any age group.

When the law sets age limits (for example, an age to drive, smoke or drink), it is not seen as ageist. These limits are for our own good.

Let's look at the elderly first. We might expect them not to be fit enough for a job, or too old to understand modern ways. This leads them to be undervalued by society. With the young, it might be a case of thinking they're too young to take on some kind of responsibility.

All religions believe in respecting the elderly – they teach that everyone is equal. Older people are wiser, therefore they should be listened to. It is a duty of the young to look after them. The young are the future and quite often children become 'adults' in their own religion at an early age. Old or young, the value of the individual is very important.

Sexism

Sexism is prejudice because of someone's gender. We often see examples of it as prejudice against women. Many religions see men's and women's roles as different, but still equal. They do not agree with prejudice and discrimination against either gender – it is unfair and therefore wrong.

A woman serving in the army

There are a growing number of female teams in previously male-dominated sports like rugby

Religious teachings

 Buddhism

Buddhism believes that as discrimination leads to suffering it must be wrong and should be avoided.

- The belief not to harm others or use harmful language (Five Precepts)
- Everyone should try to develop *metta* (loving kindness).
- Everyone is equal because everyone is welcome in the Sangha.
- Prejudice creates bad karma and has a negative effect on rebirth.
- The Dalai Lama stated that the best way to live life was to 'Always think compassion'.

 Christianity

Christianity believes that all forms of discrimination are wrong.

- God created everyone equally. (Old Testament)
- 'There is neither Jew nor Gentile, slave or free man, male or female. We are all equal in Christ.' (New Testament)
- 'So in everything, do unto others what you would have done to you.' (New Testament)
- Jesus told us to love our neighbour. (Sermon on the Mount)
- In the Good Samaritan story the man is helped because of his need, not because of who he was or wasn't. (New Testament)

The role of women in religions

Within religion there is a debate about the role of women. They are treated differently to men and there is often the accusation that women are being discriminated against despite the fact that all religions condemn any kind of discrimination. Let's look at some examples:

- In Christianity, women cannot be priests in the Roman Catholic Church.
- In Islam, all religious leaders are men, and women don't pray at the front of the mosque.
- In Orthodox Judaism, women sit separately to men, often upstairs, and do not take part in synagogue services.
- With the exception of ISKCON, in Hinduism all Brahmin priests are male.
- In Theravada Buddhism, women pray to be reincarnated as a man.

If women are denied access to certain roles, then this could be said to be discriminatory. However, these religions would just say that roles are different but equal. If women are happy with their roles and what they are or are not permitted to do, then to them discrimination is not an issue. The issue arises when women want to do something as part of their religion but are not allowed to because rules or traditions say they can't.

As time moves on there are changes being made to traditions, but women have to fight hard for those changes. They would argue that if we are all creations of God, then if, for example, a woman wants to devote herself to the service of God and serve the community of believers, would God not want her to simply because she is a woman? Perhaps a woman could deal with community issues and help people in a different way to a man? Compassion and understanding are key qualities and many women have these.

It all depends on how you view this issue. It isn't the same as other forms of prejudice where people inflict hurt and pain on others. However, if you desperately want to do something or be part of something and cannot simply because you are a woman, then it could be really hurtful.

Women cannot become Roman Catholic priests

Most Hindu Brahmin are men

There are no female imams in Islam

The Basics

1 What is meant by the words 'ageism' and 'sexism'?
2 Explain religious teaching about sexism.
3 Give some examples of ageist behaviour.
4 **Women should be allowed to be leaders in religion.**
   Explain two reasons to agree, and two to disagree.

✓ **Now you know about ageism and sexism**

Disability

Ellie Simmonds OBE won two swimming golds at the 2008 Paralympics. At London 2012, she won two more and broke the world record for 400m freestyle. She is an inspiration to all and shows we all – able or disabled – have talents.

Quite often people who have a **disability** are discriminated against. A disability includes two key areas: physical disabilities such as wearing hearing aids, being in a wheelchair, not having a limb; and mental disabilities such as having a learning difficulty or a mental illness.

Could a person in a wheelchair access your school? How often do we talk to the person pushing the wheelchair not the person in it? Have you witnessed someone call a person names who is hearing or sight impaired? It is as if they are less of a person than someone fully able-bodied. Religion believes that all people are equal and God creates people in many different ways. We are all valued despite our differences. The example at the top of the page clearly shows that people overcome difficulties and can achieve at the highest possible level.

Looks and lifestyle

The way people look is often the first thing that incites prejudiced thoughts – the clothes people wear, hair style or colour, tall or short, fat or thin. On first meeting a stranger these things might be enough for us to instantly decide whether we like a person or not. For some, these first impressions stick and they don't give people a chance. This in turn leads to discriminatory comments or actions. We could think of Sophie Lancaster in Burnley who, in 2007, was murdered because she was a Goth (see **www.sophielancasterfoundation.com**). She chose to be different and this led to discrimination of the worst kind – she lost her life!

Likewise if people choose to live a different way to us or to what we accept to be 'normal' – such as people who live together (rather than marry), gay couples or travellers – then this often leads to discrimination. Religion would not agree with any discriminatory actions. The religion may not agree with the choices people make, particularly with regards to lifestyle, but it would totally disagree with showing discrimination in such cases.

The Basics

1 **Discrimination is the worst thing a person can suffer.** What do you think? Explain your opinion.
2 **Being discriminated against because of a disability is worse than through sexism.** Do you agree? Give reasons and explain your answer, showing you have thought about more than one point of view. Refer to religious arguments in your answer.

 ## Hinduism

Hindu dharma (teaching) is that Brahman is found in everything, therefore any prejudiced thoughts or discriminative actions would be viewed as wrong.

- Hindus believe in non-violence (ahimsa), love and respect for all things.
- Compassion is a key belief with the desire to improve things for others, not persecute them.
- Hurting others can lead to bad karma, which affects future reincarnations.
- Hindus believe that the true self is the **atman** and as everyone has one this must mean everyone is equal.
- The Bhagavad Gita suggests that to reach liberation you should work for the welfare of all fellow human beings.

 ## Islam

Islam teaches that Allah created everyone as equal but different.

- This was Allah's design, so discrimination is unjustified. (Qur'an)
- Allah loves the fair minded. (Qur'an)
- The Five Pillars (beliefs and actions) apply to all people equally.
- Muhammad (pbuh) allowed a black African man to do the call to prayer in Madinah and he welcomed anyone regardless of wealth, status or creed.
- The Muslim Declaration of Human Rights states that everyone is equal.
- On Hajj (the greatest Muslim gathering on earth), everyone is equal in dress and action.

 Now you know why prejudice might happen

Racism

Racism is the belief that the colour of a person's skin, or their race, affects their ability. It is also the belief that some races are better than others. We use the word 'racist' to describe someone who discriminates against people of other races in a negative way. The slave trade was based on the belief that people of colour were somehow of less value than other people, and so could be bought and sold and treated in any way with no rights at all. It cost the lives of countless tens of thousands, and destroyed many communities. The attitude of superiority it created still exists in the world today. Look at the statistics in the UK – if you are black, you are more likely to get excluded from school, to achieve less highly than others, to get stopped by the police, to get sent to prison, to be murdered – it goes on. Our society needs to change, and racism needs to end.

Racism is illegal (see the Race Relations Act details on page 33). Most people think racism is wrong. Why should a person's skin colour or race make a difference? It shouldn't. If you are actively racist, you can pay a heavy price. You could lose your job, get thrown out of school, go to prison …

'All human beings are born free and equal … should act in a spirit of brotherhood … everyone is entitled to all the rights and freedom.' (Universal Declaration of Human Rights)

Religious prejudice

Many people today face prejudice because of their religion. This has happened throughout history because religions mark people out. Often religious people wear symbols of their religion, which makes them easy to spot. They have beliefs that shape their behaviour. When these religions are a minority in a community they stand out, therefore becoming a target for discrimination. Think, for example, of the Muslim community in non-Muslim countries after 9/11.

At the same time, religious communities can be guilty of discrimination against other minority religious groups in their own countries. In recent times, in Syria, Iraq, Thailand and the Central African Republic, religious groups have fought and killed other groups simply because they disagreed with their choice of religion.

Judaism

Judaism teaches that prejudice and discrimination are incompatible with Jewish Law. Over the years, Judaism has been the target of extreme discrimination, and therefore Jews have strong opinions on the issue.

- G-d created everyone equal. So prejudice is seen as an insult to G-d.
- The Torah tells Jews to welcome and not persecute strangers.
- The Nevi'im states that G-d expects people to practise justice, love and kindness to all.
- Treat others as you wish to be treated. (Torah)
- Jewish leaders state that Jews should live in harmony with non-Jews.

Sikhism

Sikhism believes in the principle of justice and to fight for justice where it does not exist. Equality and sewa (service to others) would clearly indicate that discrimination is wrong.

- Using the same mud, the Creator has created many shapes in many ways. (Guru Granth Sahib)
- Those who love God love everyone. (Adi Granth)
- God created everyone so all are equal and deserve the same treatment and respect. (Mool Mantra)
- The use of the langar suggests everyone is welcome – Sikh or not.
- 'God is without caste.' (Guru Gobind Singh)

 Now you know about racism and religious prejudice

Homophobia

This is prejudice against people who are attracted to those of the same gender as themselves. Homosexual men and lesbians often face prejudice (called homophobia) and are discriminated against because people do not agree with their relationships. Victims of other kinds of discrimination often receive help from friends and family who sometimes face that same discrimination. However, the families of people who are lesbian or homosexual sometimes don't know about their family member's sexuality, or may be homophobic themselves. It can be very difficult, especially for young people who work out they may be gay and only have their families to turn to, or no one to turn to. Religions have differing opinions on the subject of homosexuality, but they do agree that discrimination against these people is wrong. Sometimes, straight people are victims of discrimination as a result of mistaken assumptions.

Ellen DeGeneres and Portia de Rossi

A gay couple on a Gay Pride march

Michael Sam

Ellen Page

Religious attitudes to homosexuality

The religious attitude to prejudice based on sexuality is slightly different from the attitude to the other forms of prejudice we have looked at so far. Religions accept without question someone's age, race or gender, for example; however, they usually don't agree with homosexuality. This means that even though they don't persecute homosexuals, they don't necessarily welcome them either. Some people think that sex between two men or two women is unnatural, and wrong. This is usually because it is impossible for this kind of sex to lead to children. From most religious viewpoints the primary reason for sex is the conception of children. It is also the case that in the holy books you can read quotes against homosexuality. In Britain now, things are changing; same sex couples can legally marry. This shows that marriage is open to everyone according to the law. It means that same-sex couples have all the same legal protections any other married couples have (for example, pension and inheritance rights). However, there is no compulsion for religions to carry out the marriage ceremonies.

The Basics

1 What is meant by 'racism'?
2 Using examples, explain 'religious prejudice'.
3 Explain what is meant by 'homophobia'.
4 What are religious attitudes to homosexuality?

✓ Now you know about homophobia

The effects of discrimination

Can you work out the emotions that these people are feeling due to having been discriminated against?

'When I joined my new school after moving house it was hard to fit in because everyone knew each other. They called me names or smirked at me because of my accent. This upset me a lot.'

'I'm determined to beat this – it's been the same all my life – everyone having a go at me just because I'm gay. I will not let it stop me doing what I want or getting the job I want.'

'I went for a job – I was by far the most qualified but my skin was obviously the wrong colour. I could have done the job with my eyes shut!'

The effects of discrimination

'I'm a Muslim – my family is the only Muslim one in this area. Since 9/11 I've lost a lot of friends. No one talks to me and they treat me with suspicion. I've no one – my religion is important to me but so are people. It's hard to exist on your own.'

'I have decided that they are not going to get the better of me – I choose to dress this way; I like it and if they don't – tough! I won't let them get to me. I am all the more determined to wear what I want.'

'I can't cope with this any more – day after day of bullying. There is this gang of girls who make my life a misery. I'm black and it's always about my colour – how I don't belong here and should go back to my own country. Sometimes it gets physical too. There is no other way out.'

These are all emotional effects from the individuals' perspective. When this multiplies to people in greater numbers and becomes the norm, then it can have a devastating effect on whole minority groups.

How can religion help the victims of discrimination?

Religion can provide both practical and spiritual support to victims of discrimination. A religious book may have teachings that, when read, offer comfort and support and put things into perspective. Religious leaders can offer help and just be there to listen. They can organise meetings to highlight the problems or set up support groups. They can use school assemblies to promote tolerance and harmony.

On a spiritual level, they can pray with you or for you and if belief is strong enough, this can make you feel that you are not on your own.

Have you noticed ...

... that the religion(s) you are studying often say they want to help with suffering in many kinds of situations? The ways to help are often similar. See if you can think of these ways and how they can apply to more than one situation. Less to revise, folks!

Task

In groups, decide on a group in society that faces prejudice and discrimination. You are going to set up an organisation to work for the rights of this chosen group. Complete the following:

1   Design a logo for your organisation.
2   Write a mission statement to explain what you are about.
3   Produce a one-page leaflet to hand out to people at a meeting or rally your organisation is holding in the town centre.
4   Write a short persuasive speech to be used at this meeting or rally explaining why this particular discrimination is wrong.

 Now you know about how religions try to fight prejudice

What the law says in Britain

Fawcett
working for women's rights since 1866

The Fawcett Society traces its roots back to 1866, when the suffragette Millicent Garrett Fawcett began her lifetime's work leading the peaceful campaign for women's votes. It is the UK's leading organisation campaigning for equality between men and women.

The Fawcett Society campaigns on women's representation in politics and public life; pay, pensions and poverty; valuing caring work and the treatment of women in the justice system. It also produces research and reports and uses the media to raise awareness of inequality issues.

Check it out for yourself at
www.fawcettsociety.org.uk

fare network

The Fare network is an organisation that spans Europe, using football as a common platform, to tackle racism and help bring about a positive change in and through sport.

Set up in 1999, the network brings together existing organisations, individuals, fans, grass root clubs and minority groups willing to counter discrimination and promote social inclusion. Several campaigns and events are held throughout the year as part of Fare's work. Professional footballers, football clubs and federations have lent their support to the Fare *Football People* weeks, the largest series of anti-discrimination activities in sport.

Fare has members in 34 countries. In England, Fare works closely with Kick It Out (**www.kickitout.org**).

Stonewall

Stonewall is a charity working for legal and social equality for lesbian, gay and bisexual people in Britain and overseas. It is involved in many different campaigns – including one that tackles homophobic language in education, called Education for All.

Check it out for yourself at
www.stonewall.org.uk

There are laws in Britain to deal with discrimination. As prejudice is about the way people think, the law cannot do anything, but when that prejudice turns into discriminative actions then the law can act. However, it is not always easy to prove that discrimination has taken place.

The 1976 Race Relations Act (RRA) made it illegal to discriminate against anyone because of race, nationality or ethnic or national background in four main areas – jobs, education, housing and the provision of services. It made illegal the use of threatening or abusive language in regard to race. It also made it illegal to publish anything to stir up racial hatred.

The Commission for Racial Equality was set up to deal with cases of discrimination, and to act as a watchdog against racism. In 2000 the RRA Amendment Act was introduced as a way of strengthening the 1976 Act. It focuses on helping and protecting people in the public sector, the police service, areas of government and areas of national security. It also stresses the need to promote harmony and tolerance amongst all people.

There have also been laws passed about Equal Pay (1975), Sex Discrimination (1975), Disability Discrimination (1995) and the Sexual Orientation Regulation (2007). The Equality Act (2010) brought all these together as a single Act, protecting victims of any type of discrimination.

As well as the law, there are organisations that support victims and try to improve awareness of the discrimination certain groups face.

Age UK is the UK's largest organisation working for and with older people. In England, it is made up of a federation of over 400 charities working together to promote the well-being of all older people.

Age UK's work ranges from providing vital local services to influencing public opinion and government. Every day the organisation is in touch with thousands of older people from all kinds of backgrounds – enabling them to make more of life.

Check it out for yourself at **www.ageuk.org.uk**

Famous people – fighting to end prejudice and discrimination

Martin Luther King

Who was he?

Martin Luther King was born in the USA in 1929. As a black American, he soon became aware of the prejudice that black people faced simply because of their colour of skin. Black people were *segregated* – meaning they had separate schools, transport systems, shops, even churches. King was brought up in a Christian family and had a good education. He learned from his religion that colour shouldn't matter and his thinking was influenced by the Indian leader Mahatma Gandhi who fought for justice in a non-violent way. King is most famous for a speech he made beginning 'I have a dream ...'. The essence of this speech was his belief that everyone was equal and that people should be judged not by the colour of their skin but by the content of their character. While he had great support, he also had enemies. In 1968 he was murdered. His death had great significance and indeed sparked even more people to campaign for equal rights.

Martin Luther King

What did he do to fight racism?

This is often the focus of exam questions. The questions ask about the ways in which he protested, rather than just general information about his life.

In 1955, King organised a bus boycott to try to end segregation on the buses. It took a year to achieve but, in the end, blacks could sit next to whites rather than sitting only at the back or standing up for a fellow white passenger. In 1957, King continued to preach non-violent direct action involving marches, boycotts and sit-ins. He marched with school children in 1963 to demonstrate about the

The Civil Rights March on Washington, led by Martin Luther King

poor education and schools that black children had. He continued to make political speeches at rallies and even the US President seemed to support his ideas. His fame spread worldwide. Things were starting to change – King said 'When I die my work will only just be beginning'.

What was his legacy?

The years since King's death in 1968 have seen great change in the USA. Life is much improved for the black community. Segregation is illegal. Black people have equal civil rights with whites. However, things are not perfect and there is still a lot of poverty in many mainly black areas. America has seen the emergence of black political leaders, most notably Jesse Jackson in the 1970s and Barack Obama, who was elected as President of the USA in November 2008, and re-elected in 2012. At the time of Martin Luther King's death, the idea of a black person running what is often considered to be the most powerful country in the world would have been unthinkable. Now King's dream has been realised.

Martin Luther King Day is a national holiday in the USA around 20 January each year.

Barack Obama

Archbishop Desmond Tutu

Who is he?

As his title tells you, Desmond Tutu is a religious leader. He was born in 1931 in South Africa, a country where people lived under the Government Apartheid system. This was the total separation of the black and white communities, with the minority whites in complete control of the country. As he moved up the religious hierarchy, Desmond Tutu began to use his position to campaign against the way the black community was treated. This was potentially very dangerous because Apartheid was a government policy and if you criticised it, you faced torture and imprisonment. By 1976 he was already a bishop, and perhaps that gave him some sort of protection. He was known worldwide, and South Africa would have attracted lots of unwelcome and unfriendly attention if its government had done anything to him. In 1984 he was awarded the Nobel Peace Prize for his work. In 1986 he became Archbishop of Cape Town. He still works both within his religion and politically even today in his old age.

Archbishop Desmond Tutu receiving the Nobel Peace Prize

What did he do?

His vision was for a totally non-racial South Africa where everyone mattered because they were all humans made in the image of God. He organised a non-violent struggle using marches, boycotts and petitions, and invited the international media into South Africa to show to the world what his people were suffering. This gave the issue worldwide attention and brought international pressure on the South African white government to alter the Apartheid Laws.

An anti-Apartheid rally

What has he achieved so far?

Things have changed in South Africa. The Apartheid system was dismantled, elections were held which resulted in a black president: Nelson Mandela. Currently South Africa has a black leader. Tutu still speaks out for the rights of the poorest groups and in his book, *Voice of One Crying in the Wilderness*, he calls for action to bring social justice to South Africa, and to other African countries. For the black majority, there are still massive improvements in standards of living to be made.

See **www.tutu.org** for more information.

A shanty town in South Africa

Task

Focus on both Martin Luther King and Desmond Tutu. Make a revision list of four facts about each of their lives, four things they did to achieve their goals and two ideas for each to say what they achieved. This will give you more than enough detail for your exam if you are asked to talk about someone famous who has fought against prejudice. It might be a surprise to you to find out how little you need to learn! Usually questions about individuals are worth 3–4 marks and, as such, this is enough detail for you to learn.

Mohandas K. Gandhi

Who was he?

Gandhi is known by the name 'Mahatma', which means great soul. He was born in India in 1869 when India was part of the British Empire, and led the Indian nationalist movement against British rule. His belief in non-violent protest to achieve his aims has influenced many other leaders around the world. He studied as a barrister, and in 1893 went to work in South Africa, where he worked to gain Indian migrants basic rights. They were discriminated against, but in 1914 the South African government accepted many of his demands for the Indian people, thanks, at least partly, to his work.

Mahatma Gandhi

On his return to India, Gandhi got involved in protests against British rule. He carried out peaceful non-cooperation with the British including boycotts and marches. In 1930 he led a Salt Tax March because it was illegal for Indians to produce their own salt. He even went on hunger strike. He also focused his attention on the growing unrest between the Hindu and Muslim communities, trying to improve relations between the two sides. While much of his work was not directly to do with prejudice, what he wanted was an integrated society where everyone lived in harmony. He felt the structure of society would have to change if people were to have a better chance in life. He saw British policy as unfair on the Indian people. Although he was a Hindu, he didn't like the caste system. The lowest caste was known as 'the untouchables', yet Gandhi saw them as 'children of God' just like the rest of the human race. He fought to change attitudes to these people.

Gandhi making a speech

In 1947 British rule ended and India was split up (partitioned) along religious lines and the states of Pakistan and Bangladesh were created. Mass violence was one of the results. Gandhi had objected to Partition, saying it would be disastrous. In 1948 he was assassinated.

Why was he such an important figure?

Gandhi left a great legacy of non-violence – his values and methods were taken up in many other struggles. He famously said 'An eye for an eye … and soon we shall all be blind' to show that violence was not the answer. Likewise, Desmond Tutu said 'You cannot use methods that our enemies will use against us.' Martin Luther King said 'You should meet hate with love.' All three men share the same values of peace and compassion – Tutu and King gaining their inspiration from Gandhi.

The Basics

1 Choose one of the famous individuals from pages 34–36, and describe the work they did to fight prejudice.
2 For the same person, explain why he fought prejudice.
3 **Without Gandhi, violence would always have been the main method of protest.** What do you think? Explain your answer.

Research Task

Visit **www.bbc.co.uk/religion** to find out more details about these people. You could create a presentation about them for others to learn from.

Religion and early life

This topic is essentially about the issue of **abortion**. Some women have abortions. They are operations/procedures to end pregnancy, and the intention is that the foetus does not live to be born. The topic wants you to look more deeply into this subject. It wants you to consider when life begins; the idea of the **miracle of life**; what the law says; why some women request abortions; whose **rights** are the most important in the decision to abort; the arguments used by **Pro-Choice** and **Pro-Life** campaigners; and, of course, what the religion(s) think.

The question of when life begins is key because many people see abortion as murder or killing, and there has to be a life before there can be a murder. It does affect whether or not we see an abortion as wrong.

By law, the life begins when the baby is born. The **Abortion Act** will not allow abortions beyond 24 weeks, so is that when life begins? (Less than 5 per cent of babies born in weeks 22 and 23 survive, even with the help of extended intensive care, and many of those go on to have many health problems at least in early life.) Many people think that when the foetus looks like a baby, it should be treated as such – whether it is fully formed or not.

What we can say is that at every stage the foetus is a *potential life*.

Difficult question, then …

When exactly does life begin?

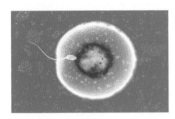

Is it at conception?

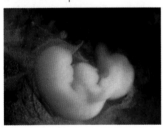

Is it when the foetus has a heart of its own, which beats?

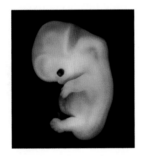

Is it when there is a backbone?

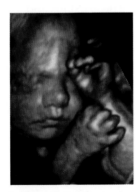

Is it when the foetus is likely to survive if born early (**viability**)?

Is it when it has been born?

The Basics

Write out the different points at which people say life begins. For each one, say whether or not you agree and explain why. Sum up by restating when you believe life begins.

Research Task

The Education for Choice organisation has a very good website that covers all the arguments about abortion and is designed to help young people, especially, make informed choices about their sexual health. Check it out, and use it to boost your notes while you work on this topic. See **www.efc.org.uk**

✓ **Now you have thought about when life begins**

About children

When a couple marry, almost inevitably at some point they think about having children. Religious people are no different from anyone else, and most will have children within their marriage.

> Why do you think people decide to have children?

You probably came up with several main reasons, such as, to show of their love for each other, to continue the family name, to fulfil a religious duty.

For most religions, having children is part of their religious duty. For Jews and Christians, a duty is to 'go forth and multiply' (Genesis), in other words to have children. Most religions see children as a gift from God, a blessing on the marriage. It is as if God has shown his approval of their union by giving them the gift of a child.

So, if this is the case – and even non-religious people can agree with many of those reasons for having a child – why do some women still feel they have to have an abortion? In effect, they are rejecting God's gift (if that is how they see it) or destroying a symbol of their love and relationship, and certainly killing. There must be some very good reasons for their decisions. It is true that most women who have abortions feel very bad about the decision they made, and suffer mentally because of it for a long time. Some never get over it. However, they all feel this was their only option, albeit a bad option. Abortion is seen as a *necessary evil*.

Before we look at some situations and you decide what people should do, let's see what the law says.

The law and abortion

The law defines abortion as 'the deliberate expulsion of a foetus from the womb, with the intention of destroying it'. It is different from a miscarriage, which has the same result (that the pregnancy ends without a baby living), because miscarriage is accidental, a turn of nature.

The law in the UK (excluding Northern Ireland) begins by stating that abortion is illegal. It then goes on to say that there are some exceptions.

Abortion can only be carried out if two registered doctors agree that at least one of the following is true:

♦ There is a danger to the woman's mental and/or physical health.
♦ The foetus will be born with serious physical and/or mental disabilities.
♦ The mental and/or physical health of existing children will be put at risk.

The abortion has to be carried out at a registered place, by a registered doctor before the 24th week of pregnancy.

A registered doctor is a doctor who has passed medical exams and is recognised by the Medical Council. So a doctor who has been struck off the official list can neither give advice, nor carry out an abortion. A registered place is a hospital or clinic that has registration with the government, and can perform such medical procedures as abortion because of that registration. Any other place is not legal.

Breaking the law carries great penalties for all those involved.

Some scenarios – what do you think?

Before you look through these scenarios, there are some rules. You can't just agree or disagree with any case, you have to explain *why* you agree or disagree. Also, you have to say what the consequences of each woman not having an abortion are because they are all asking for the abortion, even if they don't feel good about having to do that. Finally, you have to say whether you think they had another reasonable option – and why.

I know you hate having to explain your thinking! Sorry, folks, quality answers are always well explained and thought out. So let's get some practice in …

The Basics

1 What do we mean when we say a child is a 'blessing' on a marriage?
2 If children are so special, why do some women seek an abortion?
3 Copy and complete this paragraph:

An _____ is the deliberate ending of a _____, so that the foetus is destroyed. The law in the UK makes abortion _____. There are some exceptions though. Two _____ have to agree that one of these conditions is true – the _____ or _____ health of the woman is at risk; the foetus will be born with _____; and that existing children will suffer because of another baby. The abortion has to take place in a _____ place, before the _____ week of the pregnancy.

4 Explain three situations in which some people would agree with an abortion.
5 Explain your attitude to abortion, using examples to back up what you say.

Task

It is very easy to think that a religious person would automatically view abortion as wrong. Check out **www.rcrc.org** for alternative religious views.

I am a carrier of a genetic disease. My baby is at great risk of being born with that disease – the doctors have done tests, and are sure of it. If it is born, my baby will suffer greatly.

Rita

I am fourteen, and pregnant. I am too young to cope with this.

Susan

I was raped. This terrible act has left me pregnant.

Leesa

My doctors diagnosed me with cancer. They also found that I am pregnant. The doctors told me that I need the treatment if I want to live – it will be too late for me if I wait until my baby is born.

Isma

I am 46. The foetus has been diagnosed with Down's Syndrome.

Jane

I am single, and have no wish to have children, ever. I am pregnant because the contraception I was so careful to use failed. This pregnancy is neither planned nor wanted.

Tamsin

Now you have learned about the law and why some women choose to have abortions

The Pro-Life argument

Pro-Life is the term we use for those arguments that disagree with abortion – usually in any circumstances. Pro-Life **pressure groups** include ProLife, and SPUC. Since they support the foetus' right to life, their arguments are all in favour of protecting the foetus to ensure it is born.

> Read these comments and pick out the Pro-Life argument in each one.

I believe that all life is sacred, and must be protected. So, abortion is completely wrong.

God has created life and, as stewards of this world, humans have to protect life.

Abortion is the murder of another human being. Murder is wrong.

The foetus can't defend itself – so someone else has to.

When a foetus will be born with disabilities, we cannot say what the quality of its life would be, so should not decide to forbid it that life.

The foetus has a right to life, and not to be discarded as if it is just waste.

That babies are born through such difficult conditions proves the miracle of life. We cannot abandon or destroy this.

Some Pro-Life reasoning

What if Beethoven's mother had decided to have an abortion? Beethoven was deaf (and the law in the UK today allows abortion for foetuses with a disability). We would not have any of his amazing and beautiful music.

What if Einstein's mother had decided to have an abortion? What if Sir Alex Ferguson's mother had?

Any potential life could have grown up to make the same or greater contribution to the world as any of those. We should not deny that life its chance.

Task

Design a leaflet that gives the Pro-Life side of this issue. Make sure it has a clear title, and is attractive to read.
Research a pressure group that is Pro-Life – design an information sheet about that organisation.

This organisation was set up to 'secure the right to life of all human beings'. It covers all aspects of the 'right to life' argument, including embryo research, euthanasia and abortion. The Alliance believes it can do this by educating people that life should always be respected. It argues that the right to life is the most important and basic of all the rights humans have.

The ProLife Alliance started in 1996 as a registered political party and contested two general elections. It has since deregistered but continues to work primarily in the political arena, lobbying parliament and at grass roots level. A strong area of its work against abortion focuses on the media and public education. It believes that people need to know more about the reality of abortion, and the other options that are available. Its website is **www.prolife.org.uk**

✓ **Now you have thought about the Pro-Life arguments**

The Pro-Choice argument

Pro-Choice is the term we use for the arguments that defend a woman's right to choose what happens. It is usually associated with supporting the use of abortion, but it is actually about the woman and her right to decide what happens to her body. Since they support the woman's right to choose, the arguments are about the woman, rather than the foetus.

> Read these comments and pick out the Pro-Choice argument in each one.

A woman should have the right to decide what happens to her body.

Where a woman is pregnant as a result of rape or incest, it would be wrong not to allow her an abortion.

Some foetuses are so damaged that it would be cruel to allow them to be born.

If having a child is going to put a woman's life at risk, then she should have the right to an abortion.

Up to a certain point, the foetus cannot survive outside the womb, so shouldn't be thought of as a life in its own right.

If we banned abortions, women would still have them but not in a safe way. We need to protect women.

Abortion Rights is the national Pro-Choice campaign working to protect and extend women's right to choose abortion. Abortion Rights believes that the woman herself is best able to decide whether or not to continue with a pregnancy and that women need to have the option of accessing a safe and legal abortion if that is what they decide to do. Abortion Rights campaigns against restriction in the law on abortion, and for the provision of easily accessible, woman-friendly and NHS-funded abortion services. Nationally and through the work of members and thousands of supporters, it campaigns through petitions, publications, public meetings and political lobbying. Much of its work is aimed at making sure the law works, for example, stopping doctors from blocking abortion requests.

Abortion Rights was formed in 2003 from the merger of the National Abortion Campaign and the Abortion Law Reform Association. Its website is **www.abortionrights.org.uk**

Some Pro-Choice reasoning

Imagine you woke up one day to find yourself tied onto a bed in a hospital room. When you look around, you realise there are tubes attaching you to an unconscious person in the next bed. You demand to know what is going on. The doctor explains that you are the only person who can help that person to live, but they have to be linked to you for nine months, sharing your blood and taking nourishment from you. Would you be happy? Is that fair?

This can be likened to being forced to continue with an unwanted pregnancy. Surely, if you disagree with the hospital example, you have to accept women should be able to have abortions if they want them?

Task

Design a leaflet that gives the Pro-Choice side of this issue. Make sure it has a clear title and is attractive to read.
Research a pressure group which is Pro-Choice – design an information sheet about that organisation.

✓ **Now you have thought about the Pro-Choice arguments**

Religious attitudes to abortion

 ## Buddhism

Buddhist texts do not mention abortion. Most Buddhists would not favour abortion as it is seen as taking a life.

Buddhism tells us:

- Life is special and to be protected.
- The First Precept guides us to help others, not harm them, and to reduce suffering.
- Life begins at conception.
- Buddhists should show compassion (loving kindness) and practise ahimsa (non-violence).
- The main factor in the right or wrong of anything is intention.

The first and most important Precept is to not take life. Since Buddhists believe life begins at conception, abortion is killing. Those involved would have created much bad karma, based on their intentions. Abortion does not happen by accident, so the intention breaks the Precept.

Since a person's life is decided by their karma from past lives, it may be that the suffering a life will endure is necessary for their future. By carrying out abortion, we take away the foetus' chance of paying back bad karma.

All Buddhists should show compassion, including to the unborn, and practise ahimsa. Abortion is an act of violence and often doesn't give the foetus any rights, let alone compassion, and so goes against both values.

Having said that, Buddhists do recognise that at times an abortion can lead to less suffering than if the pregnancy went full term, and so accept it in those circumstances.

 ## Christianity

Many Christians believe abortion to be morally wrong. Some accept it rarely, calling it a necessary evil.

The Bible tells us:

- Life is sacred.
- All humans were made in the image of God.
- God gives and takes life.
- It is wrong to kill.
- God has planned for the life of every single one of us.

These beliefs make Christians say that abortion is usually wrong. It means killing something sacred, which God has created. Only God has that right and, by allowing abortions, we take that right out of the hands of God.

The Roman Catholic Church is completely against abortion. The *Didache* says 'Do not kill your children by abortion.' In *Vatican II*, it says 'Life must be protected with the utmost care from the moment of conception.'

However, where a woman needs urgent medical treatment, which will also mean the death of the foetus, the Church accepts the treatment. This isn't considered to be abortion.

The Protestant churches accept abortion as a *necessary evil* in some cases. For example, many would accept it for a woman who becomes pregnant after rape. However, they stress that great thought has to have been given, and the abortion has to be the absolute last resort.

Have you noticed ...

... in class discussions, abortion is one of those topics about which people have lots to say? It is a heated subject that attracts strong opinions. Make sure you have a balanced knowledge of all arguments, focusing on the specific area you are asked about. Don't just go on and on about abortion in general.

For each of the statements at the bottom of pages 43 and 44, try to come up with reasons to agree and disagree, including religious reasons. Remember the focus is the statement – it is *never* to argue whether abortion is right or wrong. Focus on the words in italics.

ॐ Hinduism

Most Hindus believe that abortion is wrong. However, in India it does happen as Hindus wish to have a male child for religious and cultural reasons, and poverty makes it difficult to manage big families. This situation is slowly changing.

Hindu scriptures tell us:

- Life is sacred and special, so must be respected.
- Those who carry out abortions are among the worst of sinners.
- All Hindus should practise ahimsa (non-violence).
- A woman who aborts her child loses her caste.
- Abortion is as bad as killing a priest, or your own parents.

Obviously, Hinduism therefore teaches that abortion is wrong. Hinduism says that the foetus is a living, conscious person, who needs to be protected. Protection is a result of ahimsa and respect. Since we all go through many lifetimes, each time creating karma for the next, when we abort a foetus we prevent that soul from working through a lifetime. This means we block that soul's progress towards union with the Ultimate Reality. It also means we make bad karma for ourselves. Some Hindu scriptures say that those who abort their children will themselves be aborted many times.

Hinduism allows abortion to save the life of the mother, as she does not need the support a motherless child would need.

The *rights* of the foetus are the most important.

☪ Islam

Most Muslims believe abortion is wrong. Shari'ah (Muslim) law does allow abortion, but it is still seen as morally wrong. It is a necessary evil.

The Qur'an and Hadith tell us:

- Life is sacred.
- Allah has planned the life of each of us.
- We are all created individually from a clot of blood and known by Allah.
- It is wrong to kill.
- God decides the time of our birth and our death.

These beliefs make Muslims say that abortion is wrong. Abortion means killing something that Allah has created, which is special. We destroy Allah's plans for the foetus, and take away Allah's right to decide the time of our death. This is disrespectful.

Muslims dispute when the soul becomes a part of the foetus. Some say at conception; some at 40 days; some at 120 days. For some, this creates a period of time when abortion may be allowed, because the foetus is still just blood and cells.

Most Muslims accept that some abortions are necessary. The most common example would be if the woman's life were at risk by or during the pregnancy. The woman's life in this case would be seen as more important to save (because of her existing family and her responsibilities to them).

Abortion is *murder*.

Judaism

Most Jews would accept therapeutic abortion (for medical reasons), but not abortion simply to remove an unwanted foetus.

Jewish scriptures and law tell us:

• Foetal life, as all life, is special.
• The foetus is 'mere water' until the fortieth day of pregnancy.
• We gain full human status only when we have been born.
• Abortion, under Jewish law, is not murder.
• The emphasis in Judaism is on life and new life, not destruction of life.

Judaism sees a need for abortion, but does not agree with abortion for just any reason. Where a woman's life is in danger, even during childbirth, her life takes priority over the foetus, and an abortion can be carried out. Some rabbis have extended the idea of endangerment to include the woman's mental health, for example in the case of rape.

The Talmud points out that the foetus is a part of the woman, not a human in its own right. Assault on her carries a severe punishment, whereas the loss of her unborn child due to that assault results in compensation only. Many rabbis now approve of abortion in cases where there is likely to be severe deformity of the foetus, for example when the mother has had rubella.

Jews are quick to point out that abortion is not acceptable, unless for therapeutic reasons. However, exactly what counts as a therapeutic reason varies depending on Orthodox, Conservative, Liberal and Reform views.

 ## Sikhism

Sikhism generally does not agree with abortion. It is seen as interference with God's creation.

Sikh teachings and scriptures tell us:

• Life begins at conception.
• All life is special and should be respected.
• Sikhs should not harm others.
• God fills us with light so that we can be born.
• God created each of us, and gave us life; God will also take that life away.

For Sikhs, there is no direct teaching about abortion. Like most things, it is up to the individual to make their own decisions, guided by God. However, abortion is believed to be morally wrong because life begins at conception and not at birth. In effect, abortion is a form of murder, since the intention to destroy life is there.

Sikhs try to live their life in worship of God, whereas abortion can be seen as going against God, the destruction of God's creation, so the opposite of that ideal for life.

When a Sikh becomes a member of the Khalsa, she or he takes vows. These include to never harm others and to do sewa (service to others). Abortion can be seen as going against both of these ideals.

Any woman who *wants* an abortion should be allowed one.

The *quality of a person's life* is more important than just being alive.

The quality of life argument

Quality of life means what someone's life is like. We try to judge whether that life is worth living because of its quality. For example, if a person is quadriplegic and in constant, extreme pain – is their life worth living? This argument is used to support abortion. It claims that if the quality of life a child would have if born is unacceptably low, it would be cruel to allow that child to be born in that condition.

Disability

In 2012, only 2692 from the 185,000+ abortions performed were for reasons of disability of the foetus – the quality of life argument. This is not a common reason for an abortion. However, the fact that it is used means that we have to think about it – there could be a question with this as its focus, and you need to be ready.

> Have a look at these situations. In each case, the woman could seek an abortion, and the law would support her. Which ones would you agree with?

1 Cheryl has been told that scans reveal her baby has not formed properly, and will be extremely badly disabled both mentally and physically if it survives the pregnancy and is born.

2 Sasha has been told her baby will be born with a severe disability because she had an illness in the early pregnancy that is known to affect the foetus.

3 Preeti has been told that her child has Down's Syndrome.

4 Cara has been told that her child's organs have not developed properly, and her child will need many operations to try to help improve the quality of its life once born. It will never have a 'normal' life.

5 Izzie has been told that her child has a cleft lip and palate.

> Imagine each woman carries on with the pregnancy and gives birth. Think about the extra points and see if you would have changed your mind if you knew them in advance.

1 Cheryl's baby will never be able to look after itself. He had to stay in intensive care for over a year after being born, and had many operations. He has to be looked after 24/7, which has made it very difficult for Cheryl and her husband with their other child, Billy, who is four.

2 Sasha's baby was born blind and deaf. She also has quite serious brain damage. She needs a lot of care, and always will. Sasha's marriage broke up because of the stress, and so Sasha has to look after her daughter alone.

3 Preeti's son is a very happy little boy, in spite of his disabilities. He went to an ordinary primary school, when he was ready for it.

4 Cara's daughter lived only six months after she was born, in spite of intensive care and several operations. Cara only got to hold her when she was dying.

5 Izzie's little boy had a series of operations to correct his cleft lip and palate. The other children at school haven't all been so nice to him though because of his scar.

> Did this extra information change anything? Does it make a difference what gender the child is? Does it make a difference if the child is likely to suffer greatly or die anyway? Do you think any of the women would choose to have an abortion if they thought their child could have a good quality of life? Whose quality of life is this about – the mother's, the child's or both?

The Basics

1 What do we mean by 'quality of life'?
2 Give two situations in which a woman might seek an abortion on quality of life grounds. Explain how these situations are about quality of life.
3 **Poor quality of life is not a good reason for abortion.** Do you agree? Give reasons and explain your answer, showing you have thought about more than one point of view.

 Now you know about the quality of life argument

Whose right is it anyway?

This is a very difficult question to answer.

It is perfect for an 'it depends …' answer – because it really does. It depends on the circumstances of the woman (alone, in a loving relationship …?), and it depends on the circumstances of the pregnancy (life or death situation, age …?). Ultimately, the decision has to lie with the mother – it is her body, she has to have the treatment, and she is the only one who truly knows how she feels.

Having said that, there are many people who feel that they should have a say in the choices to be made.

> Who do you think might possibly want to have a say in this decision? Look at the people in this picture. What do you think? Morally, should they have a say in this ultimate decision? Or is there another reason they should have a say?

What if … the man is her boyfriend?

What if … the girl is under sixteen?

What if … this was from a one-night stand?

What if … the woman's life is in danger because of the pregnancy?

What if … the woman has serious mental health problems?

What if … she is very religious?

The point of those 'what ifs' is to make you see that there is often more to a decision than a simple choice of two options. They probably made you argue a lot, and come up with even more 'what ifs'.

The more you think about it, the more complicated this becomes – until finally you might have to agree that it has to be the woman's decision ultimately.

Task

Now try these evaluative statements as a snowballing exercise (see page 26 if you haven't done one of these before). When you get your page back, you'll see a whole class-worth of ideas, with development and even examples. There are several statements so that your class can tackle different ones. You have to collect comments that agree and disagree.

- **Religions should have no say in the matter of abortion.**
- **The father should always be consulted about abortion.**
- **Medical opinion should override all other concerns about abortion.**

✓ **Now you have thought about whose decision abortion should be**

Alternatives to abortion

The whole of this topic has been about 'abortion or not'. For the exam, you might get asked about an alternative – is there another option?

This table will help to guide you through the alternatives, and suggests some pros and cons (there will be many more). Remember, though, women who have abortions tend to see no other acceptable alternative to the decision they have made, and most often they have thought about these options.

Keep it	Choose to risk own health/life	Have it 'fostered'	Have it adopted
In this option, you decide to have the baby and keep it, bringing it up yourself.	In this option, you continue the pregnancy, to the detriment of your health, even your death. The baby may or may not be born. An example would be a woman delaying cancer treatment until after the birth, by which time the treatment cannot work.	In this option, you have the baby, but then someone else looks after it – this might be for just a while. An example might be a schoolgirl, whose parents look after the baby until she is old enough or able to. The baby is not legally anyone else's.	In this option, you have the baby, and then give it up for **adoption**. Someone else becomes its legal parent. You lose all contact, unless the baby later wants to find its biological parents.
PROS Child is born, and has a life with its natural mother.	PROS Child might be born and live.	PROS Child is born, and eventually may have a life with mother.	PROS Child is born, and looked after in a loving other family.
CONS Reasons for wanting an abortion in the first place may have serious impact, such as can't love child properly, blame the child, might be unable to look after it properly.	CONS The child will have either no mother or a seriously incapacitated mother. Existing family more seriously affected.	CONS Self-esteem of child who has been given up. Confusing situation for all.	CONS Child may want to find biological parent later. Mother may find it much harder to give her baby up than she thought.

Task

Of course, without having actual examples it is very difficult to come up with what would be a valid alternative, and what the pros and cons would be. We are back to that individual circumstances thing again.

Have a look at pages 39 and 45. They are all abortion scenarios. Discuss with a partner the options on this page – are any of them better options than abortion in each case? What are the pros and cons for each? Discuss your answers as a class.

 Now you have thought about alternatives to abortion

Religion, war and peace

In this topic you need to understand the concepts of **war** and **peace**. You will also need to know the possible causes of war and examples of wars that have taken place. You will look at how modern warfare has changed and the terrible consequences for the victims of war. You will also investigate organisations that work for peace and alleviate the suffering caused by war. You will learn about religious attitudes to war including **Holy War**, **Just War** and attitudes to **pacifism**. You will also need to understand two key ideas that shape religious attitudes to war and peace – *justice* and *sanctity of life*.

I am a soldier and I believe in the sanctity of life.

Paul

I believe in the sanctity of life. I would never fight in a war.

Rami

The Basics

1 Match these words and phrases:

War	Making things fair again
Peace	Armed conflict between two or more sides
Pacifism	The idea that life is special, even sacred
Justice	People living in harmony with each other, not fighting
Sanctity of life	Belief that fighting is always wrong

2 Explain why you think Rami would not fight in a war.
3 Explain why you think Paul would fight in a war.
4 Who do you think is right? Try to give at least two reasons in your answer.

Definitions

War is armed conflict between two or more groups or nations. It involves the use of armies and weapons in a battle to achieve a goal, such as leadership of a country.

Peace is the opposite of war. It is people living in harmony with each other, and not trying to hurt each other. *Pacifists* do not believe in fighting a war under any circumstances.

Justice is fairness. It is where all people have equal rights and freedoms, and these are protected by laws made by legitimate governments. If someone goes against these rights and freedoms, then they are punished by the law, and things are made right again. A war might be fought to gain justice.

Sanctity of life is the idea that all life is valuable and special. It recognises that every human being has a right to life because we are all unique. Religious people believe that God creates all people and this makes human life sacred. A religious believer might refuse to fight because all life is sacred, or they might choose to fight to protect the lives of others.

Now you know about the key terms for this topic

A world at war

It is a sad fact that, despite our efforts to create peace and harmony, war is still very much a part of life on earth. Throughout the centuries, many thousands of wars have been fought for many different reasons. The Crusades were fought from the eleventh century for nearly 200 years by Christian soldiers who believed they were fighting for God to recapture the holy city of Jerusalem. Across the world, countries have fought each other for power, land and resources. Usually there is no simple, single reason for why a war might take place, but inevitably wars have led to misery and loss of life for millions of people throughout history.

Throughout the twentieth century, there have been many conflicts. The First World War (1914–18) and the Second World War (1939–45) saw European nations and their allies fighting for justice and freedom from invaders such as the Nazis. Many nations have fought wars of independence to gain freedom from former colonial occupation. Wars in Vietnam and Korea were waged by the USA who perceived a threat from communism. In Africa, many wars have been fought by rival groups wishing to take control of their country in the absence of legitimate government. Racial and religious differences have also led to **genocide** and **ethnic cleansing** becoming horrific features of modern wars.

In the modern world, most wars can be categorised as one of the following:

- Wars between nations – these are conflicts between rival countries or nations. For example: Gulf Wars I and II, India v Pakistan, and the wars mentioned above.
- Civil wars – these are conflicts between rival groups within a country. For example, Syria, Somalia and Sudan.
- The War on Terrorism – post-September 11 2001, the USA and its allies have declared war against extreme Islamic fundamentalists, resulting in the war in Afghanistan against the Taliban.

War in our times

About 231 million people have died in wars and conflict during the 20th and 21st centuries.

There were at least 32 armed conflicts going on in the world between and within countries in 2012.

75 per cent of all deaths in war are non-combatants.

Aid efforts, such as nutrition and education programmes, are wasted where there is war.

Visit **www.warsintheworld.com** to see how war is affecting the world today.

> Look at some of the reasons people have given for fighting or for not fighting in a war. Can you split them into the two categories? What other reasons can you add?

- For territory, to take back or gain new land
- In self-defence, when invaded, or under threat of invasion
- Life is sacred, it should never be taken.
- Wars are too expensive to fight.
- To defend a way of life – your own or other people's
- To change the leadership of a country – your own or another
- Wars lead to too much destruction.
- Many innocent lives are lost – 75 per cent of fatal casualties are not soldiers.
- As an allied force keeping an agreement with another country

The Basics

1 Describe three different types of war. Give an example of each.
2 Give two reasons, which you think are fair, for going to war. Write two sentences to explain each.
3 Give two reasons, which you think are not fair, for going to war. Write two sentences to explain each.
4 **War is always wrong.** What do you think? Explain your opinion.

✓ **Now you have thought about war in the world today**

Religious attitudes to war and peace

Buddhism

Buddhism is a religion of peace. Although Buddhist countries have armies, they exist for defence purposes, and as a secondary police force.

Buddhism teaches:

- The First Precept – to refrain from harming others; this is ahimsa, and is a core principle of Buddhism.
- The Noble Eightfold Path – making you consider others, as well as the consequences of all behaviour
- 'Hatred does not cease by hatred, hatred ceases by love.' (Dhammapada)
- 'He should not kill a living being, nor cause it to be killed, nor should he incite another to kill.' (Dhammapada)
- 'Peace can exist if everyone respects all others.' (Dalai Lama)

The message of Buddhism is one of peace, not war. Buddhists believe their actions have consequences for their future rebirths. It is wrong to harm others, yet soldiers must kill. Buddhists believe all peaceful means must be tried, because war can lead to greater problems than it solves. War is often the result of the Three Poisons (ignorance, hatred and desire), and war also encourages them, whereas Buddhism seeks to get rid of them.

The Dalai Lama is the spiritual leader of the Tibetans and his country was invaded by, and made part of, China. He believes the only resolution can be a peaceful one. He won the Nobel Peace Prize in 1992.

Christianity

The teachings of Christianity are peaceful. Jesus taught a message of love and some Christian groups have a strong pacifist tradition. However, many Christians accept that there are circumstances in which it is necessary to use armed conflict and will fight in a Just War. No Christian group would support the use of nuclear weapons.

Christianity teaches:

- 'Put away your sword. Those who live by the sword die by the sword.' (Jesus)
- 'Blessed are the peacemakers.' (Jesus – Sermon on the Mount)
- 'Love your enemies, and pray for them.' (Jesus – Sermon on the Mount)
- 'Peace I leave with you, my peace I give to you.' (Jesus)
- 'Everyone must commit themselves to peace.' (Pope John Paul II)

Christianity is a peaceful religion if we look at the teachings of both Jesus and St Paul. The Kingdom of Heaven is a place of peace and love, not violence and fighting. Most Christians throughout the centuries have believed in living in peace and harmony but are prepared to engage in war to help defend people, restore freedom and hopefully create a greater good, for example, going to war against Hitler in the Second World War.

Many Christians only agree with war in certain circumstances, for example, to repel an invading force. The Quaker Movement, however, is an example of a Christian pacifist group today. Its members will not fight in any war. Many Christians disagreed with the Iraq War (2003) because they felt the reasons for it were wrong, and that it led to many innocent people being killed. Where Christians accept war, it has to be the last resort after all peaceful efforts have failed.

Task

For the religion(s) that you are studying, use the information provided to create a booklet that explains the religious teachings about war and peace.

ॐ Hinduism

Hindus are split by caste (social division), one of which is *kshatriya* which means 'to protect from harm'. They are a warrior caste. Hindus believe in following dharma (duty), so for kshatriyas fighting is acceptable in Just Wars. However, Hinduism promotes ahimsa (non-violence) and tolerance as key virtues, which are against fighting.

Hinduism teaches:

- Kshatriyas (warrior caste) are expected to be the first to battle, and the bravest in battle; their main duty is to defend and protect others.
- Even an enemy must be offered appropriate hospitality if he comes to your home. (Mahabharata)
- Key Hindu virtues include ahimsa (non-violence), tolerance, compassion and respect, as well as protection of others.
- 'The pursuit of truth does not permit violence being inflicted on one's opponent.' (Ghandi)
- 'If you do not fight in this Just War, you will neglect your duty, harm your reputation and commit the sin of omission.' (Bhagavad Gita)

So, where a war is seen as just, in defence against an invading nation, for example, kshatriyas must follow their duty and fight. Not doing so would gain bad karma, and negatively affect future rebirths. Where it is necessary to protect others, fighting may be the only way, and so is acceptable.

However, Mahatma Ghandi stressed that justice can be achieved through non-violence. Since all life is sacred because Brahman is within all (the atman), war destroys this ideal.

☾★ Islam

One meaning of the word Islam is *peace*. Allah has 99 names known to Muslims. One of them is *As-salaam*, which means 'the source of peace'. It is said that if all people followed the Muslim way of life, there should only be peace. Muslims should work to keep the peace, and war should only occur when all peaceful means have been exhausted. Only then do Muslims have a duty to fight in the defence of Allah and the weak and oppressed.

Islam teaches:

- Greet others *salaam alaikum*, which means 'peace be upon you'.
- Greater jihad is every Muslim's personal struggle to follow Allah; the lesser jihad is Holy War in defence of Islam.
- To those against whom war is made, permission is given to fight. (Qur'an)
- Those who die in the name of Allah will be rewarded with paradise. (Qu'ran)
- Hate your enemy mildly; for he may become your friend one day. (Hadith)

When Muhammad (pbuh) was alive, the Muslims had to defend themselves by fighting. If they hadn't, they would all have been killed. Allah ordered Muslims to fight back when attacked, so Holy War became a duty for Muslims. The Muslim religion realises that sometimes to defend people's rights or to change a terrible situation, we have to fight.

In a disagreement with a nation, if talking fails to solve the problem, it becomes a duty to fight.

Jihad is a word used for Holy War, but there are two kinds of jihad – lesser and greater. The greater jihad is the struggle to always behave in a way that is acceptable to Allah – it isn't about war. Holy War is the lesser jihad.

Task

Working with a partner, write a discussion between two believers: one who will fight in a war and one who says it is wrong to fight. Remember they could both belong to the same religion or to different religions.

☰ Judaism

Judaism does not question the right to defend a just cause by war. The Talmud says that 'whoever sheds the blood of man, by man shall his blood be shed'. However, there are rules that exist for fighting war only as a last resort. It is forbidden to take delight in the war or its victory, and Jews believe that when the Messiah comes, all weapons will be destroyed and turned into peaceful tools. Peace remains the ideal.

Judaism teaches:

- The standard Jewish greeting is *shalom*, which means 'peace'.
- Get ready for war. Call out your best warriors. Let your fighting men advance for the attack. (Ketuvim)
- The sword comes to the world because of the delay of justice and through injustice. (Talmud)
- It shall come to pass … nation shall not lift up sword against nation, neither shall they learn war any more. (Nevi'im – about the future before G-d's kingdom is established)
- When siege is laid to a city, surround only three sides to give an opportunity for escape to those who would flee to save their lives. (Maimonides Code)

In earliest Judaism, war was a religious duty, and there are many descriptions of wars fought in the Bible. G-d is on the side of the righteous Israelite army, and they win. The Ark of the Covenant was taken into battle with them as a talisman. Today, war is still acceptable, but as a last resort, and only for just reasons, for example, self-defence or when the Jews or Israel are threatened.

There are rules about fighting wars, including that chances for escape and surrender must be given, that there is no scorched earth policy, and that civilians and prisoners are treated with dignity.

The ideal is peace, and justice is vital for peace.

☬ Sikhism

Sikhs have duties to fight for justice and to protect minorities. War should be a last resort, and should be fought in a just manner.

Sikhism teaches:

- The Sikh Khanda includes two swords, and Sikhs wear the kirpan (dagger) showing a willingness to fight when necessary.
- When all other methods have failed it is permissible to draw the sword. (Guru Gobind Singh)
- The Lord is the haven of peace. (Adi Granth)
- Peace is believed to come from God.

Several of the Sikh Gurus instructed Sikhs to do physical and military training. Guru Ram Das swapped prayer beads for two swords, showing a stance against oppression and injustice. Guru Tegh Bahadur led the Sikhs into battle for the right to religious freedom. Guru Gobind Singh organised the Sikhs into an effective army after setting up the Khalsa, whose members were prepared to give up their lives for their religion.

Sikhism does not look for wars to fight. Peace through justice is the ideal. However, there is an obligation to fight to get justice where necessary.

Some Sikhs are pacifists out of respect for the sanctity of life.

Task

Hold a class discussion about this statement:
Peace is an impossible dream.
Take a vote at the end of the debate. Which side won? What arguments were the most persuasive?

Fighting a war

Justice is a key idea when we talk about war. Many wars are fought to try to give justice. For example, one country may help another which has been attacked. In some countries, civil wars have occurred because the ruling government is corrupt. One problem with war is that it can lead to *injustice*, because people can get treated unfairly.

There are rules about fighting wars. Most countries have signed an agreement called the *Geneva Conventions* that outlines these rules. Having signed the agreement, armies are supposed to follow these rules when they fight. If they don't, they can be found guilty of committing war crimes. If people play by the same rules, then everything should be fairer, really.

Task

If you had to write a set of rules for war, what would they be? The bubbles on the right will help you think about rules covering all different aspects of war.

Don't forget – all sides in the war have to keep these rules. Think about how you want your soldiers and civilians to be treated.

Thinking about the treatment of prisoners

Civilians and soldiers are captured in war. How should they be treated? Do you treat civilians differently to soldiers? Why?

Look at the ways prisoners of war have been treated. Which do you think are acceptable and unacceptable? Can you give a reason for each decision?

- Use of torture for punishment
- Use of torture for information
- Use of hostage taking
- Mass execution
- Revenge punishment/ execution
- Discrimination by sex
- Discrimination by nationality and/or race
- Discrimination by religious or political beliefs
- Political indoctrination
- Use as a human shield
- Rape, maiming and pillage

- If you thought all of the treatments stated above were wrong, you already agree with the Geneva Conventions. Do you think it's a good idea to have rules about how prisoners of war are treated? Why?
- Look at your set of rules. Do your rules show *justice*? Do they show *sanctity of life*? Will they help deliver *peace*?
- Research some examples of the abuse of the Geneva Conventions in modern wars, for example, Bosnia, Iraq, Rwanda. Find out how war criminals are tried and dealt with.

Captured soldiers – what will you do with them? How will you treat them?

Hospitals in battle zones – will you allow them? Can they be attacked?

Wounded soldiers (captured or on the battlefield) – what will you do with them?

Battlefield – what counts as the battle zone?

Targets – what is it okay to shoot at or destroy?

Weapons – what types are okay to use?

Enemy civilians – can you target them? How will you treat them if you capture their town?

✓ **Now you know about fighting a war**

Holy War and Just War

We have seen that all religious traditions believe in peace not war. However, most also accept that there are times when it is necessary to go to war to avoid a greater evil. Within religious teachings there are contrasting views on war, and so religious believers must use their conscience in deciding whether or not they believe a war is morally justified.

There are three possible stances a religious believer may take:

- *Pacifist* – believing all war and killing is wrong
- *Holy War* – believing it is right to fight a war in the name of God
- *Just War* – believing it is right to fight a war in the interests of justice and the greater good

Within some religions there is clear guidance on war.

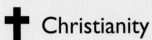 Christianity

> *Declare a Holy War, call the troops to arms. (Old Testament)*

Holy War

Within Christian history there was once a strong concept of Holy War. In the Old Testament there are many examples of wars fought in the name of God. The combatants believed that God was on their side and indeed had influence over the outcomes of battles. For example, Joshua's army was commanded to blow trumpets to bring down the walls of Jericho. The Crusades (1095–1291) were fought to capture control of the Holy Land. The Christian soldiers believed they were fighting for a sacred and noble cause. They believed that God was with them and the Muslim Turks they were fighting against were the pagan enemies of God.

Just War

St Paul said Christians should obey their rulers, who had been given power by God. When those rulers demanded Christians be soldiers, a compromise had to be found. St Augustine was the first to come up with a theory, which was eventually written in detail by St Thomas Aquinas, called the *Just War*. The message is clear – sometimes if you don't fight, you allow a greater evil to happen than a war would have caused, so you have to fight.

> *It is impossible to conceive of a Just War in a nuclear age. (Pope John XXIII)*

Christian Just War Rules

1 War must be started and controlled by a proper authority such as a government.

2 There must be a just cause for the war, it must not be aggression towards an enemy.

3 The war must have a clear aim to promote good and overcome evil.

4 War must be a last resort, every effort must have been made to resolve conflict peacefully.

5 The war must be winnable, it would be wrong to risk lives with no chance of success.

6 The war must be conducted fairly. Only reasonable force should be used and the risk to civilians minimised.

7 There must be a good outcome and peace restored.

The Basics

1 Explain the conditions of the 'Holy War' and those of 'Just War'.
2 Explain why you think some religious believers would fight in these kinds of wars.
3 **There can be no such thing as a Just War, because the innocent always suffer.**
  What do you think? Explain your opinion.

Islam and Holy War

For Muslims a Holy War is a Just War. There are rules for how Muslims should fight a war in the Qur'an, and these were written in more detail by one of the caliphs (rulers). A jihad may only be fought as a last resort and must never be against another Muslim nation.

> *Fight in the cause of Allah those who fight you, but do not transgress limits … if they cease let there be no hostility. (Qur'an)*

1 Who fights?
- Muslims have a duty to join the army and fight, if a just leader begins a war.
- Not all Muslims have to fight. Muhammad (pbuh) said one man from each two should fight, so that there are still men to defend and look after the towns and villages.
- Soldiers on the battlefield must fight – running away is wrong, because that makes it more difficult for other soldiers.
- If a town is attacked, everyone – men, women and children – has to fight back.

2 How is the war fought?
- It may only begin when the enemy attacks.
- Civilians must not be harmed, attacked or mistreated. Crops and holy buildings should be left alone.
- Prisoners of war should be treated well. Money collected for zakat can be used to pay for their food.

3 How does the war end?
- When people regain their rights.
- When the enemy calls for peace.

 # Sikhism and Just War

When Guru Gobind Singh formed the Khalsa, it was his intention to create an army of warrior saints committed to the cause of justice. Accepting the need for Sikhs to be prepared to fight, he outlined the teachings of a Just War. In Sikhism this is called *dharam yudh*, which means 'in defence of justice'.

> *His followers were to emerge as splendid warriors … having taken the baptism of the sword, would thence forward be firmly attached to the sword. (Guru Granth Sahib)*

The soldiers were to be *sant sipahi* – saint soldiers. As well as their training, they had an obligation to do *Nam Simran* and meditate daily. In other words, they had to practise their religion devotedly, as well as their military training and preparations. Guru Gobind Singh said: 'Without power, righteousness does not flourish, without dharma everything is crushed and ruined.'

✓ Now you know about religious war

55

War in the modern world

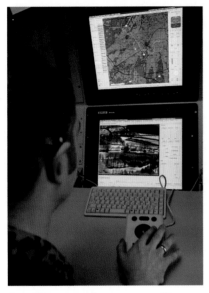

A soldier operating remote military equipment. Has war become a game?

Weapons of mass destruction

Weapons of mass destruction (WMDs) are a phenomenon of modern warfare capable of killing and maiming large numbers of people. They can cause massive destruction to both the natural landscape and man-made structures such as cities. It is almost impossible to target only military operations. WMDs are controlled from far away, either in the form of missiles or bombs dropped from planes. Whoever releases the weapon does not experience or see the effect of the weapon face to face. It is very different to soldiers on the battlefield. There are several types of WMD:

- Nuclear weapons – also known as atomic bombs, cause immediate destruction of all life and structures within their range. The radioactive 'fallout' has long-term effects.
- Biological warfare – also known as germ warfare, uses living, disease-causing bacteria or viruses such as anthrax, to cause death or serious illness.
- Chemical warfare – uses non-living toxins, such as nerve agents and mustard gas, to cause death, incapacity or illness.
- Radiological weapons – also known as 'dirty bombs', are weapons that use conventional explosives to create bombs that can disperse radioactive material. They kill people, and make the impact area useless because of contamination.

Religious attitudes

Nuclear weapons and other WMDs are unacceptable. No religion agrees with their use. They are seen as too extreme and uncontrollable. They do not fit with any Just or Holy War theories, or with ideas of moral behaviour in war.

Religious people believe in the sanctity of life, and so the effects of these weapons go completely against this belief. When the USA used a chemical weapon called Agent Orange in the Vietnam War, thousands of civilians died or were left permanently disfigured by its burning effects. The chemical has also infected the landscape and, more than 50 years on, people are still being affected with birth deformities, cancers and so on.

Religious people also believe that wars should be fought to gain justice for people. These weapons are considered unjust because they arbitrarily kill and maim civilians. During Saddam Hussein's reign in Iraq, his government ordered the use of nerve gas on the Kurds and the Shi'ah Muslims at Karbala. The weapons were being used as a tool of oppression to bring terror upon the people who opposed his rule.

Some religious believers accept the existence of nuclear weapons as a deterrent. They stop others attacking a country, but there is no intention to use them. In other words, they help to keep the peace. Most religious believers, however, think nuclear weapons are completely unacceptable. Even when not used, they cost huge sums of money, which could be better spent. Also, if the technology gets into the wrong hands, there is no guarantee they will not be used. The fact that they exist means they could be used, which is immoral.

> 'Though the monstrous power of modern weapons acts as a deterrent, it is feared that the mere continuance of nuclear tests, undertaken with war in mind, will have fatal consequences for life on earth … nuclear weapons should be banned.'
>
> Second Vatican Council

Nuclear war

The effects of the atomic bombs on Hiroshima and Nagasaki

A nuclear weapon has an immense destructive force coming from energy released by a nuclear reaction. On 6 August 1945 the Japanese city of Hiroshima was devastated by the American use of the first atomic bomb in warfare. Over 140,000 people died instantly. Three days later, Nagasaki was bombed. Since then, thousands of people have suffered illness and death from the after-effects of being exposed to radiation.

Today, many more countries have a 'nuclear capability' including Russia, the UK, China, France, Pakistan and India. The increase in the development and possession of such weapons is known as *nuclear proliferation.*

Nuclear disarmament

For the world to achieve a future without the fear of complete destruction, countries must give up their nuclear weapons. This is known as *nuclear disarmament* and is universally recognised as necessary for world peace. This could be achieved by *unilateral disarmament*, where one country gives up its weapons in the hope that others will follow. To date no country has done this, although others, like Japan, have adopted a non-nuclear stance and refused to join the arms race. The alternative is *multilateral disarmament*, which requires all nuclear powers to give up their weapons at the same time.

The case FOR a nuclear deterrent

- To discourage other countries from threatening attacks.
- Deterrents must work because nuclear weapons have not been used since 1945.
- Arms agreements can only be reached if the world powers have equal capabilities.
- The use of other WMDs is made less likely.

The case AGAINST a nuclear deterrent

- Nuclear proliferation makes the use of nuclear weapons more likely not less likely.
- Their use could never be morally justified.
- They cost the world billions, money which could be better spent on the needs of people.
- Other countries are encouraged to develop a nuclear capability.

The Basics

1 Explain, using examples, the term 'weapons of mass destruction (WMDs)'.
2 Why do some people think Britain should have a nuclear deterrent?
3 Explain why religious believers could never support the use of WMDs.
4 **Countries should destroy their weapons of mass destruction.** Give and explain two reasons to agree, and two reasons to disagree.

 Now you have thought about war in the modern world

Terrorism

Terrorism means acts of violence that are intended to create fear. A terrorist is anyone who plans or carries out such an act. Terrorist acts are often directed at civilians and, because of this, many consider them to be unlawful acts of war and violence. The United Nations Security Council regards terrorist attacks as criminal: 'Acts intended to cause death or serious bodily harm to civilians or non-combatants with the purpose of intimidating a population or compelling a government or an international organisation to do or abstain from doing an act.'

In the modern world there have been many recorded acts of terrorism. Al Qaeda's attacks on the twin towers of the World Trade Centre (11 September 2001) and the London Underground (7 July 2005) are just two that most British people remember, but these kinds of suicide attacks continue.

> Why do you think suicide bombers are prepared to kill themselves and many others?

In 2008 a group of Muslim terrorists attacked hotels, temples and public places in Mumbai, killing 164 and wounding at least 308. In Africa, there are a growing number of Islamic terrorist organisations that are responsible for many attacks.

In 2004 ETA, the Spanish separatist group, carried out the Madrid train bombings, killing 191 and injuring 1775. In the same year, Chechen separatists occupied a school in Beslan for three days, resulting in the death of 380 people. In 1995 in Tokyo the Supreme Truth cult released sarin gas in train stations killing 12 and injuring 5000.

Clearly, when people are fighting for a cause they believe in, some will be prepared to go to any lengths to have their voice heard. It has been said that 'one person's terrorist is another person's freedom fighter'. Suicide bombers are an example of the extremes some will go to.

> What do you think about this? Are people who act in this way martyrs?

The Basics

1 What is meant by the following terms?
   a Terrorism
   b Terrorist
2 Give two reasons why many religious people would consider terrorist acts to be wrong. Explain your reasons.
3 **One person's terrorist is another's freedom fighter.** What do you think? Explain your opinion.

Terrorist cloud over Winter Olympics

SUICIDE BOMBER KILLS 20 IN MARKET

Freedom fighters branded terrorists

Victims of landmines

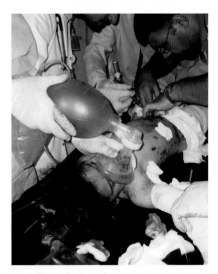
A civilian victim of war

A refugee camp

✓ **Now you have thought about terrorism**

Victims of war

In the modern world, most wars are fought in the less economically developed countries of Africa and Asia. Often these conflicts are civil wars fought between rival groups within a country. With the absence of stable government and properly trained soldiers, the civilians in war-torn countries can have their lives shattered in many ways.

Throughout the world there are over 12 million refugees. These are people who have been forced to flee their homes because of fear of massacre, genocide and other violence. Most of these people are forced to seek safety in refugee camps hundreds of miles from their homes, often in neighbouring countries.

Having lost their homes, belongings and livelihoods, refugees often have further problems to deal with. Life in refugee camps is overcrowded with only basic food, shelter and health care. Poor living conditions lead to illnesses such as cholera and dysentery. Many arrive having already been victims of torture and maiming.

Task

Imagine you have been asked to raise funds for a humanitarian aid agency. Design a full-page newspaper advert appealing for funds. Remember, you will need to tell people about why the funds are needed and what you will do with the donations.

The Red Cross and Red Crescent

In 1859, a Swiss businessman called Henry Dunant was so horrified by the slaughter he witnessed at the Battle of Solferino that he went to help care for the wounded on both sides. His actions were to lead to the organisation now known as the International Federation of Red Cross and Red Crescent Societies. Over time, the movement has grown into the largest humanitarian aid agency in the world, with a presence in almost every country.

The principle aims of the movement are the relief of pain and suffering for all people affected by conflict. The societies provide a full range of support to those in need – both immediate short-term aid and also lasting long-term aid. Some of the ways they help include setting up hospitals, establishing refugee camps, providing food, shelter and protection from attack.

The seven founding principles of the International Federation of Red Cross and Red Crescent Societies are:

1 *Humanity* – to prevent and alleviate human suffering, to protect human life and health and ensure respect for the human being. To promote understanding, friendship, co-operation and lasting peace.
2 *Impartiality* – to relieve the suffering of individuals with no discrimination as to race, nationality, religion, class or political opinions.
3 *Neutrality* – to not take sides in hostilities or take part in controversies and so retain the confidence of all.
4 *Independence* – the movement will at all times remain independent and national aid agencies that work within the movement must be able to act within its principles.
5 *Voluntary service* – it is a voluntary relief movement not prompted by gain.
6 *Unity* – there can be only one Red Cross or Red Crescent society in any one country, it must be open to all and work throughout the territory.
7 *Universality* – all societies within the movement have equal status, share equal responsibilities and duties in helping each other worldwide.

Find out more at **www.redcross.int/en**

Also look at the work of Médecins Sans Frontières at **www.msf.org.uk**

 Now you have thought about victims of war

Peace

Peace is not just the absence of war, but is a state of harmony, where justice exists for all and freedoms are respected. All religions teach the importance of peace on earth and encourage their followers to live peacefully. Throughout history, there have always been people prepared to refuse to use violence or fight in wars, even if it meant they faced imprisonment for their beliefs.

Pacifists believe that all violence is morally wrong. They will not participate in any war, regardless of the reasons for that war. *Conscientious objectors* are people who refuse to participate directly in fighting wars on the grounds of conscience. However, they will assist in non-military ways such as relief work or as medics or mediators.

Working for peace

The Golden Rule

✹ **Buddhism** – I will act towards others exactly as I would act towards myself. (Udana-varqa)

✝ **Christianity** – Treat others as you would like them to treat you. (Jesus)

ॐ **Hinduism** – This is the sum of duty: do nothing to others which if done to you could cause pain. (Mahabharata)

☪ **Islam** – None of you truly believe until he wishes for his brothers what he wishes for himself. (Prophet Muhammad, pbuh)

✡ **Judaism** – What is harmful to yourself do not do to your fellow man. (Rabbi Hillel)

☬ **Sikhism** – As you value yourself, so value others – cause suffering to no one. (Guru Granth Sahib)

The Quakers

This is a pacifist Christian group. As a Church they believe they are following the true teachings of Jesus by maintaining a completely pacifist stance. Their Peace Testimony makes clear that they will not use violence in any circumstances. It says that they denounce all violence – whatever its form. They totally oppose all outward wars and strife, and fighting with weapons, for any end, or under any pretence whatsoever. They believe that all relationships should be loving ones, including those between countries. During wars they will mediate for peace between the warring nations. They also do non-combat work such as training to be, and acting as, medics for any side, and doing work with refugees and victims of war.

> Think about these statements. How do they fit with the idea of going to war, or being a pacifist?

Gandhi

For over 30 years the Hindu leader of India, Mahatma Gandhi, used a policy of non-violence and civil disobedience to oppose British rule in India. His belief in the Hindu concept of ahimsa (non-violence) underpinned his leadership of the Hindus. Through actions such as protests, marches, speeches, sit-ins and hunger strikes, he eventually led his country to independence. He demonstrated that pacifism does not mean you have to just put up with violence and intimidation; when used effectively, it can be as powerful as any physical force.

The Dalai Lama

The Dalai Lama is the spiritual leader of Tibetan Buddhists. He is recognised around the world as a symbol of peace. When the Chinese invaded his country, Tibet, he was forced into exile. However, despite this injustice, he refuses to condone physical fighting against the Chinese. He says that hatred and violence will lead to more hatred and violence. He believes peace will only exist when everyone respects each other. He received the Nobel Peace Prize in 1992. Buddhist monks in Tibet have maintained peaceful protests against Chinese rule, despite being subjected to threats and violence.

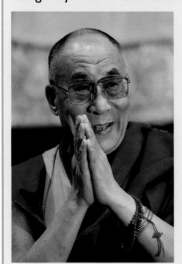
The Dalai Lama

Dietrich Bonhoeffer

Dietrich Bonhoeffer was a Christian living in Germany during the rise of the Nazi Party. He believed in pacifism and helped found the Confessing Church, which spoke out against the human rights abuses of the ruling Nazis. As the war continued, he felt that he had to be prepared to sacrifice his principles and even his life, because he believed that helping the oppressed was a test of faith. He defied Nazi rule by helping Jews escape the death camps and also worked to overthrow the Nazi Party. Even though he opposed all killing, he was part of a group that planned to assassinate Hitler because he believed it was necessary to do it for the greater good. He was eventually arrested and executed for treason by the Nazis.

Dietrich Bonhoeffer

Task

Make a PowerPoint presentation on the theme of peace. You should include: what peace means, religious teachings, beliefs and attitudes to peace, and the work of at least one person or group that works for peace. You could also select a suitable song to go with your presentation. Show your work to the rest of your class.

✓ **Now you know about peace and pacifism**

The United Nations

After the devastation of the Second World War, the countries of the world came together on 24 October 1945 to officially form the organisation we now know as the United Nations (UN). This date is celebrated around the world as United Nations Day. The main aim of the UN is the promotion of world peace. It strives to give all nations a voice in world affairs and to encourage global thinking in the determination of national policies.

This is the headquarters of the UN in New York. Find out more about the UN at **www.un.org**

The principles of the United Nations

- To maintain international peace and security
- To develop friendly relations between nations
- To co-operate in solving international economic, social, cultural and humanitarian problems
- To promote respect for human rights and fundamental freedoms
- To be a centre for helping nations achieve these aims

The UN does more than keep the peace. It also:

- provides food to 90 million people in 75 countries
- assists 34 million refugees
- fights poverty
- combats climate change
- protects human rights
- mobilises £7.5 billion in humanitarian aid
- promotes maternal health
… and much more.

International Day of Peace

Peace is the UN's highest calling.

Since 1981, 21 September has been marked out as an International Day of Peace throughout the world. In introducing this day, the UN resolution called for all nations to recognise and observe this day with a 24-hour cessation in all hostilities and a minute's silence at noon local time. In the UN headquarters in New York, the symbolic Peace Bell is rung to mark the day.

UNITED NATIONS' CHARTER

WE THE PEOPLES OF THE UNITED NATIONS RESOLVE

- ☆ To save succeeding generations from the scourge of war, which twice in our lifetime has brought untold sorrow to mankind.
- ☆ To reaffirm faith in fundamental human rights, in the dignity and worth of the human person, in the equal rights of men and women and of nations large and small.
- ☆ To establish conditions under which justice and respect for the obligations arising from treaties and other sources of international law can be maintained.
- ☆ To promote social progress and better standards of life in larger freedom.

AND FOR THESE ENDS

- ☆ To practise tolerance and live together in peace with one another as good neighbours.
- ☆ To unite our strength to maintain international peace and security.
- ☆ To ensure the acceptance of principles and the institution of methods, that armed force shall not be used, save in the common interest.
- ☆ To use international co-operation to promote the economic and social advance of all peoples.

The Basics

1 What is the UN?
2 Explain the main aims of the UN.
3 Look at the UN's Charter. Make a list of things that could be done to help achieve these aims.
4 Describe the work of the UN peacekeepers.
5 How is NATO different from the UN?
6 Explain why an International Day of Peace is important.

The United Nations Security Council (UNSC)

This part of the UN is responsible for maintaining international peace and security. In the UN Charter it states that the council should work to do the following:

1   Establish peacekeeping operations such as protecting human rights, ensuring aid organisations can function effectively, enabling the conduct of free and fair elections.
2   Establish international sanctions and regimes to prevent trade with nations which the UN has identified as abusing human rights, and to curb the flow of arms to these regimes.
3   Authorise the use of military action to protect civilians in war-torn nations (UN soldiers wear blue berets).

UN peacekeepers

All this is achieved through UNSC Resolutions. In 2014, more than 120,000 blue berets were sent to build and keep peace in sixteen operations around the world. These included Afghanistan, Sudan, Syria, India/Pakistan, Middle East, Haiti and the Congo. The blue berets are made up of professional soldiers from around the world dedicated to the UN ideal of world peace and security; they are loaned from the armies of UN countries.

What do the peacekeepers do?

♦   Monitor the implementation of peace agreements.
♦   Maintain ceasefires to enable political efforts to resolve conflicts.
♦   Help with the creation of stable and democratic governments.
♦   Monitor human rights and security reforms.
♦   Disarm former fighters and reintegrate them into their communities.

UN peacekeeping forces are mainly made up of military personnel. However, an increasing number of people with unique skills are being called upon to help, including administrators, economists, police and legal experts, landmine removal specialists, electoral observers, specialists in civil affairs and governing, humanitarian workers and experts in communication.

The North Atlantic Treaty Organization (NATO)

One way countries try to create and keep peace is by agreeing to work together towards common goals. These are laid out in documents called treaties. In 1949, 26 countries in North America and Europe signed the North Atlantic Treaty to form NATO. The agreeing nations (*allies*) are committed to supporting each other in protecting their freedom and security using political and military means. If Britain were to be threatened by another country, our allies including the USA, France and Germany have agreed to help to protect us.

NATO countries work together to promote democracy, individual liberty, the rule of law and the peaceful resolution of disputes. NATO has helped to end conflicts in Bosnia and Kosovo; provided additional support, such as enforcing the no-fly zone over Libya in 2011; and participated in peacekeeping efforts around the world. Find out more at **www.nato.int**

✓ **Now you know about peacekeeping organisations**

Topic 6 Religion and young people

In this topic, you are going to think about how young people relate to religion, and what relevance it has to them. Many young people are brought up within a faith – because their parents follow that faith and think that this is the best lifestyle for them.

We'll find out about birth and commitment ceremonies, how young people become religious and then follow a religion, how religion influences their moral development, the problems young people face as they grow up in our society and the role of schools in developing young people's religious understanding and awareness.

Young religious people

How do religious people bring up their children?

Most people want the same or better chances for their children as they themselves had. If they are religious, they believe in the truths of their religion, which will lead to heaven, paradise, enlightenment or nirvana. For religious people, this is the best possible way to live because it will bring happiness and contentment. So they want their children to follow their religion too.

- They will teach the children *how to live their faith* – how to live as a Christian or Muslim, for example, especially in a secular society.
- They will teach them *how to behave* – what the rules are for people of that religion.
- They will make sure they are made *members of that religion* through special ceremonies.
- They will make sure they learn *how to worship*, for example by taking them to their place of worship.
- They will ensure their education includes learning *about their faith*.

Our society is very secular. This means that it doesn't openly focus on religion, and why we should behave in a religious way. Many people don't even practise a religion in an obvious way, even if they follow its principles by treating other people with respect and so on. Many children today are brought up only experiencing religion on rare occasions, such as festivals, marriages and funerals. For many practising religious people, their home is a spiritual place, and they go to a religious building to carry out an act of worship with others. In a way, this means they have two different worlds to live in, which can make life difficult.

> Do you think it is difficult in Britain today to follow a religion? With a partner, discuss what makes it easy, and what makes it hard.

The Basics

1 Give three reasons why couples choose to have children.
2 Explain how religious parents would try to bring up their children.
3 Explain why it might be difficult for religious parents to bring up a child in a non-religious society.
4 **Parents should not teach their children their religion until they are old enough to decide to choose it for themselves.** Do you agree? Give reasons and explain your answer, showing you have thought about more than one point of view.

Now you how religious people bring up their children

Young people and religion

Worship

All religious traditions give opportunities for young people to participate in worship. Sometimes there are special services held especially for children and young people. These may include fun activities using dance, drama and popular music. All religions hold classes at their holy building where children can learn more about their religion. Young people can also participate directly in worship, for example, by reading from the holy book or helping with the rituals.

> Find out more about how young people participate in worship. Make a list of the things they do.

Voluntary work

Many young people get involved in voluntary work in their communities and overseas. Religions teach the importance of caring for others, which might inspire young people to help. They can help in many ways: running youth groups and Sunday schools, visiting the elderly or taking part in sponsored events. Some young people take a gap year and travel to less economically developed countries (LEDCs) to work on projects helping to improve the lives of others.

> Investigate some of the voluntary work opportunities for young people wishing to take a gap year.

Festivals

Festival celebrations are a fun time. Children learn the stories behind the festivals. They get holidays from school and lots of presents. The celebrations often have a party atmosphere, including fireworks, special food and fun games. They decorate their homes, dress up and spend time with family and friends.

> Many young people commit to faith. Some are brought up in a religious family. Others may have personal experiences that make them search for answers to questions they have about life, and religion may help them find these answers. Some young people may be influenced by others, such as their friends, teachers or inspirational people. For whatever reasons, religion can be a big part of their lives.

Social activities

All religious traditions have social activities for all ages. Holy buildings are often designed to include community rooms where all sorts of activities take place. Many young people attend youth clubs and classes at their place of worship. These give young people a chance to enjoy fellowship with their peers in a relaxed and friendly atmosphere, where their beliefs will be understood and respected.

> Make up a weekly timetable of events for a holy building, showing the activities for young people.

> Research a festival that is particularly enjoyed by children. Write a child's diary entry that explains why it was such a good time.

Youth organisations

Lots of young people join youth organisations such as the Worldwide Scout Movement. These groups engage young people in all kinds of interests and help them to develop skills they may not have the opportunity to learn elsewhere. They also include opportunities for them to participate in and learn about faith, for example, in church parades or in sessions about the beliefs and teachings of fellow Scouts around the world.

> Find out the principles of a youth organisation like the Scouts or Girl Guides and how it links to religion.

Religious holidays

Lots of young people enjoy going on special holidays called retreats, organised especially for young people by their community. They mix fun social activities with time for worship and reflection. Many young people like to travel to important places in their faith such as Mecca, Amritsar and Jerusalem. Roman Catholic churches organise trips for young people to help the sick and disabled at Lourdes. Every year, thousands travel to Taizé in France to spend time reflecting on and developing their spirituality.

> Find out about the activities that take place in Taizé. Why do you think so many young people go there?

Task

Pictures are a great help when you are trying to remember things. Collect some images for each of the categories on this page – make your work visually attractive.

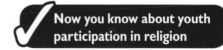

✓ Now you know about youth participation in religion

Birth ceremonies

Buddhism

There are no set religious practices for Buddhists to follow. Any ceremonies that are held come from the culture of the country itself, rather than the religion.

For some families, especially in Theravada Buddhist cultures, they want a monk to come to bless their child. The monk will visit the home, and chant some religious texts from the **tipitaka** as a blessing. To show their thanks, the couple will give gifts of food, money or other things to the monk and the monastery he belongs to.

Many Buddhists take their child to the temple soon after it is born. They want to give thanks to the Buddha for their child, so will pray and make offerings of incense, flowers, food and money to show their thanks.

Christianity

Christians have infant baptism and dedication ceremonies. If you are asked about an initiation ceremony in the exam, you could talk about either. Since there is a little bit more detail in the infant baptism ceremony, we'll look at that.

Don't forget, this ceremony differs between Christian denominations, so you might have experience of a different one.

In the Anglican Church, the parents bring their child to the church to have it baptised. This means it is welcomed into the faith, and made a member through its parents' faith. For Catholics, it also means it is washed clean of sins inherited from its ancestors.

The baby is usually dressed in white, for purity. Everyone gathers around the font for the ceremony.

The priest asks the parents and godparents some questions about their faith, and their

Hinduism

In Hinduism, there are two very early birth/initiation ceremonies. Hindus in different parts of India also have cultural ceremonies. There are a number of other ceremonies as well, a little later in the child's life.

The first ceremony is called *Jatakarma*, and happens as soon after birth as possible. At this time,

the father will put a little ghee (butter) mixed with honey on to

the baby's tongue. This is in the hope that the baby will have a good nature. The father will also whisper the name of the Ultimate Reality into the baby's ear, so that the baby is welcomed into the faith.

The second ceremony usually happens on the tenth to twelfth day after birth. It is called *Namakarana*, and is the

The Basics

Use these questions for each of the religion(s) you are studying (from pages 66–69).

1 What is a birth/initiation ceremony?
2 Describe a religious birth/initiation ceremony.
3 Give two reasons why religious people hold these ceremonies.
4 **Ceremonies held to mark the birth of a baby are just an excuse to have a party.** Do you agree? Give reasons for your answer, showing that you have thought about more than one point of view. Refer to religious arguments in your answer.

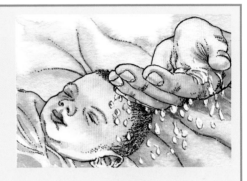

They may want the child to receive its name at the temple. Often, in such ceremonies, water is sprinkled over the child. Water symbolises cleanliness and protection from evil. Again, the parents will make offerings as gifts to the Buddha and temple.

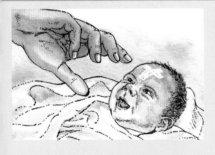

symbol for Christianity, on the baby's forehead.

Then water is poured over the baby's forehead three times – once each for God the Father, God the Son and God the Holy Spirit. The baby is being baptised in the name of each of these.

In many churches, the family will be given a lighted candle to represent Jesus as the Light of the World. It will be a reminder of their promises to bring up the child in the faith.

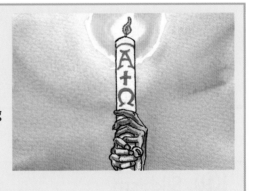

intention to bring the baby up in the faith. Then he or she takes some water from the font and makes the sign of the cross, the

a Brahmin priest will come to the home.

An astrologer will read out the child's horoscope, which he has prepared after the child was born, and the name will be announced.

Songs and hymns are sung to show happiness and thanksgiving. Many families will make a fire sacrifice (havan). They offer grain and ghee to the deities through the flames

name-giving ceremony. The baby is dressed in new clothes, and can be taken to the temple, or

of a fire, while mantras are being chanted.

Islam

There are two main ceremonies – the Tahneek and the Aqiqah.

The Tahneek Ceremony happens as soon as possible after birth.

The father whispers the Adhan into the right ear, then the Iqamah into the left. These are the two halves of the call to prayer. This means the child has been welcomed into the

faith, and the first things it has heard have been the call to prayer and the name of Allah.

Next, he takes the child and places the soft part of a date on its tongue. This is a hope for the child to be sweet natured when it gets older.

The Aqiqah Ceremony is the naming ceremony. It will take

Judaism

Boys and girls have different birth ceremonies in Judaism.

Eight days after birth, a boy should be circumcised as a mark of the covenant between Abraham and the Israelites.

A *mohel* (man trained to carry out circumcision) goes to the home of the boy. A special guest

(*sandek*) will hold the boy while the circumcision is carried out. This person may be a friend of the family or a relative, but carrying out this role is an honour, hence them being a special guest.

The father will read a blessing from the Torah. Then the mohel will bless the boy himself, and announce the boy's name.

The boy is then given to his mother to be fed.

The family and their guests will then celebrate with a party.

Sikhism

As soon as possible after birth, the father will whisper the *Mool Mantra* into the ear of the child. This means it has been welcomed into the faith. He will also put a little honey on to the baby's lips – hoping for a sweet future.

The naming ceremony will take place at the first gurdwara service after birth if possible. The couple take their child to the service, and with

them take the ingredients for karah parshad, and a romalla (a cloth used to cover the Guru Granth Sahib) as a gift for the gurdwara.

There will be readings of thanksgiving from the Guru Granth Sahib.

The granthi (the reader of the Guru Granth Sahib in the gurdwara) will stir the amrit with a kirpan, and then drop some into the mouth of the baby. He or she also says a prayer for long life and sweetness for the baby.

place a few days after birth. The baby's head is shaved, and the hair weighed. The family will

give at least its equivalent weight in money to charity. This purifies the child.

Next, verses from the Qur'an are read out loud, and the child's name will be announced. Again, the father will whisper the Adhan into its ear.

The family will pay for an animal to be sacrificed and its meat given to the poor to say thanks for the gift of a child.

Then everyone will join in a feast to celebrate the birth of the child.

For a girl, she will be announced and named on the first Shabbat (Sabbath) after her birth. This happens at the synagogue.

Many Jews follow the *zeved habit* ceremony, where a rabbi will come to bless the baby girl. The family then enjoy a meal of celebration. This happens on the seventh day after birth.

The name is chosen next. The granthi opens the Guru Granth Sahib at random, and reads the first word on the left-hand page. The parents use the first letter of this for the first letter of the baby's name. The granthi then announces that name to the congregation.

The karah parshad, which is blessed food from God, will be given out to everyone in the service. The couple arranges for a donation to be given

to the poor, as a sign of their thanks to God for their child.

 Now you know about a birth ceremony in religion

Ceremonies of commitment

Most religious traditions have ceremonies in which young people make a personal commitment to their faith. These occur at different times, but usually around the teenage years, so they are sometimes referred to as Coming of Age ceremonies. They mark the change from a child to an adult. After this, young people are expected to take full responsibility for their religious duties.

 Buddhism

There is no specific ceremony to become a Buddhist. Some will repeat the Three Refuges in front of others to mark their acceptance of the Buddhist way of life. This is because the Buddha taught that it is the way you live that is important. The believer will simply state, 'I go to the Buddha for refuge; I go to the Dharma for refuge; I go to the Sangha for refuge.'

In Theravada Buddhism, an important ceremony marks a young person's entry into a monastery. Before entering the wat (monastery), the young man must be free from debt and know the Pali phrases he must say in the ceremony. He visits the wat several times and makes gifts of incense, flowers and light, and rings a gong showing he is preparing to join the monastery. The day before the ceremony, he walks in a procession wearing a white robe symbolising his good and pure intentions in becoming a monk. His head is shaved.

✝ Christianity

Around the age of twelve, many young Christians choose to undergo a ceremony of confirmation. This is when they confirm the promises made for them at their baptism. Before the ceremony, there is a time of preparation when they will attend classes, learning what it means to make a full commitment to the

Christian faith and how they should live a Christian life.

The ceremony takes place at a special Sunday service, led by a bishop. The bishop will ask three questions: 'Do you turn to Christ? Do you repent your sins? Do you renounce evil?' Each time, the person must answer 'Yes'. The bishop then places his hands on their head and says: 'Confirm, O Lord, your servant with your Holy Spirit.' This is called the laying on of hands, and at this point the young person receives the blessing of God's Holy Spirit to guide them in their Christian life. The service then

 Hinduism

In Hinduism, sixteen samskaras (special ceremonies) mark key events in a person's life. At around the age of twelve, Hindu boys have a sacred thread ceremony to mark their full entry into their caste. The ceremony happens in a garden around a sacred fire. Puja (worship) is conducted

and then the boy's teacher presents him with his sacred thread, which is a series of cotton threads twined together.

The priest, who has taught the boy, then places the sacred thread over the boy's left shoulder and across his body to the right hip. He is now allowed to recite passages from the Vedas and conduct religious rituals. In due course,

he will also be ready for the next stage in life, marriage.

On his initiation day, he walks around the wat four times

wearing rich clothing and carrying a candle, incense and flower. He takes off the rich clothes and throws coins on the floor, to symbolise the actions of Prince Siddhartha when he left the palace for the last time. He then enters the ordination hall and asks the bhikkus (monks) to ordain him. He puts on simple yellow robes to show that he has left his worldly life behind. The abbot asks him questions and he must answer in Pali. He is then accepted into the

monastery and his religious instruction begins.

continues with Holy Communion and the newly confirmed person receives the bread and wine for the first time.

Believer's baptism

In the Baptist Church, they do not baptise children. They wait until a young person feels ready to understand the commitment they are making. In church, they announce that they are sorry for the sins they have committed and accept Christ as their personal saviour. The minister then leads them into the baptistery and dips them completely under the water. This symbolises the

washing away of sins and rising to a new life in Christ.

The Basics

Answer these questions for the religion(s) you are studying (from pages 70–73).
1 Describe a commitment ceremony and explain the meaning of any symbolic words, actions and objects.
2 Why do some religious people think it is important to have these ceremonies?
3 **Initiation ceremonies are pointless because your religion is decided at birth.** How far do you agree? Give reasons for your answer, showing that you have thought about more than one point of view.

Islam

There are no ceremonies of commitment in Islam, as a child is considered a full Muslim from birth. Islam is a complete way of life and children learn their faith in the family and in the madrasah (mosque school) as they grow up.

The words of the Bismillah mean 'In the name of God, most gracious, most compassionate'

When a Muslim child is four, they have a ceremony called Bismillah. It remembers the first time Prophet Muhammad (pbuh) met the angel Gabriel, when he was commanded to read the first words of the Qur'an from a scroll presented by the angel. The child will have memorised the passage known as the Bismillah and recites it for family and friends to hear.

Judaism

At the age of thirteen, all Jewish boys have a ceremony called Bar Mitzvah, which means 'Son of the Commandment'. In Reform Judaism girls have a ceremony called Bat Mitzvah, which means 'Daughter of the Commandment', and is completed when they are twelve. These are very important ceremonies

because they mark the change from child to adult. From this point, the young person is completely responsible for their religious duties.

There is a period of preparation during which a rabbi will instruct the young person in how to read and handle the Torah, as well as how to perform other religious obligations such as how to wear tefillin. The ceremony takes place

Sikhism

When Sikh boys and girls are old enough, they can choose to be initiated into the Khalsa through the Amrit Ceremony. However, it is very common for Sikhs to leave this ceremony until much later in life. Guru Gobind Singh invented this ceremony in 1699 and it involves making a commitment to live by a very strict moral code, including adopting all of the 5Ks.

The 5Ks

The Amrit Ceremony is conducted in front of the Guru Granth Sahib. There are five members dressed to represent the panj piare (five beloved ones). The granthi reads from the holy book and one of the panj piare recites the vows the initiates must promise to keep. The amrit, a mixture of sugar and water, is stirred with a Khanda – double-edged sword. The initiates kneel on one knee to show that they are ready to defend their faith.

They receive gifts of sweets. This marks the beginning of their religious education.

As they get older, they take on more of the religious duties. They learn how to prepare for and complete prayers so that they can fulfil Salah – the Second Pillar of Islam. Many

Muslim children keep the full Ramadan fast by the time they are in their early teens, thus completing Saum – the Fourth Pillar of Islam.

on the Sabbath (Shabbat) nearest to the boy's thirteenth birthday as part of the usual service at the synagogue. The Torah scrolls are prepared on the Bimah and then the Rabbi calls the boy to read to the rest of the congregation. The boy goes up to the Bimah and reads the passages in Hebrew for that Shabbat service.

The Rabbi then gives his sermon; part of this is for the boy to remind him of his duty to keep the commandments

throughout his life. Finally, the boy is blessed by the Rabbi with the words: 'The Lord bless thee and keep thee.' Then there is a big family celebration.

Amrit is then sprinkled on their eyes and hair to the words 'Waheguru ji ka Khalsa', which means the 'Khalsa is the chosen of God'. Those being initiated

reply, 'Waheguru ji ki fateh', which means 'victory to God'. Each person drinks some of the amrit from the bowl, to show equality and the absence of castes.

There are then prayers and hymns and the ceremony closes with the sharing of karah parshad (blessed food). After the ceremony, all Sikh men take the name Singh, meaning 'lion', and women take the name Kaur, meaning 'princess'.

 Now you know about commitment ceremonies

Young people and society

There often seems to be conflict between the older and younger people in any society. This can take the form of older people criticising the behaviour of young people. This failure of older and younger people to understand each other is known as the *generation gap*. Some of the biggest differences are about music, fashion, culture and politics.

Young people can feel *marginalised* from the rest of society. Teenagers have their behaviour controlled not only at home, but also by local authorities, the law, schools and other institutions. Unsurprisingly, young people often complain that their voices are not heard and that they are criticised unfairly, simply because they behave differently from the older generation.

All young people also have to deal with conflicts within their own social groups. *Peer pressure* (the influence of people in the same age group) can be difficult to deal with. It can be very challenging for young religious believers. In our society, believing in and living by a religion can seem outdated. Believers may find their friends do not understand why they commit to a lifestyle that prevents them from taking part in some aspects of popular culture.

> Why do some young people commit to faith if it can be so difficult?

- Family upbringing and tradition
- Personal religious experience
- To enjoy the lifestyle and believe in the religious teachings
- To give their life meaning and purpose
- To allow them to express their spirituality

> Why do you think the older people on the right have these negative attitudes towards young people? What would you say to each of them to try to change their attitude?

The Basics

1 Explain, using examples, what is meant by the 'generation gap'.
2 Explain, using examples, what it means to say young people are marginalised.
3 How can peer pressure affect young people today?
4 Make a list of the advantages and disadvantages of young people committing to a religious faith.

 Now you have thought about young people and society

Teenagers today have no respect.
George

I don't like to go out any more. The gangs of young thugs hanging around frighten me.
Mary

Youngsters today have far too much freedom.
Imran

It is too easy for young people today, there is no pressure at all.
Indira

They should have the cane in school. It never did me any harm.
Bob

If we had national service, kids would learn proper discipline.
Doris

Young people and rights

Why should I behave like an adult when they treat me like a baby?

Adults think that only their opinions count.

Why don't we get a say?

I'm old enough to make my own decisions about my life.

I can't wait 'til I'm eighteen. I'll do exactly what I like!

United Nations' Declaration of the Rights of the Child

1. All children are entitled to these rights regardless of race, colour, sex, language, religion, national or social origin, birth or status.

2. Children are entitled to special protection to enable them to develop physically, mentally, morally, spiritually and socially.

3. A child is entitled from birth to a name and nationality.

4. Children should be protected and provided with enough food, shelter, health care and opportunities to play.

5. Children who are physically, mentally or socially handicapped should have special treatment that meets their needs.

6. Children need love and understanding; they should be cared for by people who can provide them with affection and security.

7. All children are entitled to a free education that will develop their abilities, judgement and sense of moral and social responsibility.

8. Children should be the first to receive relief aid in any disaster.

9. Children should be protected against all forms of neglect, cruelty and exploitation. Children should not work before a minimum age and work should not interfere with their development, health and education.

10. Children should be treated equally and brought up in a spirit of understanding, tolerance, friendship, peace and universal brotherhood.

Imagine you have been asked to draw up a charter of rights for children. What rights would you want all children in the world to have? Compare your list with the UN Declaration of the Rights of the Child.

Do you agree or disagree with each of the points? Explain your decision. Is there anything missing? Should all countries have to agree to these rights? In what circumstances might it be difficult to ensure all children have these rights?

Read the table below. Why do you think the law has decided you have to be a certain age to do some things? What things do you agree and disagree with? Explain your opinions.

Rights of young people in the UK	
Age	**What you can now legally do!**
13	Part-time job with restrictions
14	Enter a pub, but not drink alcohol. Boys can be convicted of rape.
16	Full-time job after June, live alone, marry with parents' consent, ride a 50cc moped, pilot a glider, consent to sex, join armed forces, have an abortion without parents' consent, apply for a passport, drink beer/cider with a meal, buy a lottery ticket, use pumps at a petrol station.
17	Hold a driving licence for most vehicles, pilot a plane, emigrate, cannot be subject to a care order.
18	Adult rights in law, vote, get married, buy tobacco and alcohol, open a bank account, see your birth certificate, change your name, serve on a jury, sue and be sued, make a will, place a bet, have a tattoo, buy fireworks, be sent to adult prison.

Task

Read the views of the young people shown on this page. How far do you agree with their opinions? Explain your answers.

Discuss how young people could be made to feel more valued in society.

Now you have thought about children's rights

Young people and school

Faith schools play an important role in the community

Two-thirds oppose faith schools

Government won't fund more faith schools

The Church was the only provider of education in Britain until Victorian times. It was the influence of the Church on and within government that eventually led to government beginning to set up schools in Britain. Until then, children were simply treated as small adults who were expected to work and contribute to the family income. The Elementary Education Act of 1880 was the first step in making education compulsory for all children.

Today, the lives of young people are very different. Education is a big part of life and schools have a responsibility to prepare young people fully for, not only work, but life in general. School enables children to learn a wide range of skills, to develop socially and psychologically, to explore the world from the security of their classrooms and begin to become the adults they wish to be.

Religion and schools

Historically, religion and schools have been very closely linked as shown above. By 1944, education was compulsory for all children and the government passed an act that made the study of religion in

school part of the curriculum for all. Since then, there have been many changes to education in Britain, but Religious Studies has always been part of the curriculum.

Why Religious Studies?

Over the years, the subject of Religious Studies has changed dramatically to take account of the changing face of British society. In the past, Religious Studies concentrated on Christian teachings and beliefs. It assumed all students were believers and often reflected the teaching that happened in church Sunday schools. Today, Religious Studies in schools recognises and celebrates that students come from a wide variety of religious and secular backgrounds. It focuses on key skills and concepts that enable students to learn, understand and question some of the most profound issues facing humankind. It can help us to understand and empathise with people who live life very differently from us. By studying the different beliefs and values of others, it can help us to decide what is meaningful and important. It gives us an insight into the world we live in and our place within it.

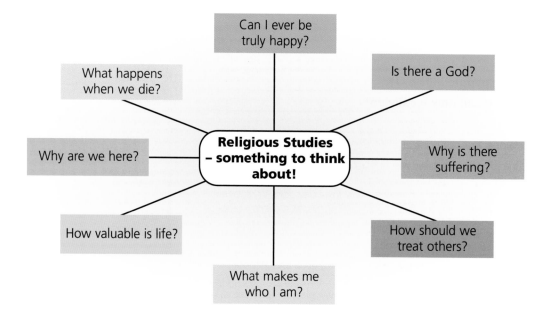

Can I ever be truly happy?

What happens when we die?

Is there a God?

Why are we here?

Religious Studies – something to think about!

Why is there suffering?

How valuable is life?

How should we treat others?

What makes me who I am?

My name is Theresa and I attend the Holy Mother Convent School. As a practising Roman Catholic, my parents felt it was important that I was able to follow my faith in school. I do all the same subjects that my friends at the local high school do, but the ethos of the school is quite different. Most of the girls at my school are also Roman Catholics, but even those who aren't take part in the religious activities in school. Every day we have assemblies that the whole school attends. We sing hymns and always conclude with prayers. Our Religious Studies lessons include preparation for confirmation and begin and end with prayers. They also include study of Roman Catholic beliefs and teachings and help us to understand our personal faith. Our school also has special assemblies when there are important holy days being celebrated, even though we are not on holiday. These sometimes take place at our local church which is good, because it means that we can attend Mass. It was really lovely being in school wearing our ash crosses on Ash Wednesday and not having to worry about being teased or questioned.

My name is Salma. I go to my local high school. As a practising Muslim, I am allowed to wear my hijab, which is a headscarf that covers my hair, although I do remove it for PE. My parents feel it is important that my education includes learning about my faith, so I also attend a madrasah (mosque school) on Saturday mornings. We have assemblies in school twice a week for each year group, but these aren't like going to worship. Usually they include a story with a moral for us to think about. Some of them are quite interesting. I like Religious Studies lessons because I get to learn about what my friends believe. In our GCSE course, we have had some great debates about things like the existence of God and arranged marriages. It's really good to be able to hear other people's views and I am confident talking about my beliefs and what they mean to me. Sometimes it can be hard in school practising your faith. Not everyone understands that when students are off for Eid, it is an important celebration, not 'bunking off'. As a Muslim, I also find the canteen menu very limiting because it doesn't include halal meat. Mostly, however, everyone is very supportive and I was thrilled when some of my classmates also fasted for a day while I was keeping Ramadan.

The Basics

1 Make a list of at least five skills you have learned in school. Choose three of them and say why you think they are important.
2 Give three reasons why you think Religious Studies is taught in schools.
3 In some countries religion is not allowed to be taught in schools. Why might that be the case?
4 Explain how a faith school may be different to a secular (non-faith) school.
5 **Religious Studies should only be taught in faith schools.** Do you agree? Give reasons for your answer, showing you have thought about different points of view.

 Now you know about religion and school

Life issues Appendix I

Revision outline

This is a revision guide for the Religion and Life Issues unit. It follows the outline of topics in the specification. If you already know all of the answers when you read through it, you will probably do brilliantly.

Use the guide as a checklist of what you know, and what you have still got to get to grips with. You could even use it as a last-minute check before you go into the exam. When you have finished all your revision, you should be able to recognise each word. Each phrase should trigger a whole lot of ideas in your head – definitions, examples and explanations. When it does, you are ready.

Topic	Words to learn	Subjects within topic – do you know …?
1 Religion and Animal Rights	Animal rights Stewardship Creation Sanctity of life Vegetarianism Companionship Animal experimentation Factory farming Zoos Hunting Fur trade Ivory trade Extinction Cloning Genetic modification	• How humans use animals to help them • How humans exploit animals • How humans and animals differ – the status of each • Religious attitudes to animal rights • Religious attitudes to slaughter methods, to meat eating, and about any food rules • Religious attitudes to animal experimentation • Religious attitudes to zoos, including their role in conservation of species • Religious attitudes to uses of animals in sport, including hunting, bull fighting and racing • Religious attitudes to farming, including factory farming • The 'rights and wrongs' of each of the ways humans use animals

Topic	Words to learn	Subjects within topic – do you know …?
2 Religion and Planet Earth	Creation Stewardship Awe Community Pollution Climate change Natural resources Natural habitat Earth Summits Renewable energies Sustainable development Conservation	• Religious explanations of how the world and life began • How the planet can be a source of awe and wonder, making us think of God • The problem with trying to help humans, but still protecting the environment • How people damage the environment • How and why people help the environment, both as individuals and in groups • The world's response to environmental problems, e.g. Earth Summits, Kyoto, etc. • Religious attitudes to the natural world • Religious attitudes to each specific topic – climate change, pollution, use and abuse of natural resources, destruction of natural habitat, and conservation • How modern living contributes to the problems, and how it needs to be part of the solution
3 Religion and Prejudice	Prejudice Discrimination Positive discrimination Equality Justice Community Tolerance Harmony Sexism Racism Religious prejudice Homophobia Ageism	• What different types of prejudice there are • Why people are prejudiced • How people show their prejudice • How tolerance, justice, harmony and the value of each person are relevant in this issue • Religious attitudes to prejudice generally • Religious attitudes to all specific types of prejudice – racism, sexism, homophobia, ageism, religious prejudice • How religions respond to prejudice and discrimination • How religions help the victims of prejudice and discrimination • What specific individuals have done to fight racism, and other prejudice • What the government has done to fight prejudice, e.g. the Race Relations Act • What positive discrimination is, and why it happens

Topic	Words to learn	Subjects within topic – do you know …?
4 Religion and Early Life	Abortion Sanctity of life Quality of life Miracle of life Blessing Conception Viability Rights Pro-Life Pro-Choice Pressure group	• When life begins – the different views • Why children are seen as a blessing • What we mean by 'miracle of life' • What we mean by 'abortion' • Why women have abortions • The arguments around 'quality of life' abortions • The law about abortion • Religious attitude to abortion • Examples of when religious believers generally would accept an abortion is necessary • What rights all those involved have or should have – mother, father, foetus • Alternatives to abortion • The work of pressure groups on each side of this issue
5 Religion, War and Peace	War Peace Conflict Justice Sanctity of life Community Pacifism Just War Holy War Victims Peacekeeping force Terrorism Weapons of Mass Destruction Nuclear weapons Nuclear proliferation	• Why religious believers believe in pacifism • The issue of sanctity of life to argue both for and against war • Examples of recent wars, applying Just/Holy War theories to them • How war makes victims of many • Organisations that help victims of war • Why religious believers might go to war • Explanation of Just War, including its rules • Explanation of Holy War, including its rules • Attitudes to war, including teachings/beliefs to support those attitudes • Attitudes to peace, including teachings/beliefs to support those attitudes • How a religious believer has worked for peace • How and why peacekeeping forces work • Attitudes to nuclear weapons, and nuclear proliferation, including beliefs/teachings to support those attitudes

Topic	Words to learn	Subjects within topic – do you know …?
6 Religion and Young People	Birth ceremony Initiation ceremony Commitment ceremony Upbringing Spirituality Moral code Faith group Commitment Belonging Brotherhood Membership Generation gap Peer pressure Faith school Assembly	• Examples of birth ceremonies from each religion you study • Examples of initiation/commitment ceremonies from each of the religions you study • How our upbringing influences our behaviour, beliefs and attitudes • Why young people belong to faith-based groups and organisations, including some examples • How and why young people come into conflict – generation gap, peer pressure, society • What rights young people have • The link between school and religion • The problems met by being a believer as a young person • The benefits found by being a believer as a young person

Mock paper

What a question paper looks like

You will be given a question paper, and an answer booklet in the examination.

Do I really need to read the cover? It's always the same, isn't it?

Well, no, not all the covers are the same, and it is easy at a stressful time to mix up what you are meant to do. Probably your teacher will have told you a million times what you have to do in the exam, but you can still forget. It is a good idea to just check through the cover – it is like a calming exercise, which helps if you are nervous. It also reassures you that you do know what you are doing.

The cover will remind you:

- How long the exam lasts – so plan and use your time well. Reassess after you have answered each full question – you might have gained or lost time. Don't spend too much time on one question, but don't rush yourself either. You start with four questions to answer in 90 minutes – about 22 minutes a question.
- That you get a choice of any four of the six questions on offer. If you answer them all, you'll be given marks for the best four, but it might not be the best use of your time. Some people find they have lots of time left when they have finished what they should do, so they do extra questions to pass the time!
- To use blue or black ink/pen. This makes your paper easier to read and mark. This is especially important when exam papers are going to be marked online – you need your writing to be clear and bold, so no one has to struggle to read it.
- That you should do any notes or practice work on either your answer booklet, or on extra paper. Sometimes, people write correct things that they then don't put into their real answer. If you hand in all your working out and notes, the examiner can credit you for anything you missed out. They are obliged to read it all. In your answer booklet, write on the lines only – don't go into the margins or above/below the box as the examiner won't see what you have written, which might cost you marks. The OMR system which scans your booklet into the computer for the examiner to mark online isn't designed to pick up anything outside the writing area.

So much for the cover, what about the inside?

There will be six questions, and the chances are that each one will have a picture or bit of writing to start with. The pictures are meant to stimulate your brain, and start you thinking. In other words, they are meant to help you by triggering the relevant ideas for that question.

In the first question that follows, the questions are split 2/3/2/5/6 marks. There has to be a 3- and a 6-mark evaluative question, but the other 9 marks could be split up a different way – 1/2/6, or 2/3/4, or 4/5, for example. So be prepared (through the practice in this book) for that. What is definite is that all six questions will be split in the same way, so if one question is split 2/3/3/4/6, they all will be (through possibly in a different order, e.g. 2/3/4/3/6).

For practice

Choose any **four** questions from these six to answer.

Each question is worth **18 marks** in total.

If you wanted to practise one topic – testing your knowledge – you could give yourself a 22-minute time-test.

---

1   **Religion and Animal Rights**

This is the stimulus. The idea is that it helps you with the question, triggering ideas.

(01)   Give **two** reasons why some species of animal are endangered.   (*2 marks*)

Be sure to give two different reasons.   *You must explain why some animals are endangered. Don't just give the names of the animals.*

(02)   **Religious believers should never use products that come from animals.**
What do you think? Explain your opinion.   (*3 marks*)

Products include meat, and food items with animal ingredients, as well as goods from leather, bone, etc.

(03)   Explain briefly **one** way religious believers can help to reduce animal suffering.   (*2 marks*)

You must explain the way they can help. This must be a practical answer.

(04)   Explain religious attitudes to animal rights. Refer to beliefs and teachings in your answer. (*5 marks*)

You must apply beliefs and teachings to the question – don't just say 'life is sacred'. You have to say how that belief impacts on animal rights.

(05)   **There is nothing wrong with hunting animals.** Do you agree? Give reasons for your answer showing that you have thought about more than one point of view. Refer to religious arguments in your answer.   (*6 marks*)

Use the DREARER formula (see page 174), and remember to put a conclusion at the end of your answer.

2   Religion and Planet Earth

Use this in (06).

(06)   Give **two** reasons why pollution is harmful to the environment.   *(2 marks)*

(07)   Explain briefly **one** way religious believers can help to reduce pollution.   *(2 marks)*

This could be what is done by an individual or by a group. Don't forget, religious believers are the same as everyone else, and so do the same things you would.

(08)   **Religious believers should have a place at Earth Summits.** What do you think? Explain your opinion.   *(3 marks)*

Earth Summits are gatherings of world leaders, so think about why religious believers should have a say there.

(09)   Explain religious beliefs and teachings about the created world.   *(5 marks)*

You need to give about four teachings and explain each one.

(10)   **Human lifestyles do not have to change to protect the planet.** Do you agree? Give reasons for your answer showing that you have thought about more than one point of view. Refer to religious arguments in your answer.   *(6 marks)*

This is about the way we live. Think about different lifestyles to give yourself more scope to answer – do people in poor countries really have the same impact on the environment that you do?

3   Religion and Prejudice

(11)   Give **two** reasons why it is important for all people to have equal rights.   *(2 marks)*

> Focus on *equal rights*, not just
> the idea of being equal.

(12)   Explain briefly why some religious believers agree with positive discrimination.   *(2 marks)*

> You must write about *positive*
> discrimination, not just discrimination.

(13)   **Prejudice against religion is worse than other types of prejudice.** What do
you think? Explain your opinion.   *(3 marks)*

> Give three reasons to agree, or disagree,
> or a mix of both.

(14)   Explain religious attitudes to discrimination against women. Refer to beliefs and
teachings in your answer.   *(5 marks)*

> Be careful not to label religious practice separating
> men and women as justifying discrimination.

(15)   **There will always be prejudice and discrimination.** Do you agree? Give reasons for your
answer showing that you have thought about more than one point of view.
Refer to religious arguments in your answer.   *(6 marks)*

> 6-mark questions are often easier if you take an 'It depends …' approach.
> 'It depends …' opens your brain to lots of answers on each side of the argument.

4   Religion and Early Life

(16) Give **two** reasons why some religious believers want to have children.   *(2 marks)*

Don't include answers about people who
have children by accident.

(17) Explain briefly what it means to describe a baby as a *miracle of life*.   *(2 marks)*

Make sure you only write a couple of
sentences/ideas to answer this.

(18) **Religious beliefs should not interfere with a woman's right to choose abortion.**
What do you think? Explain your opinion.   *(3 marks)*

This question is about the right to choose,
not whether abortion is okay or not.

(19) Explain why there are different religious attitudes to abortion. Refer to beliefs and
teachings in your answer.   *(5 marks)*

This question isn't primarily about abortion,
but about why there are different religious
attitudes to it. Think about different abortion
situations that will help you to show these
different attitudes.

(20) **Fathers should have rights when decisions are being made about abortion.** Do you
agree? Give reasons for your answer showing that you have thought about more than
one point of view. Refer to religious arguments in your answer.   *(6 marks)*

Who else has rights? Include all of
them in your answer.

5   **Religion, War and Peace**

{ VICTIMS OF WAR FACE NEW HORRORS }

*Always pay attention to the stimulus –
it will help you with the question.*

(21) Give **two** problems faced by people living in a country at war.   *(2 marks)*

*Try to give problems caused by war, not just
everyday ones that anybody faces.*

(22) Describe briefly the work of one organisation that helps the victims of war.   *(2 marks)*

*It would be really easy to write too much –
just say two things the organisations do.*

(23) **Religious believers can do nothing to create peace on earth.** What do you think?
Explain your opinion.   *(3 marks)*

*In the 3-mark evaluation questions, it is
okay to answer from just one point of view.*

(24) Explain the religious teaching known as the Just War theory.   *(5 marks)*

*This theory has a series of key points – just
work through them in your answer.*

(25) **No country should have Weapons of Mass Destruction.** Do you agree? Give reasons
for your answer showing that you have thought about more than one point of view.
Refer to religious arguments in your answer.   *(6 marks)*

*If you don't refer to religious arguments,
you can't get more than 4 marks.*

6   **Religion and Young People**

(26) Give **two** ways in which religion can help young people as they grow up.   *(2 marks)*

> Simply name two ways. There is no
> need to waste time explaining them.

(27) **Religion should only be taught in faith schools.** What do you think?
      Explain your opinion.   *(3 marks)*

> Although you could answer this just from one side, it is
> usually easier to write a better answer by arguing from
> more than one point of view because you can think of
> more arguments – just don't write too much!

(28) Explain briefly what is meant by the term *the generation gap*.   *(2 marks)*

> Sometimes giving an example is a good way to explain –
> and helps you when a term is actually difficult to explain!

(29) Explain, in detail, an initiation ceremony in **one** religion you have studied.   *(5 marks)*

> This is asking you to describe what happens. You
> need to get it in the right order and give details.

(30) **Children are only religious because their parents are.** Do you agree? Give reasons
      for your answer showing that you have thought about more than one point of view.
      Refer to religious arguments in your answer.   *(6 marks)*

> If you don't give more than one point of view,
> you can't get more than 4 marks.

Life issues Glossary

Abortion deliberate expulsion of foetus from womb with the intention to destroy it

Abortion Act (1967) the UK law on abortion, which was amended by the Human Fertilisation and Embryology Act (1990)

Adoption where one/two people take on someone else's child legally as their own

Ahimsa (☬) 🕉 non-violence

Ageism prejudice against someone because of their age, leading to discrimination

Allah ☾ One God, Islamic term for God

Animal experimentation use of animals to test products and medicines, and to advance medical knowledge

Animal rights the idea that animals should have rights because of respect for life

Atman 🕉 inner 'self'/soul

Bible ✝ Christian holy book

Brahman 🕉 Ultimate Reality

Buddha ☸ Siddattha Gotama, the enlightened one, founder of Buddhism

Climate change global warming, which is characterised by freak and extreme weather, and which is seen as the major issue for the planet

Cloning taking the DNA from something and using it to produce a replica of the original being

Conservation helping to mend environmental damage, or to protect the environment

Creation idea that God created the world from nothing

Destruction causing the loss of something, e.g. cutting down trees which destroys natural habitats

Dhammapada ☸ Buddhist teaching, also spelled as Dharmapada; teachings of the Buddha

Disability lack of ability relative to the standard for a group, e.g. most people have no hearing difficulties, so someone who is hearing impaired can be considered to have a disability

Discrimination acting on prejudice

Emissions the release of gases and pollutants into the atmosphere that can cause environmental damage and health problems

Eternal life 🕉 concept of life everlasting

Ethnic cleansing when a group tries to remove a minority group from an area either by murdering them all, or forcing them to leave, so that a single ethnic group remains

Extinction the wiping out of a species, so that none can be found in any surveys over a set period

Factory farming farming as a business, where animals are intensively farmed, also known as battery farming

Fostering where a people legally look after someone else's child for a period of time, but do not take the child as their own

Genetic modification changing the DNA of something to be able to change the species, e.g. a pig to make its body parts compatible with humans for transplant; a crop to make it grow more quickly

Genocide the targeting and attempted wiping out of a whole ethnic group, e.g. the Holocaust

Guru Granth Sahib (☬) Sikh holy book

Guru Nanak (☬) founder of Sikhism

Holy War ☾ conditions under which Muslims should fight war

Hunting chasing animals to kill for food, fur, sport

Jesus ✝ founder of Christian religion; believed to be the Son of God by Christians

Judgement Day ✝ ☾ ☘ belief that at the end of time, all humans will be raised from the dead to be judged on the actions of their life by God

Just War ✝ (☬) conditions under which Christians/Sikhs should fight in war

Karma (☬) 🕉 the consequences of our words, deeds and actions

Kashrut ☘ food laws

Khalifah ☾ stewardship; belief that Allah has given us a duty to look after the world

Khalsa Sikh who has taken vows of faith

Kurahit prohibitions ('Do not ...') for Khalsa Sikhs

Langar Sikh community kitchen, set up by Guru Nanak

Miracle of life idea that getting pregnant, carrying to full term and giving birth is a very special, even miraculous event

Muhammad (pbuh) Prophet of Islam, final prophet to the world (Seal of prophets)

Natural habitats areas of natural vegetation and associated wildlife

Natural resources the things we use, such as coal, gas, oil, which are found naturally

Noachide Laws early set of laws found in Torah

Pacifism belief that all violence is wrong

Peace absence of war; harmony between groups/ nations

Pollution when too much of something is dumped into the atmosphere, on to land, into water, so that the environment is affected

Prejudice pre-judging people, usually unfavourably, before getting to know them

Pressure group a group set up to put pressure on society/government to make change, e.g. AbortionRight

Pro-Choice arguments to support a woman's right to decide what happens to her body, e.g. abortion

Pro-Life arguments to protect the right to life, in this book, of the foetus

Poverty deprivation of the basic needs that give quality of life, e.g. food, water, shelter, money

Quality of life argument about what a person's life should be like for it to be worth living, used within abortion debate

Qur'an holy book of Islam

Racism prejudice based on colour/race

Right the right to something, e.g. in the case of abortion a foetus' right to life, or the father's right to be involved in the decision

Sanctity of life idea that life is special and sacred

Sentient being idea that all life has sensory ability, i.e. can see, hear, etc.

Sexism prejudice based on gender

Shari'ah Law law of Islamic countries, based on the Qur'an, Hadith and Sunnah

Stewardship belief that humans are given the duty/task to look after the world for God; in Islam, khalifah

Suffering pain and discomfort felt as a result of something, can be caused by nature or by humans

Sunnah the words and deeds of Prophet Muhammad (pbuh) collected into a book

Sustainable development developing technologies that can be continued, and which do not cause more long-term harm than good

Tipitaka Buddhist scriptures, means 'Three Baskets' after three groups of scriptures

Ummah brotherhood – all Muslims are part of the Ummah

Vegetarianism non-meat diet; those who also do not eat dairy products are vegan

Viability capacity for survival, i.e. when a foetus is likely to survive if born, in the UK at 24 weeks

War two or more sides or nations in armed conflict against each other

Waste unwanted or undesired material or substance produced by human activity, also referred to as rubbish

Zoo place where animals are kept on show for the public to see, most are from other countries and climates

Religion and Morality

Topic 7: Religious attitudes to matters of life (medical ethics)

This topic is about life – just like it says. It focuses on the beginning of life, and on maintaining life, including research to improve the quality of life. So there are two very distinct halves to it, and you need to understand the two halves separately. The religion binds it all together because it gives you an idea of the attitudes that religions have to life, and from that you can work out the rights and responsibilities humans have regarding life. For some people, this is a frightening topic because it seems to have lots of science in it, and a lot of people don't find understanding science easy or comfortable. But let's make it simple – you are studying religion, and only need the most basic knowledge of the science. Don't worry – you'll be fine …

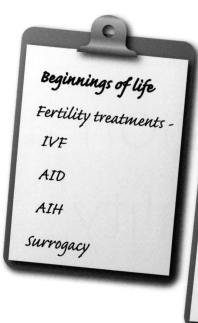

Beginnings of life

Fertility treatments –

IVF

AID

AIH

Surrogacy

Maintaining life

Genetic engineering

Embrology

Stem cell research/technology

Saviour sibling/designer baby

Cloning

Transplant surgery

Blood transfusion

Human experimentation

Now you should have a working definition of each subject or most, anyway.

Can you think why we might want to keep any of them as part of our medical system?
Can you think of why we should be wary of any of them as part of our medical system?

Those questions are crucial. The exam might ask you what these different subjects are – if it does, then it will probably only be for a small number of marks. However, it is more likely to ask you what the benefits and issues of each are, because that is where the religion and ethics come in (and this is a religion and ethics exam!). It is most likely to ask you what religions think about them, which is a mix of the benefits and issues with religious teachings. We will do all of that in the next few pages.

 Now you know the elements of this topic

Ethical issues and religious attitudes

Religious people need to make a judgement on what they can or can't do or use. They often have to ask the questions that are on this page. In the exam, when you are asked about religious attitudes to something, use these as starters for the points you make.

Why is life sacred?

It is important to remember that all religions believe that life is sacred and special. This is either because it is created by God as the most important part of the whole creation, or because it is one part of a long journey to enlightenment.

Who has the right to create life?

The fact that humans can now create life without having sexual intercourse is viewed differently depending on religious beliefs. For some religious people, the *only* way to a pregnancy should be sexual intercourse. This means the pregnancy has been created by God through the act of sex. For some, helping a couple become pregnant is fine, as long as only the couple's egg and sperm are used. This means that scientific methods are acceptable, but any use of donors is not. For others, medical science is seen as a gift of God, or an alleviation of suffering – so it is always acceptable, even when donors are involved.

What about maintaining life – whose right is that?

Well, God created life and gave man **stewardship** and dominion over his creation, according to many religions. So God must permit scientific knowledge and medicine as part of humanity looking after life. If a religious person believes in rebirth or reincarnation, then they would see medicine as helping people and easing suffering – both of which are important. So, when we talk about whether it is okay for humans to maintain life through **blood transfusion** and transplantation, then most religious people would say it was.

What about 'Frankenstein technologies'?

Frankenstein was a doctor from a famous story, written by Mary Shelley. He created a human from the body parts of dead humans, and then brought it to life using electricity. The result was a monster. Some religious people see some of the medical technologies as being like what Frankenstein did, and therefore, wrong. Things like **cloning** are seen as man taking God's place. There is also the worry about whether clones can have a soul. Some people believe that stem cell technology and embryo research mean that the potential life (the embryo created in a laboratory) doesn't deserve the same respect or rights as an embryo in the womb, or as a person. Each of those technologies means that many embryos are simply discarded or destroyed – and that is bad, because it can be seen as killing, or at the very least disrespecting life!

The Basics

1 Explain why life is sacred.
2 Explain how religious believers see the right to create life in different ways.
3 Explain why religious believers accept medical knowledge and advances.
4 **Medical research is an expensive waste of money.** What do you think? Explain your opinion.

 Now you have thought about some of the ethics

Science starting life

Having children is part of nature. Many couples feel they should have children to complete their relationship. Many people have what we call a *maternal* or *paternal* urge – they want to have children, and it is a very important thing for them. When they can't have children, some look to doctors and medicine for help – even when it costs a lot of money and the success rate is low.

The course lists specific types of **fertility treatment** that you have to know about. The exam could ask you about any of those types – what they are, what benefits or problems there are, or what the religions think about them. Let's find out what they are. There are other forms of fertility treatment, but the exam doesn't specify those, so you don't need to know them. Anything extra could impress those reading, but it isn't needed.

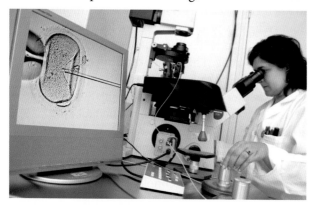

IVF

IVF stands for *in vitro fertilisation. In vitro* means 'in glass'. It makes the point that the egg and sperm are collected and brought together in a Petri dish. A number of dishes are prepared and are kept warm for a few days. The sperm fertilise the eggs, and the eggs begin to develop until each egg has become about eight identical cells, and is called a blastocyst. Several of these are then artificially placed into the woman's womb in the hope that a normal pregnancy will result.

IVF is used when the woman cannot conceive naturally. There is about a 25 per cent success rate. The egg and sperm could have come from the couple and/or donors. The egg and sperm will have been kept frozen ready for use and once fertilised any unused blastocysts must be destroyed within fourteen days by law.

Surrogacy

This is where another woman carries a pregnancy to full term for a couple. Conception is usually by one of the artificial methods on this page. It can be done using the couple's and/or donors' egg and sperm. The resultant child is then brought up as the child of the couple. **Surrogacy** is used in cases where the woman cannot medically carry a pregnancy. The surrogate will have agreed to bear the pregnancy. In the UK, although surrogacy occurs, it is illegal to pay someone to do it.

AID/H

AID/H is artificial insemination by donor/husband. Doctors collect several semen samples, which the man has produced by masturbating. The semen contains the sperm that are needed to fertilise the egg. The doctor uses a syringe to put the samples into the woman's womb when she ovulates, in a position in the womb which makes it more likely for fertilisation to happen. Hopefully, the egg will be fertilised. AIH is used when the husband has a low sperm count – the procedure helps his sperm to fertilise his wife's egg. AID is used when the husband has no sperm count (he is infertile), or he has a genetic disease that he does not wish to pass on (this means his sperm are fertile, but the risk of passing on the disease is too great). The success rate of this treatment is very low (currently about 15 per cent).

✓ Now you have learned about fertility treatment

Religious attitudes to fertility treatment

Don't forget to use the quotes on pages ix and x as well as the more specific information given here.

 ## Buddhism

- Buddhists practise ahimsa – loving kindness and non-violence to all sentient beings.
- All lives are shaped by karma, and suffering in this life is from that karma.
- Life exists from conception.

Having families has never been a major focus of Buddhism. However, those who want to but can't conceive children, suffer because of that.

Buddhists see fertility treatment as showing **compassion** (loving kindness) to people in this situation. It is possible to see their predicament as a result of previous karma though – which they need to work through. There is concern over the throwing away of excess embryos, as this can be seen as killing.

 ## Christianity

- Go forth and multiply. (Genesis)
- God knows each of us intimately, and has set a plan for our life. (Old Testament)
- Infertility is a call from God to adopt. (Roman Catholic teaching)

There are a variety of Christian views. Some accept all fertility treatment as part of God's gift of medicine, and even an extension of Jesus' teachings of love. Roman Catholics, however, see it as wrong, because children should be conceived by a couple within the confines of marriage. This is believed to be natural law. Many Christians hold a midway view. They accept fertility treatments, but see use of donor materials as adultery.

 ## Hinduism

- The householder (grihastha) stage of life should lead to children in a family.
- All men come into the world burdened by ancestor debt. The only way to repay this is by fathering a son.
- Karma shapes our lifetimes, and we have to face difficulties to repay bad karma from the past.

Children are very important in Hinduism, especially boys. There is a pressure to have children, and if that means through artificial means, fine. Levirate marriage (conceiving a child with a second wife/husband) is accepted in Hinduism, so use of donor materials would be. Fertility treatment can also be seen as a compassionate way to help people, as is surrogacy.

 ## Islam

- Allah gives life to whom he chooses. (Qur'an)
- 'Marriage is my tradition.' (Muhammad, pbuh)
- Do not come near adultery or fornication for it is shameful. (Qur'an)

Islam sees marriage and having children as a **duty**. There is the belief that Allah blesses couples with the gift of children, suggesting it is his will if someone is unable to have a child. Most Muslims will accept fertility treatments, though, seeing the knowledge as a gift from Allah. However, use of donor materials is seen as both adultery and fornication, so is considered wrong.

Judaism

- Go forth and multiply. (Genesis)
- Do not commit adultery. (Exodus)
- There are several stories of women being 'helped' to conceive when obviously infertile in the Tenakh, such as 2 Kings 4:14–16.

Judaism accepts fertility treatment as long as no donor material is used. The egg and sperm must be from the couple. Use of donor sperm is considered to be adultery, which breaks one of the Ten Commandments. It also requires a man to 'waste seed' because the child will not be his – another rule broken. There is concern over the potential social problems for the child and parents when it learns how it came to exist.

 Sikhism

- 'May you have seven sons.' (a traditional wedding blessing)
- Any third person within a marriage is seen as adultery.
- God gives life, which is an expression of his will. (Guru Granth Sahib)

Sikhism encourages couples to have children, and that is seen in the marriage blessing. For those Sikhs who cannot have children, any fertility treatment must not involve donor materials. This is considered to be a kind of adultery – one of the Four Abstinences. Although God chooses who will be born (which can mean accepting infertility as God's will), many Sikhs accept fertility treatment as God-given knowledge.

The Basics

1 Explain what is meant by IVF, AID, AIH and surrogacy.
2 Why do some people seek fertility treatment?
3 Outline the attitude of one or two religions to each kind of fertility treatment.
4 Why do many religions not accept fertility treatment that uses donor materials?
5 **People should just accept being infertile as God's will.** Do you agree? Give reasons and explain your answer showing you have thought about more than one point of view.

Task

Use the information from the religion(s) you have studied to argue this point:
Religious people should never use fertility treatment.
Make sure you have two points of view in your answer, and have explained your arguments, supporting them with religious quotations.

✓ **Now you have learned about religious attitudes to fertility treatment**

Helping others

The second portion of this topic is about how medical science tries to help people, and the religious attitudes to that.

All religions say that people should help each other. For some, looking after others is a duty from God – Christians, Muslims, Jews and Sikhs might say this. For others, it is helpful to their spiritual development to help others – Buddhists, Hindus and Sikhs might say this. Then again, it could be seen as an act of worship, or devoting yourself to God's work. So you'd expect religions to support medical science and its continued improvement. It isn't always the case, though, and there are areas of the newest medical advances that religious people are either concerned about or disagree with.

Think about these scenarios. For each one, discuss with a partner whether you think the medical treatment is morally or ethically right: in other words, is it a good or bad thing in each case. The treatment to discuss is in bold.

Sam has been hit by a car. He needs an operation and many **blood transfusions**.

Caleb has very weak heart. He needs a **transplant** to save his life.

Jack's granddad has Parkinson's disease. Doctors say that **stem cell therapy** could help him to recover.

Jay and Shilpa's young son has a genetic disorder. They need tissue from a perfect match donor. Doctors have said they can **genetically engineer** the DNA of a new baby the couple could have, to provide the donor materials needed to help their son.

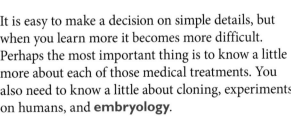

Do you still reach the same decision when the extra information below is available?

- Sam's family do not believe it is right to have blood from someone else.
- Caleb's doctors have said the only available heart is that of a genetically modified pig.
- Stem cells come from embryos that are a few days old. The embryos are then discarded.
- Jay and Shilpa don't want another child – a new baby would be produced only to save the child they already have and want.

It is easy to make a decision on simple details, but when you learn more it becomes more difficult. Perhaps the most important thing is to know a little more about each of those medical treatments. You also need to know a little about cloning, experiments on humans, and **embryology**.

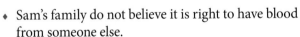

Now you have thought about how medicine can help others

Medical research

The Human Embryo and Fertilisation Act (2008)

The 1990 Act covered three main areas. Firstly, it regulated any fertility treatment that uses donated eggs or sperm, or embryos created through IVF. Secondly, it made rules about the storage of eggs, sperm and embryos. Thirdly, it gave guidelines and rules for any **experiments** on early stage human embryos. In 2000–2001, the Act was amended to allow the use of a dead man's sperm (when collected in his lifetime), and to allow doctors to create embryos to use in research on **therapeutic cloning**. These amendments were made for the purpose of improving medicine in the future, and the better understanding (and so tackling) of disease. In 2008, further amendments to the Act ensured the regulation of any embryo not *in utero*, banned sex-selection for non-medical reasons and recognised same-sex couples as the legal parents of children conceived through donated materials.

The whole point of the law was to set up rules for scientists to work within. It tries to show respect to embryonic life – when embryos are destroyed after fourteen days their development has been minimal. It also tries to show respect to people's lives by trying to find cures and ways to help people.

Embryo research

Embryo research is only allowed on embryos younger than fourteen days. Scientists use this research to try to learn more about the development of embryos, and also to learn more about disease, especially genetic diseases. The hope is that this research will help to find cures. It is impossible to study embryos when they are in the womb, so the only way is to use 'spare' embryos from fertility treatment or to create embryos just for research.

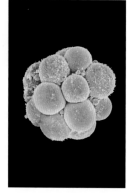

A human embryo less than fourteen days old

Stem cell research

Within embryos are stem cells. These are cells that can develop into any part of the human body – they have the ability to become anything. They are being used to 'grow' organs like kidneys, and also to help repair parts of the brain in sufferers of Parkinson's disease. Once the stem cells have been removed, the embryos die.

Genetic engineering

Everyone has DNA – it is what makes each of us unique. It contains all the reasons for why, who and what we are – it is like human programming. This programming is made up of 100,000 genes. Some of those genes are dangerous and even fatal – they make us susceptible to diseases, or even to being born with a disease. Scientists have worked on gene research and can modify the genetic make-up of cells to successfully treat hundreds of genetic disorders and diseases. This is called **human genetic engineering**.

Cloning

This is asexual reproduction – in other words creating a human foetus from one person, using an egg and cells. The foetus is an exact replica of the human it was cloned from. Dolly the sheep was the most famous example of cloning. It is illegal to clone humans.

✓ **Now you have learned about medical technologies**

Thinking about medical technology

Task

In the exam, you could be asked why religious people agree or disagree with any of the medical technologies on the previous page.
Read the conversation between James and John below. They are discussing these technologies. Pick out their arguments to agree or disagree with each type of technology.
Copy and complete the table at the bottom of the page as you work through their conversation, using the information from the previous page as well.

James: Did you read about those scientists? They are cutting up embryos to do research on. That's experimenting on babies!

John: Yeah, but they can only do it up to fourteen days, so it's just a blob of cells really. And anyway, they are finding out stuff that will help people in the future.

James: It's still a baby, I think – well, a 'going-to-be' baby. I think that is cruel and says their life isn't worth anything.

John: They have no nerves, so there is no pain. I think it is better to sacrifice them and learn, than to let babies be born with illnesses and stuff.

James: I bet you agree with stem cell research too then, don't you?

John: Certainly do. Those cells are like magic – they change into whatever you need them to be. Doctors will be able to grow organs, or help people with brain damage. The embryos are leftovers from IVF, so they would be destroyed anyway – I reckon it's a better use to take their stem cells out. Helps people that way.

James: It is still being disrespectful of life – even if it is only potential life. Life is supposed to be special and sacred. So what about cloning then?

John: Oh, I'm not sure about that. No sex, but there is a baby – doesn't seem right.

James: IVF is no sex, but a baby – and you agree with that.

John: Cloning is different. They don't even use two people to make the embryo. I think all babies should come from a mum and dad, not a mum and a bunch of her own cells! And what about the problems the clone could have? They have the same genetic age as the cells that made them – imagine being a baby with the genetics of a 50 year old! You'd get all the ageing stuff way too early!

James: But it would mean you could make **designer babies**, like to provide a perfect match for someone who was ill with a disease. I think that is a good thing about it.

John: Well, in that case, you should accept genetic engineering. Scientists get the embryos and take out the DNA, fix it and put it back. That way the baby doesn't have the disease in the first place.

James: We are back to experimenting on embryos. I'm confused about what to think now!

Technology	What is it?	Benefits	Problems
Embryo research			

 Now you have thought about the medical technologies and their ethics

Transfusions and transplants

Most people have absolutely no worries at all about this. They support both. In effect these procedures don't take life, don't mess with the living, and do help others. But, what are they?

Transfusions

This is usually about blood and blood products (like plasma or platelets). If someone has to have an operation, they may need extra blood to replace the blood they lose during the operation. If someone has an accident and loses a lot of blood, they may need it to be replaced. This is what blood transfusions are all about. The blood that people are given must, in most cases, match the blood group they have. There are a number of different ones, and some are more common than others. Get the wrong blood group and it could be fatal. Blood transfusions for humans have been happening since 1818, and blood groups were only discovered in 1900 – so transfusion was a very risky procedure until then.

> There are always appeals for people to give blood. Why do you think blood services have to keep asking for more blood?

Transplantation

Organ transplantation happens because the organ in someone's body is failing, has failed or is so damaged that it needs to be replaced. The first transplant procedure was done in 1905, and was corneal grafting (replacing part of the eye). The first organ transplant was done in 1954 – it took that long to get it right! Nowadays, organ transplantation is very common. Most organs are donated by the dead, who have carried a consent form, or whose families have agreed their bodies can be used to help others. Organs such as the heart, liver and kidneys are common transplant organs, but really most of the body can be used. Some people give up organs while still alive, for example, giving up one of their two kidneys, or donating a part of their liver. This is usually for a relative – so is an act of love – but there are cases in other countries where people sell the organ because they need the money. That is illegal in the UK. Recently, doctors have been able to genetically modify certain animals so that organs from their bodies can be used in humans – this is called xenotransplantation.

> There are always appeals for people to carry donor cards. Why do you think the number of appeals increases all the time?

NHS
Blood and Transplant
www.blood.co.uk

Task

1 Would you give blood? Explain your answer.
2 Would you join the NHS Organ Donor Register? Explain your answer.
3 More people have joined the NHS Organ Donor Register than give blood – why do you think that is?
4 Would you accept an organ from an animal if you needed one? Explain.
5 Do you think people should have to carry a card to *not* be an organ donor? This would mean that the body of anyone who dies could be used to help others. Explain your answer.

donor card **NHS**

NHS Organ Donor Register

Now you have thought about transfusions and transplants

Religious attitudes to maintaining life

Don't forget to use the quotes on pages ix–x and 95–96 to boost your knowledge here.

 Buddhism

- In many lifetimes, the Buddha gave up his own life to save that of others, for example, lying down before a starving lioness so that she could eat him and then feed her cubs.
- The Bodhisattva vow – to help all who need help.
- Cherish in your hearts boundless goodwill to all beings. (Buddha)

In terms of transfusions and transplants, Buddhism leaves it to the individual's choice. It is a good thing in that you help others, usually selflessly. There are concerns about experimenting on embryos and about other technologies linked with embryos. One monk has said that until we know for sure the embryos feel no pain or have no consciousness of what is happening to them, we should not do experiments on them. However, it is the case that this work should help many people in the future, and so – in that sense – many Buddhists will cautiously accept the technologies.

✝ Christianity

- All life is sacred, and should be respected because it is given by God.
- Jesus helped others.
- Love one another. (Jesus to his disciples)

Roman Catholics believe that any research using embryos is wrong and against natural law. A foetus should be given the same respect a person would have – and we wouldn't do this to people. Other Christians are similarly unhappy because they believe all life is sacred. However, many can see the potential benefit in the future to many people, and when the embryos used were to be discarded anyway, they see this as making something good from bad. Cloning is seen as playing God and therefore wrong.

Organ donation and blood transfusion are seen as acts of kindness. In fact, Pope Benedict XVI called it a 'free act of good will', and he himself has agreed to be a donor after his **death**. Most Christians agree with both, though Jehovah's Witnesses have now pioneered bloodless surgery because they disagree with having blood from someone else (the life is in the blood).

 Hinduism

- Hinduism has stories where human body parts are used to help others.
- All things, including humans, are expressions of Brahman.
- Daya (compassion) and dana (charity) must be practised by Hindus.

There is nothing in the scriptures that prevents Hindus from being blood or organ donors. In fact, it fits well with their duties and efforts to attain moksha (liberation/freedom from the cycle of rebirth). It is up to the individual, though, to make the decision.

When it comes to things like cloning, this is not seen as creating souls (Hindus believe souls migrate into bodies) so is okay. Where embryo research uses live embryos, Hindus see this as wrong, because it is experimenting on human life.

Islam

- Whoever saves a life, it would be as if he had saved the life of all people. (Qur'an)
- Shari'ah Law prohibits the mutilation of a body.
- Do not take life – which Allah has made sacred – except for just cause. (Qur'an)

Embryo research on *live* embryos is wrong. It is a life, which is sacred. If the tissue used in experiments is from a miscarried foetus or an abortion, then it would be acceptable to use it in research, which could benefit others. Cloning is playing God, and is therefore shirk (blasphemy).

There is a dilemma in Islam that we should not cut up dead bodies, but still have a duty to save life. **Transplant surgery** is seen as saving life, so Shari'ah Law allows it as the lesser of two wrong things. Blood transfusion simply helps others, so is encouraged, even though it is not a common practice among Muslims in the UK.

 ## Judaism

- If one is in the position to be able to donate an organ to save another's life, it is obligatory to do so. (Rabbi Moses Tendler)
- A basic principle of Jewish ethics is the infinite worth of a human being.
- It is forbidden to mutilate a body, and the whole body must be buried.

Genetic engineering is acceptable in Judaism if it is to get rid of disease, but not to improve G-d's creation (blasphemy). Research using live embryos is wrong. Embryos that are left over from IVF, for example, could be used, rather than creating embryos (sacred life) to experiment on.

Jews have an obligation to preserve human life. So, most rabbis would permit both transplants and transfusions. However, the time between certified death and removal of a heart is unclear, so heart transplants are not acceptable (the removal could have caused the death).

Sikhism

- Sewa – service to others as an act of worship.
- Life begins at conception, and is given by God.
- Caring for the sick has been part of Sikhism from the earliest days of the faith.

Sikhs do not agree with experiments on live embryos because life begins at conception. They would accept genetic engineering where it prevents disease, but not to improve or alter the body God has created. Cloning could either be helpful or against God – depending on the intention behind it.

Transplants and transfusions both help others. Service to others is a duty and whether by donating, or by being the surgeon who carries out the procedure, a Sikh does sewa. Since Sikhs believe that the body is just waste after death, it can be used to help others.

Many Sikhs believe that God gave humans this knowledge, so to not use the knowledge for the good of humans is wrong.

The Basics

1 Explain each of these terms – embryo research, genetic engineering, cloning, transplants, blood transfusions.
2 For each of them, explain the attitudes of the religion(s) you have studied.
3 Why might a religious person disagree with any of them?
4 **Medical science is playing God.** What do you think? Explain your opinion.

 Now you know the religious attitudes

Humans and experiments

For the course, you have to think about whether it is right to experiment on humans, and what religions would say about that.

Scientists already do experiments on humans. They do observational tests, for example, to watch behaviour. They carry out surveys, and get people to keep logs of their feelings, emotions, temperature, pulse and so on. They interview people and collate the results. None of these causes any harm to people.

Scientists also test new drugs on humans. The humans usually volunteer, and are usually paid (in the UK) for being the guinea pigs. These drugs have already gone through years of checking and animal testing first, so it really is at the last point before public use – it is meant to be safe and useful when it gets to this stage. Again, there should be no harm to humans.

What we can see is that generally speaking, testing on humans is always meant to be safe. The tests are always carried out with the consent of the person.

Having said that, there are historical cases of testing having been done without consent, for example, the Nazis in the Second World War, or the Japanese in China in the first half of the twentieth century. No one thinks that these tests were right. The people were victims of abuse. But what if people agree to the tests, and they go wrong? One famous example of this was in March 2006, when some volunteers had extreme reactions to the drugs they were testing. All recovered, but it was headline news.

INFORMED CONSENT TO EXPERIMENT

Principal investigators Dr. R. J. Portman and Dr. K. R. Singh

By signing below, I am indicating that I am at least 18 years of age, and I have read and understand the procedures described above. My questions have been answered to my satisfaction, and I agree to participate in this study.

Signed ....

Task

Your teacher will give each group one of the phrases below. Write on an A3 sheet. Take three minutes to write as many points in agreement or disagreement as you can onto the sheet. Swap the sheet with another group. You then have four minutes to add extra points, and/or extend any of the points already on there. Swap the sheet with a third group. You then have five minutes to read the comments, then add from your group or extend what is already on there. Swap with a fourth group, and check the different ideas that have come out about the statement those groups have thought about.

Why do scientists do experiments on humans?

If people agree to be guinea pigs, and if they are paid and they know what will happen, is it okay to test on them?

Should there be limits and regulations to testing on humans?

Science needs answers for the future, so people should be used as test subjects with or without their knowledge.

Why is testing on humans not as controversial as testing on embryos?

Testing on humans is like saying life isn't sacred or special.

Which is more important – testing on people or embryos?

Now you have thought about testing on humans

This topic is about the last part of life. It includes attitudes to the elderly, and the issues they face. It then goes on to look at attitudes to people at the end of their life, including **euthanasia,** life support and **hospices**. Finally, it is concerned with how religions view **life after death** – what they think will happen to us.

Two concepts key to the whole of this topic are **sanctity of life** and **quality of life**. You need to know what they mean.

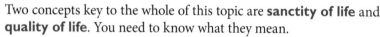

Sanctity of life

This is the idea that all life is special. Many religions believe life is sacred because God created it (Christianity, Hinduism, Islam, Judaism and Sikhism). Some religions believe life is special because it is the way we can achieve enlightenment (Buddhism and Hinduism). No one in the world believes that life is worth nothing. All the legal systems put murder as the worst **crime** you could commit, with the toughest **punishments**. Life is special, and deserves to be protected and cherished – not given up on. All religions believe that.

Quality of life

This is a description of how good someone's life is. It includes how comfortable they feel, how easy it is for them to live through each day, perhaps how much they have in terms of money and possessions. For this topic, it is about whether or not life is worth living because of the medical situation a person finds themselves in. Giving someone a good quality of life is part of the most basic teaching of all religions – that we should treat others as we wish to be treated.

> Look at the scenarios on the right. In each case, is it about sanctity of life or quality of life? Or both? Explain your thoughts each time.

- John is a serial killer. He murders people who are dying of terminal illnesses.
- Sarah visits her mother often to make sure she has everything she needs and is comfortable.
- Dave is very ill with cancer, and is constantly in a lot of pain. He is in a hospice.
- The local priest blesses those who are ill or dying, and visits them often.
- Kulpna is a doctor in the Intensive Care Unit. She makes decisions about life support.

 Now you have thought about the sanctity and quality of life

Getting old

Like it or not, most of us get old. We certainly all know old people – and by that we mean people beyond the age of **retirement**. Many of those people actually feel quite young, and would feel insulted to be classed as old. For this course, let's stick to 'those beyond the age of retirement', which means the over 65s – people who get a state pension and various other benefits because of their age. People who reach 75 get extra support. More and more people are living to be older – our life expectancy has increased a lot in the last century.

> What issues are there for **senior citizens**? With a partner check out the examples below, and pick out the positives and the negatives.

George: I fought in wars and won medals. In my lifetime I have seen many things and learned so much. I can pass on that knowledge and wisdom which comes from experience. I don't get much respect from people though – even after what I did for my country. Young people especially don't get it – they can be quite rude and ageist to me.

Susan: My health isn't as good as it used to be, and I need lots of medicines. My family are a big help to me, so that I can still live in my own home with their support and with visits from nurses regularly. I feel like I am the centre of my family – they all still come to me for a chat and advice. I've become what my gran was – the matriarch!

Benjamin: I hated it when I had to retire. I worked for the government, so I had no choice. I suddenly had nothing to do with my day. I have got more used to it now, and I have lots of hobbies which I enjoy. Some of them are hobbies I had as a boy, and only now have the time (and money) to go back to.

Brian: My pension isn't as good as my wages were, so I have less money than I used to. Sometimes money is very tight. I was glad that the government gave us some extra heating money this year – I don't think I could have afforded to keep my home warm and eat if I hadn't got that.

Esther: I am very active even though I am 80. I keep myself fit and healthy by walking and going to the OAP sessions at the local gym (they are free!). I don't think old people's voices are heard – we are just written off as a bit mad and out of touch. Some of us are but I think we are still worth listening to a lot of the time!

The Basics

1 What issues do you think old people face in Britain today?
2 Make a list of the good things about being old.
3 **Old people are no use to society.** What do you think? Explain your opinion.

 Now you have thought about being old

Caring for the elderly

Our society cares for the elderly in a variety of ways. The exam could ask you about how we do that, so let's think – you already know this, so use your knowledge.

> For each scenario below, work out whether there is any support and what that support is.

Fred lives on his own, in his house. He has a state pension and his family visit him with extras every week.

Nora lives in a **care home for the elderly**. She eats in the dining room with the others. Specially trained people work in the home, and provide all the care and support the people need. Her family visit when they can.

Jane lives in sheltered accommodation. This means there is a warden who lives in another part of the building, and if she has a problem she can get his help quickly. A community room in the building means she gets to spend time with other people of her age. There is a doctor's surgery and a coffee room in the building as well. Her food is delivered by Meals on Wheels.

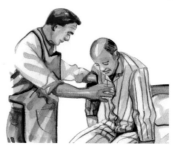

Andrew lives in his own house, but has carers to help him every day. One helps him get up and washed, and sorts out his breakfast. Later his pre-ordered meals will be delivered and another carer will come to prepare them for him. Finally the carer helps him to go to bed.

Religious attitudes to the elderly

 Buddhism

- We may carry our mothers on one shoulder, and our fathers on the other, and look after them for a hundred years … we will still be in debt to them. (Buddha)
- Old people are a demonstration of anicca (impermanence), so we learn from them.
- May all beings be happy. (traditional Buddhist blessing)

 Christianity

- Honour your father and mother. (Ten Commandments)
- Listen to your father who gave you life and do not hate your mother when she is old. (Proverbs)
- You shall rise up before the grey headed, and honour the aged. (Leviticus)

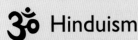 ## Hinduism

- Whoever honours his father, honours the Creator himself. Whoever honours their mother, honours the earth itself. (Mahabharata)
- The whole purpose of human existence is to benefit other people through one's life, possessions, thoughts and words. (Bhagavata Purana)
- Let your mother be a god to you. Let your father be a god to you. (Taittiriya Upanishad)

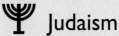 ## Judaism

- Honour your father and mother. (Ten Commandments)
- Do not cast me off in old age, when my strength fails me. (Psalms)
- See that they [parents] eat and drink, and take them where they want to go. (Talmud)

Islam

- Your Lord orders that you … be kind to parents. (Qur'an)
- May his nose be rubbed in the dirt who found his parents approaching old age [and he] did not look after them. (Hadith)
- Your Lord has commanded that … you be kind to your parents. You should not even say 'Uff!' or criticise them … say 'Lord bless them, they nurtured, cherished and sustained me in childhood'. (Qur'an)

Sikhism

- It is the greatest sin to quarrel with parents who have given you birth and brought you up. (Adi Granth)
- When a man acts in an unkind way towards his parents, his religious actions are worthless.
- Countless wrongs does the son, his mother forgives and remembers none. (Guru Granth Sahib)

The Basics

1. It is quite obvious that all religions believe we should show respect to our parents. For each religion you are studying, explain how we can show respect to the elderly, and use quotations to say why.
2. In what ways do people support the elderly in our society?
3. Are there any forms of support that you think are unfair or wrong? Explain why.
4. **Religious people should care for their relatives as their first duty.** What do you think? Explain your opinion.

 Now you have thought about caring for the elderly

Care for the dying

Everyone dies – we all know that. For some, death is sudden, or swift. For others, it comes at the end of a long and/or painful time. There is an argument about whether we should have the right to choose to die if we want to, and about how the dying should be cared for. For the exam, you need to be able to argue about both.

The hospice movement

Hospices are homes for the dying. People may go there until they die, or to give their families respite from looking after them for a while. On average, people stay there for two weeks, whether as a respite or until death.

Originally, hospices were places for travellers, the sick and the needy to stay. They were set up by Christians. Over time, some of them began to specialise in looking after those who were dying.

When someone is dying, they can't be cured – only cared for. If that care covers all aspects of their being, they will not wish for euthanasia. This is the basic idea of hospices.

The aims of hospices

1 To relieve the physical symptoms of illness, in other words, to get rid of as much pain as is possible. This includes things such as massage, meditation and relaxation. Often, medical treatment for the dying is very specialised – we call it palliative care.

2 To care for the emotional and spiritual well-being of the patient. Many dying people have unfinished business, which is a worry to them – the hospices help them to sort things out. Many patients are angry ('why me?') and hospices help them to come to terms with dying. Many patients need to be listened to, and given time – relatives often can't cope with this, but the hospices do.

3 To support the families of patients because they suffer too. Hospices provide many support networks and services for them, even after the death of the patient.

4 To educate others about caring for the dying, and to work out new, better ways to care for them – invaluable in the future, so that the experience built up in hospices can be used in other places.

Religious groups see hospices as the way forward for terminally ill people. God wants us to care for these people, to look after them, to express God's love for them; not to kill them.

Research Task

Find out about a hospice local to your school. Learn something of the work it does, the values behind its work, the number of people it helps each year, whether it specialises in certain illnesses or age groups. Produce a report on that hospice for others in your class.

The national charity organisation for hospices: **www.helpthehospices.org.uk**
You can learn much about the hospice movement from its website.

St Ann's Hospice

every day makes a difference

Registered charity number 258085

This hospice was opened in 1971, and serves the Greater Manchester community. Its aim is to improve the quality of life of people with life-limiting illnesses. It aims to do this while supporting families and carers.

In a year, the hospice cares for over 3000 people, and about 40 per cent of patients return home after their stay. This costs almost £9 million, meaning that the hospice has to raise over £16,000 a day, which it does through voluntary contributions.

Cancer-related illness accounts for the majority of patients. Each patient is cared for on an individual basis, and at all times care aims to meet their personal needs. This is what makes the support so unique and effective.

Care is based on the simple idea that, though having a life-limiting illness or dying, each patient is still a living person with unique spiritual and emotional needs as well as physical ones. The hospice tries to care for these.

Supporting families

When someone is dying, there is a huge burden on their family. They have to try to support and care for their dying relative, but at the same time cope with their own feelings. Many people feel sad at the pain and loss, angry that this is happening, worried about the future, and they struggle to cope with everything.

How do religions support the families of the dying?

Hospices try to support families, by having network support groups work through them. They will put families in contact with agencies who can help them.

You have already read that the hospice movement was set up by Christians. Many hospices today retain those religious links – just check out a list of hospices on the internet or in a phone book and you will see how many are named after saints and other religious characters. Religions, of course, support the members of their communities who are dying, and also support their families.

Members of the religion can pray for the family and the dying. They can give comfort with readings from the holy book. They can be there to give emotional support, or just spend time with them. They can listen to them, and help them come to terms with what is happening. They can provide practical help to do things for the family – shopping and so on.

The Basics

1 Explain what a hospice is.
2 What are the aims of a hospice?
3 Describe the work of one hospice.
4 How do religions support the families of those who are dying?
5 How can religious believers comfort the dying?
6 **Hospices are the best way to help the dying.** What do you think? Explain your opinion.

 Now you have learned about hospices

Euthanasia

Euthanasia is mercy killing. It is helping someone to die, who is suffering from a terminal illness, or whose quality of life is less than they can bear, usually because of a degenerative disease. Euthanasia is done because of compassion – loving kindness.

The debates surrounding euthanasia have a long history! Hippocrates, a doctor from Ancient Greece, openly stated he would not prescribe drugs to help someone end their life. His stance has become the Hippocratic Oath, sworn by doctors in the UK, which says 'I will give no deadly medicine to anyone if asked, nor suggest such counsel …' In 1516 CE, Thomas More defended euthanasia as the last treatment option for doctors to give, if the patient wanted it.

In the twentieth century, in most Western countries, groups exist to try to make euthanasia legal. In some countries, it is legal. The debate rages on.

Active euthanasia is when the dying person is killed to put them out of their suffering. What happens ends their life – their illness does not kill them.

Passive euthanasia is when the dying person is allowed to die through taking away the medical support they have – the illness is allowed to kill them.

Task

Look at these scenarios. Which ones are active euthanasia and which ones are passive?
1 Ben's doctor injects him with a medicine that stops his heart so that he dies.
2 Carl's doctor turns off his **life-support machine** which is keeping him alive.
3 Lisa decides to stop taking the medicine that is slowing down the growth of her brain tumour, so that the tumour will kill her sooner.
4 Jean's husband puts a pillow over her face and suffocates her when her illness has become too painful to bear.

The law on euthanasia in the UK

Euthanasia is illegal in Britain. It can be seen as assisted suicide, so breaking the Suicide Act 1961, which forbids anyone from helping someone else to die and carries a fourteen-year jail sentence. It can also be viewed as manslaughter or, at worst, murder, which carries a life sentence.

Doctors do switch off life-support machines when patients have no sign of brain activity, and they do administer drugs to ease pain, which also shorten life. Neither of these is seen as euthanasia in the UK.

The Basics

1 What is meant by euthanasia?
2 Using examples, explain the difference between active and passive euthanasia.
3 Explain why doctors might feel unhappy about active euthanasia.
4 What is the law in the UK regarding euthanasia?
5 **Everyone should have the right to die if that is what they want.** Do you agree? Give reasons and explain your answer, showing you have thought about more than one point of view.
6 **Euthanasia is murder.** Do you agree? Give reasons and explain your answer, showing you have thought about more than one point of view.

Why euthanasia – or why not?

The exam often asks why religious people agree or disagree with euthanasia. Religious people are just the same as anyone else, and their reasons may be religious or secular. Work through the reasons on the right and decide which ones agree with euthanasia and which ones go against it.

> Can you add any other reasons why people might agree or disagree with euthanasia?

- No one has the right to take life – only God.
- Everyone has the right to decide when they have had enough.
- It is an act of kindness to help someone die if that is what they really want.
- To allow euthanasia would encourage it – then people would force it for their own desires, for example, making a rich parent feel like a burden.
- Euthanasia is another form of murder.
- For some people, the only help we can give them is to help them die.
- There can be miracle cures, and good can come out of terrible situations, so we should not seek euthanasia in case the situation is meant to be.
- We should show love by caring for the dying in their last days – not by killing them.

The life-support issue

Doctors will switch off life-support machines. This is done with the consent of the family, and is always when the patient has no hope of recovery. Essentially, the machine is keeping the person alive by making their lungs breathe, monitoring their heart and feeding them intravenously.

Switching off the machine is not seen as euthanasia in the eyes of the law, and doctors cannot be prosecuted. It is a recognition that medical treatment has failed – the patient is in effect already dead.

Not everyone agrees with switching off these machines. One famous example is that of Tony Bland. He was a Liverpool fan severely injured in the Hillsborough disaster (96 fans were crushed to death at an FA Cup semi-final in 1989). He suffered broken ribs, punctured lungs and severe brain damage. He was on a life-support machine until 1993 when the courts granted his parents' wish to have his treatment ended so that he could die. Tony's life-support machine was switched off on 22 February, and he died on 3 March.

Life and SPUC both disagreed and mounted campaigns to stop the life-support machine being switched off. They claimed that it is not our place to end life, but to protect and save it.

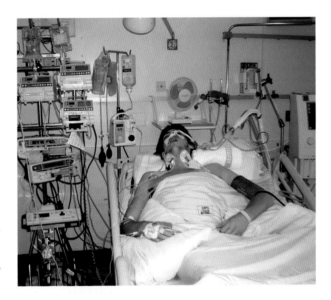

The Basics

1 Explain why some people agree with euthanasia as an option.
2 Explain why some people disagree with euthanasia.
3 Explain different attitudes to life support.
4 **Life support is another way of playing God.** What do you think? Explain your opinion.

✓ Now you have thought about euthanasia

Religious attitudes to death and euthanasia

 Buddhism

Buddhists believe all life is special. It deserves protection. Death is inevitable – just part of the journey. It is wrong to speed up that death though, because everyone has karma to work through, and the suffering leading up to death may be part of that karma.

- I will abstain from taking life. (First Precept)
- At the hour of death, a king and a beggar are equal because no amount of **wealth** or relatives can affect or prevent death. (Lama Zopa Rinpoche)
- A primary guiding principle in Buddhism is the relief of suffering.
- 'In the event a person is definitely going to die … is either in great pain or has virtually become a vegetable, and prolonging his existence is only going to cause … suffering for others, the termination of his life may be permitted according to Mahayana Buddhist ethics.' (Dalai Lama)

Many Buddhists would not support euthanasia – life should be protected and suffering is part of our karma. However, it is important to make death as comfortable as possible, so Buddhism supports the hospice movement, which helps people to have a 'good' death. Our state of mind is important when we die because it is a key to shaping our next lifetime. If we are angry, anxious and upset, then this will have a negative impact. If we face death with acceptance, then the rebirth is better. Having said that, the intention of every act is key – and euthanasia is usually done out of compassion, and with the wishes of the person who dies, so is a 'good' death.

 Christianity

Life is sacred because it is created by God. We should protect life as much as possible. Generally, although Christians talk about being with God after death, there is no wish to hasten death. The hospice movement is seen as the compassionate and proper way to help those who are dying while they wait for God to take their life.

- God created life in his own image. (Genesis)
- You shall not kill. (Ten Commandments)
- I, your God, give life, and I take it away. (Old Testament)
- It is the teaching of the Catholic Church that life be respected from conception until natural death.
- Doctors do not have an overriding obligation to prolong life by all available means. (Church of England)

Attitudes to euthanasia are diverse in Christianity but most Christians do not agree with it. It is seen by many, such as the Roman Catholic Church, as a failure of the systems available – and even as murder. Many Christians believe it is our duty to look after people when they are dying, not just kill them – which suggests they are not worthy of life. The Church of England accepts passive euthanasia, where nothing can be done for the patient, but does not agree with active euthanasia. The Dutch Protestant Church believes that the patient can lose all quality of life, and that God would not wish for their suffering to continue. These Christians accept active euthanasia, and even bless people before the procedure is done.

For some questions on religious attitudes, see pages 113–14.

Hinduism

Hindus believe that our atman (soul) lives through many lifetimes, and that each life is shaped by the words, actions and thoughts of the previous ones. This means that any suffering in this life is intended so that bad karma from previous lifetimes can be worked through. Cutting short this life by euthanasia just puts off that task – so is generally seen as wrong.

- Ahimsa (non-harming) is a basic principle of Hinduism.
- Compassion (loving kindness) and respect (including for all life) are other key principles of Hinduism.
- The result of a virtuous action is pure joy; actions done from emotion bring pain and suffering. (Baghavad Gita)
- The one who tries to escape from the trials of this life by taking their own life will suffer even more in the next life. (Yajur Veda)

There is great respect for age and the wisdom associated with it in Hinduism. This protects many older people from even the suggestion of euthanasia, but it does not mean that some of them will not choose to die rather than be a burden on their family (as they see it). It would be accepted that they refuse food or medicines, but it would be wrong for them to be euthanised. Active euthanasia can be seen as trying to escape problems, so it is wrong for the person to seek euthanasia. Also, if the person trying to help them die is doing so because they can't cope with their own feelings, then that is wrong. Hindu principles are to look after, care for and support the dying until their natural death.

Islam

In Islam, any form of self-harm or self-killing is wrong. Basically, it is the decision of Allah when a person should die, which means any interference into what is Allah's plan is wrong.

- Neither kill nor destroy yourself. (Qur'an)
- No one can die except by Allah's leave, that is a decree with a fixed term. (Qur'an)
- Whoever kills a man … it shall be as if he had killed all mankind. (Qur'an)
- Do not take life – which Allah has made sacred – except for a just cause. (Qur'an)
- Euthanasia is zulm – a wrong doing against Allah. (Shari'ah Law)

The Muslim attitude to euthanasia is very straightforward. Life is sacred, made by Allah. It will be ended when Allah decides – not when the person themselves or their family or a doctor decides. There is a story of a man who was helped to die because of the great suffering he was in. The man and his 'helper' were both denied paradise as a result. No one knows the plans of Allah. This is called al-Qadr or the predestination of Allah's will. In other words, Allah has planned for this experience and it must be important. So no one should make that decision to end life – it will happen when Allah wills it. This does not mean that a person couldn't refuse the medicine that is keeping them alive longer. In many cases, passive euthanasia would be accepted – where there is absolutely no hope.

The Basics

Using pages 112–15, read through the religion(s) you have studied and answer the following questions:
1 Use teachings to explain their attitude to life.
2 Use teachings to explain their attitude to when we die.
3 Use teachings to explain whether or not they agree with euthanasia.
4 Describe their beliefs about life after death.
5 **There is no such thing as life after death.** Do you agree? Give reasons for your answer, showing you have thought about more than one point of view. Refer to religious arguments in your answer.

See page 114 for more questions.

Judaism

In Judaism, life is sacred. Death should be a calm experience where possible. Attitudes to euthanasia vary – but are mainly focused on the type of euthanasia. The experience of the mass murder of the Holocaust also influences attitudes to unnatural death.

- You shall not kill. (Exodus)
- G-d gives life, and G-d takes away life. (Psalms)
- For everything there is a reason, and a time for every matter under heaven: a time to be born, and a time to die; a time to plant and a time to pluck up what has been planted. (Ecclesiastes)
- If there is anything which causes a hindrance to the departure of the soul then it is permissible to remove it. (Rabbi Moses Isserles)
- One who is in a dying condition is regarded as a living person in all respects. (Talmud)

For Judaism, the question is whether euthanasia shortens life or shortens the act of dying. The latter would be acceptable, so that the person can have a 'good death'. Life and death belong to G-d, though G-d would not want to see us suffer. It is important to protect and support life, to care for the dying, but it is wrong to end life through active euthanasia, because that is G-d's role. In the Holocaust, millions of Jews were murdered as Hitler attempted to wipe out the entire population of the Jews in Europe. This makes it even more important to safeguard and respect life, and euthanasia can at times be seen as throwing that life away.

 Sikhism

Life is sacred, and all souls are on a journey through many lifetimes, according to Sikhism. Liberation from rebirth is the eventual goal, but each life has been shaped by the words and actions of previous ones. As a result, suffering is part of the karma being worked through from a previous lifetime.

- God sends us and we take birth. God calls us back and we die. (Guru Granth Sahib)
- A sign of divine worship is the service (sewa) of others. (Adi Granth)
- The sign of a good person is that they always seek the welfare of others.
- Sikh gurus set up **hospitals** and medical treatment for Sikhs – this has continued to the modern day.
- All life is sacred and should be respected. (Guru Granth Sahib)

There is no place for mercy killing in Sikhism. The Sikh gurus set up hospitals and treatment centres for the sick and dying. Many Sikhs work within the health service, which they see as sewa – service to others. Active euthanasia, then, would be considered wrong. The suffering involved in terminal illnesses is from the karma of previous lifetimes, and has to be worked through. A Sikh's role in these cases is to care for the dying, rather than speeding up their death. That care is the respect that their sacred life deserves until God decides they should die.

Task

With a partner, come up with as many reasons to agree and disagree with these statements as you can. Be sure to include religious arguments in those reasons.
- **Euthanasia should be available to anyone who wants it.**
- **Religious people should never accept euthanasia.**

For some more questions on religious attitudes, see page 113.

Life after death in the religions

 ## Buddhism

Buddhists believe in rebirth. There is no permanent soul, rather a mix of ever-changing skandhas – emotions, feelings, intelligence and so on. After the death of the body, this mix fuses with an egg and sperm at conception. The thoughts, actions and intentions of each life shape the quality of the next. The goal is to achieve enlightenment, and stop being reborn.

 ## Christianity

Christians believe in the physical resurrection of the body. At death, the body waits until Judgement Day. Catholics call this Purgatory. At judgement, each person will face God and Jesus to evaluate their deeds. If they were good in life, they will go to heaven, which is paradise and wonderful forever. If they were bad, they will go to hell for eternal punishment.

 ## Hinduism

Hindus believe in reincarnation. Their atman (soul) lives through many lifetimes, each one shaped by the thoughts, words and actions of their past lifetime(s). Its goal is to achieve enlightenment and become one with the Ultimate Reality and stop being reincarnated.

 ## Islam

Muslims believe in resurrection and **Akhirah**. At death, the body waits in the grave (barzakh) and sees the events of its life. This can be quick or very slow and painful. On Judgement Day, people are sorted according to their beliefs and actions. The wicked are cast into hell; the truly good go straight to Paradise. All others cross Assirat bridge, carrying the book of their deeds (sins make it heavier). The bridge is sharp, and so they are purified from sin before going to Paradise.

 ## Judaism

Judaism focuses on this life, rather than the next. Some teachings mention a heavenly place. Jews talk of the 'world to come', which is when the Messiah will come to rule the earth in peace. That is life after death because the dead will be woken to live through that time.

 ## Sikhism

Sikhs believe in reincarnation. The soul is born into many lifetimes, whose quality is decided by the words, thoughts and deeds of the previous lifetime(s). The point of each life is to serve and worship God, so that eventually the soul can be reunited with God (Waheguru) and stop being reincarnated.

Task

The exam has several times asked the question 'Explain how believing in life after death might affect people's behaviour in this life'. Discuss this with a partner – how would you answer it? Consider – what decides on a soul going to heaven or hell? What behaviours might be sure to send someone to heaven or hell? Alternately, if believing in rebirth/reincarnation, what decides on a better next life? And, what behaviours would do that? Now write a great answer.

 Now you have learned religious beliefs about euthanasia and life after death

Last thoughts about the end of days

The exam could ask you what is meant by *death*, and it is a difficult term to explain without using the word 'dead'. Also, there is some debate about it, and it is part of the reason why switching off a life-support machine is so contentious.

What is death?

Is it when your heart stops?

There is definitely no heartbeat in a dead person! However, there is an illness where a person's heart stops then restarts. Also, we see on hospital programmes on TV that there is a procedure to restart a heart when it stops. Finally, for some operations the heart has to be stopped at a certain point. In all these cases the person keeps living.

Is it when we stop breathing?

Dead people don't breathe. However, people can hold their breath. Other people need ventilators to breathe. We don't say those people are dead.

Is it when our organs pack up?

If none of our organs worked, we would not be alive. However, thousands of people live with damaged or not working organ(s).

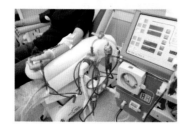

Is it when our brain stops functioning?

Doctors check the brain stem for electrical activity when a decision about life support is being made. Once the brain stem has stopped working, you can't recover from whatever problems you have. Machines could keep your body alive, but you won't ever regain consciousness, or be able to function.

So, we could say that no heartbeat, no breathing, no organs working and no brain stem activity are all characteristics of a dead person. The point of death, though, seems to be when the brain is no longer able to send instructions to the rest of the body to do all the things it needs to do. If any of the characteristics is *permanent*, then the person is dead – so if asked the question 'what is death?', you could say 'when the heart stops *permanently*', for example.

Many people believe we should have the right to decide when we die – if only in the case of a painful and terminal illness. This is called *self-determination*. Check out the website Dignity in Dying – **www.dignityindying.org.uk** – for a look at this argument.

> Whose right is it to choose death?

> Pick out the reasons below that say why people should be able to choose what happens with their life, and those that don't. Can you think of any more?

> *My life belongs to God. I don't have the right to decide when I die.*

James

> *Letting one person choose death opens the door to people forcing relatives to choose death too.*

Sasha

> *If I can refuse medical treatment, I should be able to ask for help to die.*

Kyle

> *I decide on everything else in my life, so why not death as well.*

Grant

> *My body, my life – it should be my right to die.*

Rebekkah

Topic 9

Religious attitudes to drug abuse

When asked to list drugs, people often list **illegal drugs** – heroin, cocaine, marijuana and so on. They tend to forget those drugs that we meet on a daily basis – alcohol, caffeine and tobacco.

You will find out later that it is actually the use of alcohol and tobacco, legal drugs, which causes the most deaths, crime and violence of any drugs in our society.

Only a complete fool would take drugs!

Some drugs are okay if you don't overdo it.

Everybody uses drugs.

Why do you think this is the case?

Discuss the views of the young people above. What reasons can you think of to agree and disagree with each of them?

What is a drug?

Simply put, a drug is any substance that, if consumed, will affect the way our bodies and mind work. Drugs can be divided into four categories depending on the effects they have. There are stimulants, depressants, hallucinogens and opioid analgesics.

Stimulants (uppers) work by acting on the central nervous system to increase the activity of the brain. *Depressants* (downers) do exactly the opposite; they also work on the central nervous system, but they slow down the brain activity. *Hallucinogens* act on the mind, distorting vision and hearing. *Opioid analgesics* have a painkilling effect.

Make a list of drugs you know the names of. Can you categorise each by one of those four terms?

For this unit, you have to be aware of the range of drugs used legally and illegally in society. You need to understand the different reasons people have for using drugs and the effects that drug use has on them and society in general. You need to be aware of the debate about the **classification** and legal status of some drugs. You will look at the problems **drug abuse** causes and evaluate the effectiveness of methods aimed at reducing drug taking.

You need to learn to put this knowledge into a religious perspective. To do this you must understand some religious teachings about the body and mind. You need to apply these teachings to the issues so that you can effectively explain religious attitudes, for example, to the use of social and **recreational drugs**. What is the response of religious believers to drug users?

A good place to start is to think about the religious teaching on the *sanctity of life*.

If someone believes all life is a gift from God, valuable, holy and having a purpose, what do you think they will say about drug use? Will they say all drugs are wrong? Will the teachings affect the rules that religious people live by? If so, how?

Cocaine Heroin GAS CANNABIS Crack Coffee LSD Alcohol Anabolic steroids Aspirin Tobacco Ecstasy Magic mushrooms Skunk Aerosols Paracetamol Morphine POPPERS Amphetamines Antibiotics

✓ **Now you have begun to think about drugs**

Drug use

The reasons people take drugs are almost as varied as the drugs that are available. Most people, at some point during their life, will use drugs for medical reasons. Drugs prescribed by a doctor, or bought over the counter at a chemist, are intended for a good purpose – to make us well. No one is going to reasonably say that this is wrong, and all religious traditions support the use of medically prescribed drugs. This unit is concerned with the reasons people take legal and illegal drugs for non-medical use.

Legal drugs, such as alcohol, caffeine and tobacco, are part of our social life. Just look at how many coffee bars, pubs and clubs there are in towns and cities – this shows that these drugs are simply part of our society. However, the 2007 ban on smoking in public places is recognition of the dangers that nicotine use poses to users (smokers) and non-users (passive smoking).

The dangers posed by some drugs are such that the government has deemed it necessary to make their sale and use illegal through the Misuse of Drugs Act, 1971. Drugs such as heroin, cocaine, amphetamines and cannabis pose serious threats to the users and society in general. Consequently, far fewer people use illegal drugs because they not only have health risks, but are against the law.

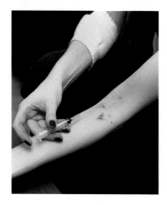

	Strongly agree	Agree	No opinion	Disagree	Strongly disagree
Anyone caught experimenting with illegal drugs should be expelled from school/college.					
You need alcohol to make a social occasion go well.					
Smokers should have to pay their own health care bills.					
Cannabis should be legal.					
Alcoholics are a drain on the country financially and in social terms.					
Glue sniffing is harmless adolescent fun.					
People should take medication only when they desperately need it.					
Society has a duty to help heroin users give up heroin.					
People who work with young people have a duty to be a positive role model when it comes to drugs.					
The drug you take depends on your cultural and social background.					
Children under fourteen should not be allowed to drink caffeine-based drinks.					
The government should make smoking and chewing tobacco products illegal.					
If people stopped smoking and drinking, the government would lose millions.					
What you do in the privacy of your own home should be your business and no one else's, as long as no one is hurt.					

Task

Complete the questionnaire, saying how much you agree or disagree with each statement. Discuss your answers in class. Try to come up with three reasons to agree and disagree with each.

Why use drugs?

Ask ten people why they first took a drug and you will probably get ten different answers. The same could be said of twenty people. If your parents drink or smoke, ask them why they continue – they will probably give you the same reasons as anyone who takes drugs. What about you? Do you use any drugs? Have you ever stopped to think about why you do? Is it your choice or are you simply giving in to the pressures and temptations around you?

Task

Make a list of reasons why people use drugs. You may be asked exactly that question in the exam. Are there different reasons for using different types of drugs? Try to give some examples of drugs taken for specific reasons.

I like the risk

Boredom

REBELLION

It's fun

My friends do it

Easy to get them

Curious

Can't give it up

Makes me feel grown up

Escape

There's no real harm

Enjoy it

So, someone whose life is tough, and has lots of personal problems, may turn to drugs. But not everyone does – why not? Some people seem to have everything and yet they turn to drugs – why? Some people just enjoy the habit. Clearly, drug use is very much a personal issue.

The reasons that drugs are used can be classified into broad areas:

- *Experimental* – to see what it's like.
- *Recreational* – some drugs are used in a social setting.
- *Experiential* – some drugs are used because of their effects, for example, they make us feel better or calm us down.
- *Addiction* – some drug takers become addicted and cannot stop themselves using the drug. Their bodies cease to function properly without it, so giving it up often needs specialised help.

Can you fit any drug into any of these areas? Or does it depend on the drug? We'll come back to this later in the topic.

The Basics

1 What is a drug?
2 What are legal drugs? Give examples.
3 What are illegal drugs? Give examples.
4 Make a list of reasons why some people use drugs. Remember to explain the reasons fully.
5 **Taking drugs is a personal choice – it should have nothing to do with anyone else.** Do you agree? Give reasons and explain your answer.

 Now you have begun to think about why people take drugs

Tobacco

Tobacco fact file

- About 10 million adults in the UK smoke – 21 per cent of all males and 19 per cent of all females.
- Two-thirds of smokers started before they were eighteen.
- It is illegal to sell tobacco products to anyone under the age of eighteen.
- About 27 per cent of men and 22 per cent of women are now ex-smokers.
- About 100,000 people die every year from smoking-related illness – that's 274 a day.

- Smoking causes 30 per cent of all cancer deaths; 80 per cent of lung cancer deaths.
- One in two smokers will die because of their habit.
- Smoking rates are higher among poorer people – 14 per cent of managerial/professional workers, 33 per cent of those with manual/ routine occupations.
- Over 4000 different chemicals can get into your bloodstream because of smoking; these include DDT, tar, nicotine, arsenic, phenol, ammonia, naphthalene and cadmium.

Kicking the habit

The government has invested large sums of money in raising awareness about the damaging effects of smoking. Tobacco products are **taxed** heavily and some of this money is used to fund NHS quitting programmes. In 2011–12, the Government earned £12 billion in tobacco taxes; it spent £1.5 billion on 'stop smoking' schemes. But why should people give up?

> Why do people smoke? Are the reasons different from those for taking illegal drugs? Why is it more acceptable to smoke than use other drugs? Do you think smokers understand the risks?

Cost – If you smoke, work out how many cigarettes you smoke a day. How many packs a week is that? Multiply by 52 for the weeks in the year. Now multiply by £7, which is about the average price for a packet of cigarettes. That is one year's cost to you. In 2013, a 20-a-day habit cost more than £2500 for the year. What else could you spend that money on?

Health – Yours and that of the people around you. Smoking is one of the most dangerous things anyone can do to damage themselves. But smoking is also very harmful to others because of the effects of passive smoking. In 2010, £2.7 billion was spent by the NHS dealing with smoking-related illness. Just think how much could be done with that money if no one smoked.

Environment – Smoking pollutes the environment. This was known as early as the seventeenth century when James I famously banned smoking in court because of its disgusting odour. Think of the litter that smoking produces and the trees cut down to make the cigarettes and their packets in the first place.

Smoking – the effects

> So, what does smoking do to you?

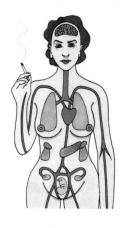

Short term
- Body odour and bad breath
- Stained fingers and teeth
- Dry skin and wrinkles
- Reduced sporting performance

Long term
- Coronary heart disease
- Emphysema – affects breathing/ lungs
- Cancer of the mouth, throat, lungs, bladder
- Pregnant women who smoke risk the health of their baby

Passive smoking

Smoking doesn't only affect smokers.

Think about three main factors for giving up. How might it benefit others if someone stops smoking?

Anyone in a smoking environment will be subjected to passive smoking. They will breathe in the fumes of the cigarette tip while it is burning and also the fumes that are exhaled by the smoker. It is estimated that across the world 600,000 deaths a year are caused by passive smoking.

Passive smoking can irritate the eyes, nose and throat. It leads to headaches and nausea. It increases breathing problems for asthmatics and increases the number and severity of the attacks they suffer.

Passive smoking can have a greater effect on children because they are still growing. It can also affect the normal growth of their lungs. For adults, it increases the chances of developing heart disease and a number of cancers.

Make a list of the potential dangers of smoking in the home.

When a pregnant woman smokes, the unborn baby smokes too. Anything the mother takes in passes through the umbilical cord and into the baby. Babies born to smokers often show symptoms of the effects of smoking. They can be premature and underdeveloped. They are more likely to suffer respiratory illnesses as their immune systems have been affected by the mother smoking.

No smoking
It is against the law to smoke in these premises

Much of Europe has now introduced no smoking policies in all public buildings. The smoking ban was implemented throughout the whole of the UK in 2007. When it was introduced many people complained that it was against civil liberties and people should have a right to smoke if they chose.

What do you think? Is it a good idea to prevent people smoking in public buildings? Would you extend the law to include all public places, even outside? Why do you think some pubs, clubs and restaurants objected to the ban?

The Basics

1 Why do some people smoke?
2 Explain some of the health risks of smoking.
3 Give three reasons why you think it is hard for smokers to quit.
4 How do you think the taxes raised from cigarette sales should be used?
5 What is passive smoking?
6 **Religious people who smoke are doing nothing wrong.** What do you think? Explain your opinion.

Action on Smoking and Health (ASH) is a campaigning, public health charity that works to eliminate the harm caused by tobacco. It challenges the tobacco industry, which it feels is not honest about the effects of tobacco. Obviously, the future of tobacco companies relies on people being smokers. It is their business to increase the number of smokers, not decrease them. Check out ASH and the truth about tobacco at **www.ash.org.uk**

ash.
action on smoking and health

✓ **Now you have begun to think about smoking**

Alcohol

Most adults have tasted alcohol and over 60 per cent of adults in the UK enjoy a drink at least once a week. Many young people have tasted alcohol, and it is part of growing up as far as some people are concerned. The law states that it is illegal to sell alcohol to, or buy alcohol for, anyone under the age of eighteen. The only exception is in licensed premises where sixteen- and seventeen-year-olds can have a drink with a meal. Even those over eighteen can't just drink what they want, where they want. Many cities and towns have alcohol-free zones to prevent people drinking on the streets. The heavy fines retailers can incur mean that increasingly shops are refusing to sell alcohol and tobacco to under 21s and insist on ID being shown by anyone they think may be under this age.

Alcohol fact file

- It is estimated that 3.3 million children in the UK live in a family with alcohol problems.
- Alcohol misuse costs the NHS up to £2.7 billion every year.
- 12 per cent of school pupils drink each week (down from 26 per cent in 2001 – but those who drink, drink more).
- Alcohol misuse is a factor in 30 per cent of suicides each year.
- Nearly half of all household fires are linked with someone who has been drinking.
- 43 per cent of pedestrians killed in road accidents had been drinking; 16 per cent of all road deaths are alcohol related.
- Over 55,000 drivers every year test positive for alcohol.
- Heavy drinkers/smokers are 150 times more likely to get cancer of the throat/mouth.
- 47 per cent of all victims of violence said their attacker was affected by alcohol.

What do these facts tell you about the dangers of alcohol misuse?

Why do you think these regulations exist?

The Basics

(Use this double page to help you answer these questions.)

1 List some of the reasons why people drink.
2 What are the short-term effects of alcohol use?
3 How does alcohol misuse affect:
   a the drinker
   b their family
   c society in general?
4 **Religious people should never drink alcohol.** What do you think? Explain your opinion.
5 Check out the website **www.drinkaware.co.uk**

Discussion point

The government collects taxes (duty and VAT) from the sale of legal drugs. What do you think should happen to this money? Why do you think legal drugs are taxed so highly?

Alcohol – the effects

Alcohol affects people in different ways. Things like your size and weight, what you drink and how much, whether you have eaten and the mood you are in when you drink, can all influence the effects you feel from alcohol. After just a couple of drinks most people will become more relaxed and talkative, which is why many people think it is a stimulant. In fact, alcohol is a depressant. It slows down your system and reflexes, which is why many people have accidents when they are drunk.

The long-term effects

You can have a great time when drinking, which is why many people do it. However, like most things it needs to be in moderation to ensure that there is not a heavy price to pay. Alcohol abuse can have a very damaging effect on the drinker, their family and society. This is why many religious traditions do not agree with drinking alcohol.

Regular alcohol abuse can have serious physical and psychological effects. These include:

- Decrease in brain tissue and function
- Impotence and infertility
- Heart disease and failure
- Liver disease and failure
- Anxiety and depression
- Obesity – alcohol has a high calorific value
- Skin reddening and poor circulation

The short-term effects

- Increased aggression
- Loss of control and judgement
- Inability to work
- Addiction and dependency

Clearly these effects can be very damaging to anyone who drinks heavily or becomes an alcoholic. But what about their families? How might they suffer? And what about society in general? Does alcohol misuse affect others?

Task

Design an advert to warn people about the dangers of caffeine.

ANXIETY · INCREASED HEART RATE · LOSS OF CONSCIOUSNESS · IMPOTENCE · DIARRHOEA · HANGOVER · RELAXED · CONFUSED · DEHYDRATION · VOMITING · INCREASED AGGRESSION · TALKATIVE · IMPAIRED JUDGEMENT

What sort of risks might someone take when their judgement is impaired?

Alcohol Concern is the national charity on alcohol misuse. It works to reduce the incidence and costs of alcohol-related harm and to increase the range and quality of services available to people with alcohol-related problems and their families. See **www.alcoholconcern.org.uk**

 Alcohol Concern
The charity making sense of alcohol

A quick glance at caffeine

Caffeine is a stimulant found in tea, coffee and many soft drinks and energy drinks. It is a stimulant often used to ward off drowsiness and increase alertness. Most people enjoy caffeine drinks and never think of them as a drug. However, too much caffeine can cause restlessness, insomnia, upset stomach and excitability. It is possible to become addicted to caffeine and suffer the 'caffeine jitters'.

✓ **Now you have begun to think about alcohol**

Let's talk drugs

Coke – Charlie – snow – c – base   rock – wash – stone   E – Mitsubishis – Rolexes – dolphins – MDMA

gear – H – brown – skag – smack

Mushies

microdots – dots – trips – tabs – Acid

Draw – weed – hash – puff – ganja

spliff – skunk – wacky backy

POPPERS – RAM – THRUST – ROCK – HARD – KIX – TNT

Speed – uppers – billy – phet – sulphate

sustanon 250

Roids – anavar

This is only a quick look at drugs. Check out websites such as **www.talktofrank.com** and **www.release.org.uk** to find out more. Local police forces and **young offenders'** teams are usually happy to come into school and give talks about drugs too.

Drug classification

The law regarding illegal drugs comes under the Misuse of Drugs Act, 1971. It lists three classes of drugs, and gives penalties for possession (having the drug for personal use) and supplying (having more than is needed for personal use, therefore intending to sell it).

> *Hang on! What about cannabis?*

- Class A drugs: For example, cocaine, crack, ecstasy, heroin. Up to seven years' **imprisonment/fine** for possession; up to life imprisonment/fine for supplying.
- Class B drugs: For example, amphetamines, Methylphenidate (Ritalin). Up to five years' imprisonment/fine for possession; up to fourteen years' imprisonment/fine for supplying.
- Class C drugs: For example, anabolic steroids, tranquilisers. Up to two years' imprisonment/fine; up to fourteen years' imprisonment/fine for supplying.

Cannabis is usually smoked but can be used in food preparations. It makes the user relaxed and talkative. There is a debate surrounding the illegal status of cannabis. It has been classified as B then downgraded to C and is now class B again. Why all the fuss?

> *I think cannabis should be legal. It is a natural plant and is less harmful than tobacco. It's no different from having a drink to unwind and relax. People have been smoking it for centuries, even religious people who claim that its effects help them achieve a higher spiritual awareness. It's daft making it illegal because it criminalises loads of people that use it and wastes police time. It's also known to have pain-relieving effects. People should be able to make up their own minds.*

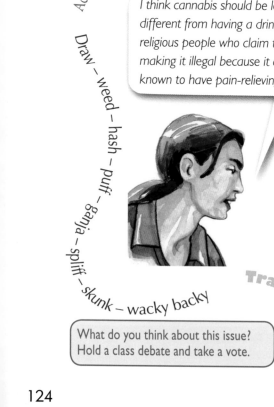

> *Cannabis should be class B. It is a dangerous drug. Long-term abuse can lead to mental health problems and increased risk of cancer, because it is mixed with tobacco. The use of cannabis also encourages people to try harder drugs for the rush, that's why it's called a gateway drug. Classifying cannabis warns people of the dangers.*

Trangs – moggies – maxxies – jellies

What do you think about this issue? Hold a class debate and take a vote.

✓ **Now you have begun to think about types of drugs**

The risks ... why we stop, or don't start

Why we don't take drugs

Ben, 22 — *I sold the Christmas presents for my four-year-old, to buy drugs; my family kicked me out.*

I got a criminal record for possession. — **Sara, 19**

Jamie, 27 — *Sniffing drugs destroyed my nose. I had to have plastic surgery to hide it.*

Made me keep hallucinating. I still get panic attacks. Doctors say I've done permanent damage. — **John, 34**

Steve, 32 — *I weight train and used steroids. Gave me road rage, no one could cope with me. I didn't like what I'd become.*

My kid saw me shooting up. — **Lynn, 24**

Lee, 15 — *My mate fell into the canal. I was too gone to help. He drowned. I watched.*

We had to sack her. She became too unreliable, even a risk. — **Len, 48**

Gill, 27 — *I've seen what it's done to my mates – it's not happening to me.*

Just never been interested. — **Dave, 26**

Sue, 18 — *Seems a waste of money to me – gone in minutes with nothing good to show for it.*

✓ **Now you have begun to think about why people don't use drugs**

Release was set up in 1967, and is the world's longest-running drugs charity. It tries to provide a range of services dedicated to meeting the health, welfare and legal needs of drug users and those who live and work with them. It provides information and legal support. Check out its work at **www.release.org.uk**

Release
Drugs, The Law & Human Rights

There are lots of different types of risks to taking drugs – legal or illegal.
Try to come up with a list of risks before you read those on this page.

Health risks – short- and long-term, disabling and fatal

If you desperately need a fix, you aren't going to check someone's HIV status before you share their needle, are you? And when you are off your head, how can you protect yourself?

Financial problems – drugs cost money

If you are addicted, you need to take the drug, so the money has to be found. Hard drugs, such as heroin, lead people into hurting others to get the money they need. How do you cope when your mum steals your stuff to pay for her habit?

Uncertainty – you never know exactly what you are taking

Drugs are rarely pure. The side effects could include death. Did you really intend to pay for cement powder and cocaine?

Criminal risks

Getting a record can get you the sack or restrict the jobs you can do. It can also be a block to travelling. How many parents would complain if they knew a teacher had a criminal record for drugs?

The Basics

1 Explain, using examples, how illegal drugs are classified.
2 Why do people take illegal drugs?
3 Explain, using examples, three ways that illegal drugs can harm a user.
4 In what ways do illegal drugs affect more than just the user?
5 **People should be free to use whatever drugs they choose.** Do you agree? Give reasons for your answer, showing that you have thought about more than one point of view.

The body and mind

In today's hectic world it is easy to forget how important it is to look after ourselves. Every year thousands of people have time off work or school because of illness, often when it could have been avoided if they had only listened to the warning signs their bodies were giving them. Lack of sleep, poor diet and misuse of drugs are just some of the ways people abuse their bodies.

All religious traditions teach that we are all special and unique in some way. This is summed up in the teaching of the *sanctity of life*. The physical body is seen as a shell that carries the real inner person. Within all religious traditions there are beliefs and practices that encourage believers to care not only for others, but for themselves. This means that where drugs are concerned, if they are for medical purposes most religious people would be happy to use them. However, for other drugs they would follow the specific teachings and guidance of their faith to decide whether or not they are acceptable.

Make a list of ten things that many people do that are bad for their physical and/or mental well-being.

 ## Buddhism

Health is the greatest of gifts. (Dhammapada)

 ## Christianity

You should learn to control your body in a way that is holy and honourable. (New Testament)

 ## Hinduism

Yoga destroys suffering for him who is moderate in eating, leisure activities, work, sleep and wakefulness. (Bhagavad Gita)

 ## Islam

We give through this Qur'an all that gives health and is a grace to those who believe. (Qur'an)

 ## Judaism

This [G-d's teaching] will bring health to your body and nourishment to your bones. (Psalms)

 ## Sikhism

The pain of selfishness is gone. I have found peace, my body has become healthy. (Guru Granth Sahib)

Research Task

Research some examples of religious beliefs and practices that help believers to keep a healthy mind and body. Use the headings in the spider diagram on the next page to help you.

Task

Now, write an information leaflet: Healthy Mind and Body – A (name of religion) Guide.

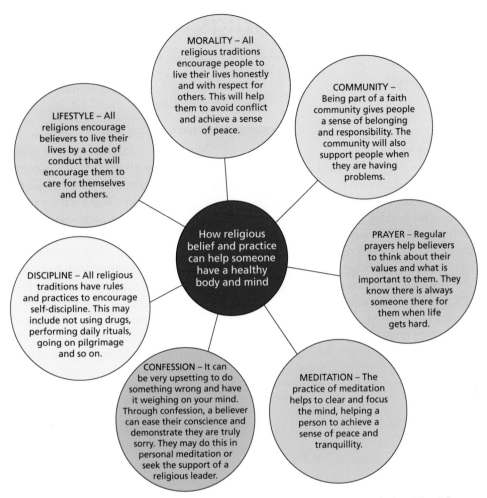

MORALITY – All religious traditions encourage people to live their lives honestly and with respect for others. This will help them to avoid conflict and achieve a sense of peace.

COMMUNITY – Being part of a faith community gives people a sense of belonging and responsibility. The community will also support people when they are having problems.

LIFESTYLE – All religions encourage believers to live their lives by a code of conduct that will encourage them to care for themselves and others.

How religious belief and practice can help someone have a healthy body and mind

PRAYER – Regular prayers help believers to think about their values and what is important to them. They know there is always someone there for them when life gets hard.

DISCIPLINE – All religious traditions have rules and practices to encourage self-discipline. This may include not using drugs, performing daily rituals, going on pilgrimage and so on.

CONFESSION – It can be very upsetting to do something wrong and have it weighing on your mind. Through confession, a believer can ease their conscience and demonstrate they are truly sorry. They may do this in personal meditation or seek the support of a religious leader.

MEDITATION – The practice of meditation helps to clear and focus the mind, helping a person to achieve a sense of peace and tranquillity.

How might religious belief and practice help someone have a healthy mind and body?

How can drug addicts be helped?

Lots of options are available, which include:

♦ Replacement drug therapies – addicts can be helped to get over withdrawal symptoms from addictive drugs, by the use of nicotine patches, methadone and so on.
♦ Counselling – many addicts have underlying reasons why they use drugs. Support and guidance can help them resolve these issues.
♦ Voluntary self-help – groups like Alcoholics Anonymous are made up of people who have first-hand experience of addiction. Members support each other in their struggle to quit.
♦ **Rehabilitation** centres – specialist units run by health care professionals. These can be residential and use a range of treatments, therapies and counselling.
♦ Charitable organisations – many secular and religious organisations working with the poor and homeless also help addicts.

Find out about drug rehabilitation centres and their effectiveness.

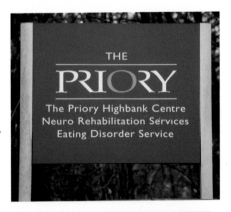

THE
PRIORY
The Priory Highbank Centre
Neuro Rehabilitation Services
Eating Disorder Service

✓ **Now you have begun to think about health and well-being**

Religious attitudes to drugs

 Buddhism

As a Buddhist, I am striving to reach enlightenment. This means that I should live my life according to the Middle Way that the Buddha taught. Anything that would cause me to stray from this path would not help me in my spiritual journey. The Buddha gave many guidelines on how to live life well and become enlightened. The Five Precepts advise me to not take drugs because they cloud the mind and would make it difficult to achieve enlightenment. They also remind me that I must not harm others and that under the influence of drugs many people cause harm to others directly and indirectly. This is also why I do not smoke. Not

only is it a health risk to me, but passive smoking harms others.

As a Buddhist I am free to choose my own path in life, but I prefer not to use any drugs, including alcohol. The Pali Canon may be an ancient text, but we now know the dangers of alcohol that it refers to are very true. For example, loss of wealth, intelligence, health, morality and good reputation. Following the Eightfold Path I am reminded that the work I do must be positive and helpful, so I personally would not want to work in the tobacco or alcohol industry. The path also reminds me to have right awareness and meditation – using drugs would prevent me from doing this.

 Christianity

As a Christian, I follow the teachings of the Bible and the example of Jesus. There aren't any direct teachings saying drug use is wrong, so I rely on interpretations of the scriptures to guide me in the decisions I make. I would never want to use illegal drugs because they are harmful to myself and others, as well as being against the law, which the Bible says I should follow. Genesis tells me that God created me and that I am special and unique. St Paul says that my body is a temple of the Holy Spirit, so I should keep it sacred. Personally, I don't smoke because of the health risks, but I have Christian friends who do. I have also read that Rastafarians and people

in the Ethiopian Coptic Church use marijuana as a means of heightening spiritual awareness, but this is an exception among Christians.

Alcohol is permitted in Christianity. St Paul advised his friend Timothy to drink some wine to aid his digestion and, of course, wine is used during Holy Communion. In fact Jesus drank wine and in John's Gospel the first miracle Jesus performed was to turn water into the finest wine at a wedding in Cana. However, there are many teachings that warn against drunkenness and misusing alcohol. Proverbs says that getting drunk will just make you loud and foolish and Ephesians cautions that drunkenness will ruin you, so like many Christians I drink only in moderation.

Task

All religious traditions accept drugs are necessary for medical use. They also teach that the law should be followed and so dealing in or using illegal drugs is wrong.

List some reasons why religious believers would:

1 use prescribed or over-the-counter drugs (hint: benefits)
2 not use illegal drugs (hint: consequences).

ॐ Hinduism

As a Hindu I live my life striving to achieve moksha. This is release from samsara, the circle of rebirth and suffering. To achieve this I must fulfil my dharma, so I choose not to use drugs of any sort. My tradition does not say that I have to do this; there are no teachings against using drugs. Hinduism is a very personal spiritual journey; many Hindu holy men do use natural

plant substances that have hallucinogenic effects to achieve a heightened spiritual awareness. This is only really practised among ascetics who have chosen to live a very different type of lifestyle, removed from the rest of society.

In modern Hinduism each person chooses whether they wish to smoke or drink alcohol. The teachings do tell us, however, that anything that causes you to lose your mind is foolish and does not bring spiritual rewards. Meditation and worship cannot be performed correctly under the influence of drugs and taking them into a temple would be very disrespectful. If I am to succeed in life and follow a spiritual path I need to be healthy in mind and body.

☾★ Islam

As a Muslim I do not use alcohol or illegal drugs as they are haram – forbidden. Prophet Muhammad (pbuh) called intoxicants the mother of all vices. The Qur'an says that my body is a gift from God and is on loan to me until Judgement Day. I have a responsibility to look after it and not abuse it with drugs. Drugs cloud the mind and are khamr, which means to cover. The effects of illegal drugs would make it impossible for me to perform salat (prayer) and meet my other **responsibilities** in life. Some of my Muslim friends do smoke tobacco, but are encouraged not to do this around others because of its harmful effects. Certainly, they must resist the temptation to smoke during Ramadan as it is forbidden to let anything pass through the mouth during daylight hours.

The Qur'an describes alcohol as the work of Shaytan. Prophet Muhammad (pbuh) once told a story of a man who drank and then proceeded to blaspheme, kill and commit adultery. The prophet said that whoever drinks, Allah will not accept their prayers for 40 days. Many Muslims will not work where there is alcohol or enter a house where it is present. In Muslim countries there are very severe punishments for people who drink or are involved with any type of drug trafficking.

Task

1 What religious teachings would encourage believers to help drug addicts?
2 How might religious believers help drug addicts?
3 Research the work of a religious organisation that works with young people who are vulnerable to drug misuse and crime. For example, Centrepoint, Outreach for Youth, Street Pastors.

Judaism

Genesis tells me that I have been created by G-d and it would be wrong to do harm to His creation. My body is on loan and needs to be cared for until the Day of Resurrection. Illegal drugs would cause harm to my body and would also harm others. I have a responsibility to live correctly in society and contribute positively to my community. I could not do this if I were under the influence of drugs. I do not smoke, but I do have Jewish friends who do. However, it is harmful to yourself and others and many rabbis would encourage followers to avoid tobacco.

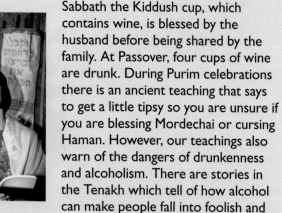

Alcohol is permitted in Judaism and wine forms an important part of many ceremonies. Every Sabbath the Kiddush cup, which contains wine, is blessed by the husband before being shared by the family. At Passover, four cups of wine are drunk. During Purim celebrations there is an ancient teaching that says to get a little tipsy so you are unsure if you are blessing Mordechai or cursing Haman. However, our teachings also warn of the dangers of drunkenness and alcoholism. There are stories in the Tenakh which tell of how alcohol can make people fall into foolish and immoral behaviour. Wine is a gift from G-d, but it is to be enjoyed sensibly.

 Sikhism

As a Khalsa Sikh I have made a commitment to avoid all tobacco, alcohol and anything that alters my body. The Kurahits prohibit any such things. When Guru Nanak was offered an opiate he replied that he was hooked on praising God. The Khalsa way of life requires discipline. Each individual must choose this path for themselves so the commitments made are an important part of achieving spiritual success. Using illegal drugs would damage the body and make the mind unfit

for meditation on God's name. It would be wrong for any Sikh to use them.

The Reht Maryada tells a story about Guru Gobind Singh uprooting a wild tobacco plant. When he was asked why he would do such a thing, he replied that if alcohol destroys a generation, tobacco destroys several. The dangers of tobacco are such that all Sikhs should avoid its use. As a Sikh my body is a temple for God and should be treated with respect. Alcohol can lead to sinful actions and it clouds the mind. A Sikh should be devoted to serving God and others and this requires a healthy mind and body.

The Basics

1 Explain, using beliefs and teachings, religious attitudes to:
   a smoking
   b alcohol
   c illegal drugs.
2 **Religious people should not use recreational drugs.** What do you think? Explain your opinion.
3 **There is nothing wrong with people using drugs as long as they don't harm anyone else.** Do you agree? Give reasons for your answer, showing that you have thought about more than one point of view. Refer to religious arguments in your answer.

 Now you have begun to think about religious attitudes to drugs

This topic is about **law and order**. It is about what we mean by crime, why people commit crimes and the way society deals with offenders. It is also about why we punish offenders, and the debate about the death penalty. Key to the topic are religious teachings and beliefs about human nature, repentance and forgiveness. You will have to show your understanding of religious attitudes to crime and punishment.

> MAN JAILED AFTER SETTING UP CANNABIS FARM

> BOY OF 16 PUNCHES MAN TO DEATH

> MAN DIES IN SUSPECTED HIT AND RUN

> MUM KILLS AND BURIES HER OWN CHILD

> THREE ARRESTED IN COUNTER TERRORISM STING

> CAR THIEVES TO DO COMMUNITY SERVICE

> WOMAN CHARGED WITH FRAUD AFTER STEALING MONEY FROM HOSPITAL

All societies have laws to guide people's behaviour. They should **protect** individuals, protect property and make society a safe place for everyone. When someone breaks the law they commit a crime. In the UK millions of crimes are committed each year. Many other crimes are not reported or followed up because they are considered trivial or the victim is too embarrassed or scared to say anything. Most crimes are committed by people under 25 years of age. Men are more likely to commit crimes than women. At some point in our lives most of us will experience the effects of crime.

There are two kinds of laws in the UK. *Bye-laws* are made by the elected councillors and apply to a local area. They cover things like parking restrictions, alcohol-free zones and environmental concerns such as litter and dog fouling. Breaking a bye-law can result in a fine, but you don't get a criminal record. There are also some strange bye-laws out there. For example, there is a law against dying in the Houses of Parliament!

Parliamentary laws are made by the government and apply to everyone in the country. These laws also put crimes into two categories. *Non-indictable offences* include minor crimes and driving offences. These are usually dealt with in a magistrates' court. *Indictable offences* are much more serious crimes. These are dealt with in criminal courts with a judge and jury, and usually carry much harsher potential penalties.

> Why do you think there are local laws and national laws – why not just one set of laws?

For this course, you need to know about these types of crimes:

- *Crimes against the person* – offences causing direct harm to a person, for example, murder, rape, GBH
- *Crimes against property* – offences that damage or deprive people of their property, for example, arson, burglary, trespassing
- *Crimes against the state* – offences that potentially endanger everyone or affect the smooth running of society, for example, terrorism, treason, perjury
- *Crimes against religion* – not part of criminal law, but part of this course. These crimes involve breaking rules that are set by a religion and only apply to that religion and its followers.

The Basics

1 Write a definition in your own words for all of the key words on this page (in italics).
2 Using examples, explain the four types of crime.
3 **Religion should dictate the law.**
   What do you think? Explain your opinion.

✓ **Now you are beginning to think about different kinds of crime**

Causes of crime

Task

No one likes it when someone does something that hurts or upsets them, so why do people commit crimes? Make a list of reasons with a partner as to why you think people break the law.

What crimes are being committed here? Why might these people be breaking the law?

You probably have lots of different ideas about why crime occurs – if there were only a few crimes, it would be easy to find solutions and put an end to crime and the misery it can cause. For some criminals, there is a trigger or immediate cause that leads them to break the law. For example, an argument in a pub might lead to a physical assault, or a group of bored youths may steal a car and go joyriding. However, there may be much deeper causes that lead, or even force, people into a life of crime. For example, drug addicts need to pay for their habit. This might lead to theft, prostitution or drug dealing – all criminal offences.

It is important to know why someone commits a crime, because the punishment they receive needs to be effective. For example, a drug addict who steals is not going to give up just because they received a fine or had a short spell in prison. To prevent them reoffending they need help to overcome their addiction. If a murderer has deep psychological problems, there is no point locking them up in a regular prison where they will continue to be a danger to themselves and others.

Social reasons

Some people break the law because they may want to fit in with a gang or are pressured by peers. They feel they need to show off or prove themselves in some way.

Environmental reasons

Where people live and their home background can influence some people into crime. **Poverty** and deprivation have been linked with some criminal activities.

Psychological reasons

Human nature can cause people to commit crime; they may simply be greedy, aggressive or jealous. Some people, such as sociopaths or kleptomaniacs, commit crimes because they have more deep-rooted problems.

Drug addiction

Crime figures routinely show that drug addiction is the highest single cause of crime. Under the influence of alcohol or illegal drugs a person's judgement is impaired. Much gang crime is drug related and individual addicts are often drawn into crime to fund their habit.

✓ **Now you have thought about why people commit crime**

Crime and punishment exercise

Task

Look at the list of crimes below. Can you identify the name of the crime being committed in each case? Now look at the list of punishments available under the English law. Which punishment do you feel is the most suitable in each case? For each one, say how you would punish the offender and why. What do you hope your punishment will achieve? Can you suggest any other punishments that you think would be more suitable?

Punishments

Life imprisonment

Fourteen years' imprisonment

Five years' imprisonment

Seven years' imprisonment

Two years' imprisonment

Six months' imprisonment

Suspended prison sentence (only enforced if they reoffend)

Community service

Curfew order

Anti-social behaviour order (ASBO)

Fine

Disqualification from driving

Attendance centre order

Electronic tagging

Probation order (required to meet probation officer weekly)

Restraining order

Exclusion order

Compensation order

Police caution

Crimes

1 A young woman who killed her husband after years of domestic abuse by him
2 A man who raped two women
3 A woman who assaulted a nurse who was treating her for a head injury she got while drunk
4 A schoolgirl who stole items worth £65 from a department store
5 Four football fans who kicked a rival fan to death during a street brawl after the match
6 A schoolboy who covered a bridge near a railway station with graffiti
7 A woman who defrauded £50,000 from her employers
8 A person who sold drugs in a school playground
9 A woman who drove her car for eight months without insurance or an MOT
10 A student who did not purchase a TV licence
11 A man who sexually abused a number of children
12 Someone who set up a cafe for people to smoke cannabis on the premises
13 A man who mugged at least seven people
14 A gang of men who held up a train at gunpoint and stole millions in bank notes that were being taken for destruction
15 A drunk driver who hit a pedestrian leaving them permanently confined to a wheelchair
16 A man who killed at least nine people
17 A young man who raped a woman he had been dancing with all night at a club and had walked home

Task

Make a list of reasons why people who commit crimes are punished.

 Now you have begun to think about punishment

The aims of punishment

Society sets up rules, and we have to obey them or face the consequences. However, what one person thinks is very wrong, another person might consider less wrong. That is why we have a judicial system that sets tariffs for punishments to guide judges in the sentences they hand down.

A judge will also know other information before they give a sentence. For example, if the person has offended before, and information from psychologists and perhaps about their home background. What kind of information might have influenced your decision when choosing a suitable punishment?

> Did you think about the reasons why you were punishing someone in the exercise on the previous page? How might this have influenced the decisions you made? There are six main aims of punishment and you probably came up with all of them in the punishment exercise.

Vindication

People who break the law must be punished; otherwise there is no point in having the laws in the first place. If there were no penalties for breaking the law there would be little motivation to keep it. For example, someone who parks in a car park and does not display a valid parking ticket may get a fine, because the rule says you must have one. It doesn't matter that the car park is nearly empty, you are only going to be ten minutes and you don't have change – rules are rules and we can't choose which ones we are prepared to follow.

Deterrence

A punishment is meant to be unpleasant so that the offender is *put off* or **deterred** from committing crimes in the future. A burglar who gets sent to prison for five years will hopefully not want to experience that again. Also, if we know what the punishment is going to be, many others would be put off committing

MURDERERS TO SERVE FULL LIFE SENTENCES

the crime in the first place. For example, the penalty for drink driving in the UK is a minimum twelve-month driving ban, a hefty fine and potentially a prison sentence, so most people don't do it.

Protection

Some criminals pose a danger to people and society in general. The laws exist to protect people and their property. One way this is done is by locking up criminals who commit serious offences such as murder, child abuse and arson. Criminals who have serious psychological problems that mean they are unlikely ever to be able to conform to the laws of society are housed in special prisons called high security psychiatric hospitals. These prisoners are also being protected by being locked up – as some of them would be a danger to themselves outside prison.

Retribution

This is a punishment inflicted on someone as vengeance for a criminal act. The aim of the punishment is to repay the person for what they have done, so that the punishment matches the crime – an eye for an eye. When people break the law, someone somewhere is hurt, even if they are just upset or angry. Most people follow the law so it isn't fair that a few criminals just ignore the rules and do as they please. Society uses punishment to make the offender pay for what they have done. In some cases **retribution** can be very severe. In the UK criminals can receive lengthy prison sentences; in other countries they also use capital or corporal punishment.

BRING BACK HANGING FOR MURDERERS

Reformation

Obviously society cannot simply lock up everyone who breaks the law and throw away the key. Many punishments are given to try to change the nature of the person who has offended (**reform** them). This is because most people who break the law are still going to be part of society. It is important to try to make these people realise the effects their action had on others in order that they will act for the better in future. For example, someone convicted of joyriding might have to do **community service** in a physiotherapy unit dealing with victims of road traffic accidents. In prisons there are usually education and work programmes to

support offenders in their rehabilitation. This helps to prepare them to rejoin society as a constructive member. Religious groups especially feel this is an important aim of punishment.

Reparation

COMPANY ORDERED TO PAY RECORD DAMAGES TO INJURED WORKER

Reparation means to make up for what you have done. Someone who breaks the law must be made to make amends and compensate their victim or society for their wrongdoing. For example, if an offender damages property they may be made to pay for the damage they have done to make up for the hurt and inconvenience their actions have caused. In the UK, as well as the criminal courts there are also civil courts. These often deal with cases where one person or group will sue another for the damage or injury they may have incurred because of the other's negligent, selfish or criminal activity. For example, people who injure themselves at work may sue their employer.

The Basics

1 Give an example of a crime and a suitable punishment to demonstrate each aim.
2 Only the harshest of punishments are effective. Give and explain three reasons to agree, and three reasons to disagree.
3 **Protection is the most important aim of punishment.** Do you agree? Give reasons for your answer, showing you have thought about more than one point of view. Refer to religious arguments in your answer.

✓ **Now you have thought about the aims of punishment**

Punishment

Look at pages 134–35 on the aims of punishment. What aims are met by each of the punishments below?

Punishments in the UK	
Custodial sentences	**Locking the offender up**
Prisons (adult)	There are different categories of prison in the UK. High security prisons are category A and B and house the most dangerous offenders; category C prisons are used for those serving shorter sentences; and category D are open prisons for those who can be reasonably trusted not to try to escape.
High-security psychiatric hospitals (e.g. Broadmoor)	These are used to house offenders with serious psychological disorders, such as psychopaths and sociopaths, who are a threat to the safety of others and themselves.
Young Offender Institutions	These are used to house young offenders (15–21 years of age). Education is an important part of the prison routine.
Non-custodial sentences	**Alternatives to prison**
ASBO	An anti-social behaviour order sets restrictions that the offender must stick to, e.g. a curfew, not go to certain places.
Community service (community payback)	Offenders must do unpaid work in the community as a punishment, for up to 300 hours. They do not have a choice, although their offence and experiences may influence magistrates.
Curfew	Offenders must return home by a set hour. This is often used with tagging.
Electronic tagging	An electronic device attached to the offender's leg means that their movements can be monitored.
Fines	A set amount of money must be paid for the offence.
Probation	Offenders must meet regularly with a probation officer who monitors their behaviour.
Restorative justice	Young offenders must attend sessions where they think about/discuss their crime, why it was wrong and its effect on the victim.

Fact! Prisons spend on average just £1.96 on each inmate's daily food

Fact! 47 per cent of prisoners have no qualifications

I work for the Prison Reform Trust and have direct experience of how damaging locking people up can be. It's easy to say that prison life is easy when you have never been inside one. The reality is quite different. Conditions in some prisons are very poor; inmates can be locked in their cells for 23 hours a day. Problems such as over-crowding, lack of exercise, poor diet, boredom, violence and drug abuse are a daily experience. I think it is really important that prisoners have the opportunity to reform and the hope of reward for good behaviour.

Parole means that a person can be released early, having served some of their sentence. When on parole they must live within the law and are supported by a parole officer, who will help them to reintegrate into society. The parole order may require them to have treatment, for example, for drug abuse. The aim is to help them avoid reoffending and become active and purposeful members of society.

Fact! There is one suicide per week in English and Welsh prisons

The **Prison Reform** Trust was founded in 1981. It works to create a more humane and effective penal system. It provides advice, information, educational work, research and campaigning. Its work has been very effective in achieving change in prisons, as well as in the policies and practices of the penal system. Find out about this charity through its website at **www.prisonreformtrust.org.uk**

Fact! It costs £60,000 per year to keep someone in a young offender institution

Fact! February 2013 saw 1320 under-eighteens being held in prisons

I'm in this young offender institution coz they want to change me, reform they call it. I have to go to sessions and talk about the stuff I've done and how it affects others. I've done loads of stuff. I've had warnings, three ASBOs, paid fines and done community service a couple of times too. I didn't do the last one though coz it was boring. I'd have gone if it was working on cars or something like that. Me and the gang like taking cars and hanging out in the street. I'm only in here coz a copper saw me flashing a blade. I miss home and my mates and hate all the rules.

Fact! In late 2012, 7657 people were serving life sentences

I was imprisoned twenty years ago for armed robbery. It wasn't my first offence, I had done time before. I thought it was important to be hard and to stand up for myself. I got into a disagreement with a prison warden and ended up with another sentence for GBH. I should have been paroled by now, if it wasn't for that. Somehow it just doesn't seem important any more. My wife divorced me by mail a few years back. Joey and Tina were just toddlers when I was sent down. I didn't see them grow up. I sometimes wonder what they are like now. Simple things like having a beer in the pub, driving a car, cuddling on the sofa are just distant memories. I'm used to life in prison, the routines, not having to make decisions and I've learned to just do as I'm told!

Fact! 52 per cent of young offenders had been permanently excluded from school

Fact! 54 per cent of women prisoners have children under sixteen at home

I'm doing two months in prison because I allowed my teenage daughter to stay off school. I didn't think it would come to this. I was so frightened when they brought me here and embarrassed by the admittance procedures. I cried constantly for the first three days. It is hard to adjust to having your life run by someone else. I can't stop worrying about the kids. My mum isn't well so they have had to go into foster care. I know I'm going to lose my job too, because they don't know I'm in here, unless they have read the local papers. Going home will be really bad, everyone will know and they probably think I'm an awful mother.

The Basics

1 Use the information on these pages to describe the potential long- and short-term effects of prison sentences on the offender.
2 Explain why non-custodial sentences might be more effective for young offenders.
3 Explain three reasons why young offenders are dealt with differently to adults.
4 **A life sentence should mean life in prison.** Do you agree? Give reasons for your answer, showing you have thought about more than one point of view.

✓ Now you have begun to think about the effects of punishments

Capital punishment

Capital punishment is the death penalty. In most countries this is reserved for the most extreme offences, usually murder. Worldwide, other crimes such as blasphemy, adultery, drug offences, corruption, fraud, smuggling, treason, hijacking and war crimes are capital offences.

> Are any crimes so bad they merit the death penalty? What do you think?

Why use such an extreme punishment?

The crimes are seen as so bad that no other punishment would be suitable. People who commit such horrific acts must face the most severe punishment, so that justice is seen to be done and others are deterred from committing these crimes. It is the principle of 'an eye for an eye' and is seen as the law of equality of retribution in Islam. A murderer shows no respect for human life, so the state shows no respect for the murderer's life. Many holy books name certain offences as being punishable by death.

USA executions (1976–2014)	
Lethal injections	1194
Electrocution	158
Lethal gas	11
Hanging	3
Firing squad	3

In 1977 the USA allowed individual states to choose if they wished to use capital punishment. Presently 32 states have readopted the death penalty – Texas is responsible for over one-third of all executions that take place. To date there have been over 1360 executions in the USA since 1976. Right now there are over 3000 people awaiting execution in America's death row cells. Amnesty International has said that the USA is savage, barbaric, cruel, prejudiced and uncivilised. This is because the USA has executed: people who offended as a child; people who have mental illnesses; blacks sentenced by all-white juries where the prosecution has removed potential black jurors from the trial and many other seemingly unfair cases. If this is what can be said about what is considered the most democratic country in the world, what might be the situation in other countries?

Check out more about the death penalty in the USA at **www.amnestyusa.org**

Facts and figures

- 140 countries have abolished the death penalty in law or practice.
- 58 countries retain and use the death penalty.
- This century 88 per cent of all known executions have taken place in China, Iran, Iraq, Saudi Arabia and the USA.
- Between 1976 and 2003 the USA executed 22 children (under the age of eighteen at the time the crime was committed) – more than half of those executed worldwide.
- In March 2005 the USA abolished child executions, affecting over 70 juvenile offenders on death row in twelve states.
- In the USA, since 1973, over 130 prisoners on death row have been released after their convictions were overturned.
- Methods of execution worldwide include: firing squad, hanging, lethal injection, stoning, beheading, gas chamber, electric chair, crucifixion (Sudan).

> Discuss the information above. What issues does it raise about the death penalty?

Did you know? Over 1100 people have been killed by lethal injection in the USA, some of them dying in excruciating pain. Victims have been seen gasping for air, convulsing, grimacing in agony and have received chemical burns 30 cm long. Some executions have lasted as long as an hour.

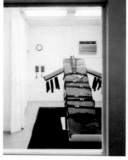

Did you know? In California in 2008, the legal system cost $137 million per year. Without the death penalty it would have cost just $11.5 million.

Find out more about the work of Sister Helen Prejean and the move to abolish capital punishment in the USA. Watch the films *Dead Man Walking* and *The Green Mile*.

The arguments for capital punishment

- An 'eye for an eye, life for a life' means that murderers should pay with their life.
- Capital punishment acts as a deterrent – it puts people off committing horrendous crimes.
- It brings **justice** for the victims and their families.
- Life sentences do not mean life; murderers walk free on average after sixteen years.
- Terrorists murder indiscriminately and they cannot be reformed.
- It's a waste of resources housing criminals for their entire life.
- It's natural law; the death penalty has been used for centuries around the world.
- It demonstrates that society will not tolerate some crimes.
- This is the only way to totally protect society from the worst murderers who it is believed cannot be reformed.

The arguments against capital punishment

- Retribution is uncivilised; two wrongs don't make a right.
- Most murders are done on the spur of the moment, so capital punishment would not deter.
- Victims' families still grieve; killing the murderer doesn't end the pain of loss.
- It is a contradiction to condemn murder and then execute (kill) a murderer.
- Executing terrorists would make them martyrs.
- Legal systems can fail and innocent people can be executed.
- All life is sacred and murderers should be given the chance to reform.
- It is inhumane and degrading to put anyone through the mental torture of death row.
- Legal systems are full of inequalities and prejudices.

Should the UK reintroduce hanging?

Amnesty International was founded in 1961 by Peter Benenson, a British lawyer. Today it is the world's biggest human rights organisation, informing the world about human rights abuses and campaigning for individuals and political change. Amnesty disagrees completely with execution, seeing it as cruel, inhumane and degrading. In its reports about the death penalty in the USA, it has highlighted the degrading nature of the system, giving examples of prisoners being taken from intensive care to be executed, wiring up prisoners who were still awaiting last minute appeals, executing people who were clearly mentally ill, and a paraplegic being dragged to the electric chair. Campaigning against and monitoring the use of the death penalty worldwide is just one part of Amnesty's work. The organisation campaigns to end all human rights abuses and recognises the inherent value of all human life. Find out more about Amnesty International by checking out its website at **www.amnesty.org.uk**

The Basics

1 What is capital punishment?
2 Explain three reasons why the death penalty is used.
3 Use the information from pages 141–43 to explain religious attitudes to the death penalty.
4 **It is never right to execute a murderer.** Do you agree? Give reasons for your answer, showing that you have thought about more than one point of view. Refer to religious arguments in your answer.

Now you know arguments about capital punishment

Human nature

To understand religious attitudes to crime and punishment, it is helpful first to consider human nature. Laws exist to control behaviour and make society work. But do they assume anything about what people in general are like? Which of the following ideas about human nature do you most agree with?

1 People naturally try to be good and act in a way that will make others happy.
2 People are naturally selfish and will act in a way that will make them happy.
3 People are neither good nor bad; their actions are shaped by their experiences.

All religions have rules and laws that believers must follow. These rules give people a framework and guidance to help them live their lives correctly to achieve their spiritual aims. For example, the Ten Commandments apply to Jews and Christians, and Sikhs follow a code of conduct called the Reht Maryada. When a believer does something that breaks one of their religious laws they commit a *religious offence* (sometimes called a sin). Just as in society when someone breaks a law they are punished, there is also the belief in religious traditions that believers who sin will be punished in some way. Ultimately their afterlife could be affected – going to hell or being reborn in a lower life form.

Deciding what is right and wrong can be a tricky business. Religious people have several sources of authority to guide them. They should, however, always be guided by their **conscience**. This is sometimes described as the voice of God inside your head telling you what is right or wrong. Have you ever felt guilty, ashamed or disgusted with yourself because of a wrong action? Conscience is what causes these feelings.

Religious traditions accept that everyone makes mistakes, but they also teach the ideas of *repentance* and *forgiveness*. To repent is to recognise that we have done something wrong and to be truly sorry. It involves learning from the mistake and doing our best not to repeat it. Forgiveness is accepting that a person is sorry for what they have done wrong and allowing them a second chance.

Religious people are also guided by *duty* (things that must be done) and *responsibility* (understanding that we are in control of our own actions). They have duties and responsibilities to themselves, others and (except for Buddhists) God. Correct living means self-discipline and putting others first. Human nature then can be developed and guided for good in the world. Fulfilling your duties and responsibilities leads to spiritual rewards in the afterlife.

Task

Find out about the main law codes of the religions you are studying.

The Basics

1 What is meant by the terms: right and wrong; human nature; religious offence; sin; conscience; repentance; forgiveness; duty; responsibility?
2 Explain how the behaviour of religious people is guided by their faith.
3 **Religious people should always forgive wrongdoers.** What do you think? Explain your opinion.

Now you have thought about human nature

Religious attitudes to crime and punishment

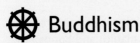 Buddhism

Buddhism teaches that people should follow the laws of the country in which they live. The Noble Eightfold Path relates to living life correctly. Each of the steps in the path starts with the word 'right' and emphasises the importance of correct action. A life of crime would not be right livelihood and criminal activity would be against the First Precept because it causes harm to other people. Furthermore, the motivation behind crime is often linked to selfish human traits and desires. Breaking the law would lead to bad karma and this would affect future rebirths, preventing a person from achieving enlightenment.

Buddhist teachings:

- Suffering is caused by attachment to the material world.
- The three poisons (greed, hatred, ignorance) are the cause of evil actions.
- The law of karma – the sum total of good and bad actions
- Buddhists should practise metta (loving kindness) and karuna (compassion).
- The story of Milarepa illustrates that all people are capable of change.

Buddhists teach that all people can change and bad actions will have karmic consequences. Buddhists would agree that the public needs to be protected from dangerous criminals. However, imprisonment should provide opportunities for the offender to reform and be helped not to create further bad karma. The principles of non-harming and compassion mean Buddhists would not agree with punishments that were unduly severe or would cause direct harm to the offender. The Angulimala society provides support for prisoners.

 Christianity

Christianity teaches that the laws of a country should be followed unless they are unjust. The Ten Commandments are reflected in the laws of the UK. St Paul taught that the state should be obeyed because God has given permission for it to exist. For Christians, law breaking means they are committing sins as well as crimes. This could affect them in the afterlife because they believe they will be judged by God. In Roman Catholic Christianity there is also the belief in purgatory. This is a place of suffering and torture where souls must be cleansed before they can enter heaven.

Christian teachings:

- 'Love your neighbour' (Jesus) – Christian love (agape) should be shown to all people.
- Pray for those who persecute you. (Jesus)
- The Ten Commandments – a law code that guides behaviour
- Forgive your brother 70 x 7 times (Jesus) – meaning that a Christian should always be prepared to forgive those who wrong them.
- The Lord's Prayer – recognises that everyone sins and needs forgiveness.

Christians accept that offenders must be punished. Punishments should be fair and just and offenders should be treated humanely. The Quaker Elizabeth Fry devoted her life to prison reform. Amnesty International, which was founded on Christian principles, works worldwide to campaign for the protection of prisoners' human rights. The story of Adam and Eve (The Fall) shows that everyone sins. Christians believe that people should have the opportunity to repent for their wrongdoing and make amends. It is important to follow the example of Jesus and be prepared to forgive others. Most Christians do not agree with the death penalty. Some, however, follow the Old Testament teaching of 'an eye for an eye'.

Task

1 Look up the story of Angulimala. What does it teach about Buddhist attitudes to crime and punishment? **www.angulimala.org.uk**
2 Look up the Parable of the Lost Son and the story of the woman caught in adultery. What do they teach Christians about repentance and forgiveness?

ॐ Hinduism

Hindus believe that all people should follow the law and that rulers have a responsibility to ensure justice is carried out and people are protected from offenders. In the Hindu scriptures dharma (duty), caste and the belief in karma are important influences on attitudes to crime and punishment. Every Hindu is born into a caste and has a duty to fulfil. Criminal activities bring bad karma and would cause a person to be reborn into a lesser life form. The principle of ahimsa (non-violence) would also be broken, since crime causes harm to others physically and/or emotionally.

Hindu teachings:

- Karma – all evil actions result in bad karma that influences rebirth.
- Reincarnation and moksha – the cycle of rebirth (samsara) depends on karma. Moksha can only be achieved through good actions.
- 'An eye for an eye makes the whole world blind.' (Gandhi)
- 'When a person claims to be non-violent … he will put up with all the injury given to him by a wrongdoer.' (Gandhi)
- Murdering a Brahmin is the most serious of crimes. (Laws of Manu)

Hindu teachings make clear that just punishments should appropriately provide retribution, deterrence and reformation. In the past the severity of punishment was greater the lower the caste of the offender. In modern times many Hindus follow the example of Gandhi and would expect offenders to be treated humanely and that punishment should make provision for the offender to learn from their mistake and reform. The Laws of Manu make clear that the death penalty is acceptable for crimes such as murder, theft and adultery, but in India today only murder and treason are capital offences.

☪ Islam

Muslim law (Shari'ah) is both secular and religious. It is based on the Qur'an, Hadith and Sunnah of the prophet. An offender therefore breaks Allah's laws as well as man's law. To outsiders Islamic law can appear to be harsh. However, Islam is a complete way of life and all Muslims have a responsibility to each other and the community. For example, there is no reason to steal because zakat is provided for the poor. Criminal activity is an offence to Allah and will be punished on earth and in the afterlife.

Muslim teachings:

- A thief, whether man or woman, shall have their hand cut off as penalty. (Qur'an)
- The woman and man guilty of adultery or fornication, flog each one of them. (Qur'an)
- We ordained for them; life for life. (Qur'an)
- Day of Judgement – Allah will decide who goes to paradise or hell.
- If a man is killed unjustly, his family will be entitled to satisfaction.

Crime in Islam can be divided into four groups. *Hadud* – the worst crimes: murder, blasphemy, theft, adultery, false accusation, treason, highway robbery and drinking alcohol. There are capital and corporal punishments for these offences. *Jinayat* – involve killing or wounding and the victims have the right to claim compensation. The law of compensation allows offenders to pay diya (blood money) in exchange for a lesser punishment. *Ta'azir* – are lesser crimes, and punishments are decided by a judge who will consider social pressures and change. *Mukhalafat* – covers laws related to the smooth running of the state, such as driving offences, and a judge decides the punishments. Punishments should ensure that justice is served. Islam accepts there may be mitigating circumstances to be considered and allows for the forgiveness of offenders.

Task

1 Find out how Gandhi (see page 36 of this book) led a campaign of peaceful civil disobedience against British rule in India. Write a report on your findings.
2 Find out more about the use of capital and corporal punishment in Islamic countries. Write a report on your findings.

Judaism

The Torah is the Jewish law book and includes 613 *mitzvoth* (rules). These outline the conduct expected of all citizens. They include secular and religious guidance. All Jews are expected to follow the law and keep their religious duties and responsibilities. There is also guidance on repentance for wrongdoing. Jews believe that G-d will forgive and be merciful if a wrongdoer makes *atonement* – repents their sins and makes amends. They can do this through prayer, fasting and charitable giving. The *Bet Din* (Jewish court) makes decisions about religious matters.

Jewish teachings:

- The Ten Commandments
- G-d created the world with justice and mercy so that it would last. (Midrash)
- The Lord does not enjoy seeing sinners die, He would rather they stop sinning and live. (Nevi'im)
- If anyone takes the life of a human being they must be put to death. (Torah)
- Yom Kippur – the Day of Atonement when Jews make confession and atonement for sins

Judaism teaches that society should be protected and that people should be deterred from committing crimes. Punishment should be just and rehabilitate the offender. The Torah does allow execution for some crimes and emphasises the need for corroborative evidence from two independent witnesses. The teaching of an 'eye for an eye' is about making amends. The death penalty exists as a deterrent and it is rarely used; Judaism considers it important for offenders to have the opportunity to atone for their crimes.

 # Sikhism

Sikhs regard the law as important for ensuring justice and the protection of weaker members of society. All people need God's guidance to avoid the evils of anger, greed, lust, pride and attachment to worldly possessions. Human nature means that sometimes people fall into sin, but they should have the opportunity to repent and make up for their mistakes. Khalsa Sikhs follow a strict code of discipline (Reht Maryada) when they commit to the community. If a Sikh were to break this code they would have to make reparation before the rest of the community. In society, Sikhism teaches its followers to be law abiding, but to be prepared to fight against injustice and oppression.

Sikh teachings:

- Law of karma – evil actions result in bad karma and lower rebirth.
- Kurahits – religious vows guiding personal conduct
- Kirpan – a symbol of the fight for justice and truth
- If someone hits you, do not hit him back; go home after kissing his feet. (Guru Granth Sahib)
- He who associates with evil-doers is destroyed. (Guru Granth Sahib)

Sikhs believe in *nirvair* – trying to be without hatred. They accept that it is important to punish criminals in order to protect society and reform the offender. They do not accept physical or mental torture, as they respect the dignity of all human life and the essence of God within all. Many Sikhs support human rights organisations like Amnesty International and would offer support and counselling to convicts. Sikhs are told to follow their conscience and many would not support the death penalty because of the belief in the sanctity of life. However, some may regard it as a useful deterrent and just punishment for some crimes.

Task

1 Look up the Ten Commandments. Explain how they guide religious and secular behaviour.
2 Look up the Sikh Kurahits. Write a report on how they would influence a Sikh's life.

The Basics

Use pages 141–43 to explain the attitude of the religions you are studying to:
1 the law
2 the punishment of offenders
3 capital punishment.

Religious attitudes to rich and poor in British society

When we think about rich and poor, we don't necessarily think of people in Britain. We assume most people are fairly wealthy and if not there is help available both from the government and other organisations. However, although there are less extreme problems in Britain than in less developed parts of the world, problems do exist.

In this topic we will look at the issue of the causes of wealth and poverty in Britain, and how people gain wealth and indeed lose it. Secondly, we will focus on attitudes to money from the point of view of the six world religions. Thirdly, the course will have a look at responses to this issue and who is responsible for helping such people in Britain.

You must *not* write about the poor in other countries in your answers in this topic – that is the next topic!

So, let's get started. Why are some people poor in Britain? They may have been born into a poor family, may have lost money on **gambling**, may be out of work, may have had a poor education, may have lost their business, may be addicted …

Homelessness

On the streets of our cities a growing number of people sleep rough. It is impossible to work out exactly how many people are homeless because the numbers change constantly and not everyone who is homeless is on an official list. According to Government statistics for 2014, there were over 160,000 homeless people (rough sleepers, people legally recognised as homeless by councils) with up to 400,000 more 'hidden homeless' (people who sleep rough, squatters, people who sleep on other people's floor, people in hostels and so on). Why is the problem so big? The cost of housing in Britain has risen dramatically over the last twenty years and many council houses (social housing) have been sold off.

In the UK, there are 40,000 (overnight and long-term) hostel beds available for the homeless. Some are used by the young homeless, many of whom left home because of difficult family situations, abuse or because they simply did not feel wanted. They get involved in crime to survive, often abuse drugs or alcohol and leave education. Many have mental health and behavioural problems. They cannot get a job because you need a fixed address to get a job and to get a fixed address you need a job! Many homeless people are ex-armed forces. When they leave the forces they find they cannot cope with an ordinary job or home life and end up on the streets. It is estimated that in 2010, the homeless problem cost councils £345 million, plus the NHS £64 million – there will have been other costs as well.

Task

Research **homelessness** in Britain. Search Google or use these websites to start you off: **www.shelter.org.uk**, **www.bbc.co.uk/ news**, **www.oasisaquilahousing.org**, **www. crisis.org.uk**
Produce a leaflet or PowerPoint® or organise a class debate on the issue. You could think about the following statement: 'In Britain, one of the world's richest countries, nobody should be homeless.'

✓ **Now you know about homelessness**

Gambling

As people have become more affluent in Britain more people have become involved in gambling. Some are serious gamblers and others might just have a 'flutter' on the odd occasion. However, at the other end of the scale, there are many people who are poor and use gambling to try to win money they need. The problem is that for every time they win, there are many times when they don't. Also, when someone does win there is the buzz to carry on.

In the long run this gets them into a far worse financial situation, but the chance of winning big money keeps them gambling.

It is probably true to say that it is possible to gamble on anything. Traditionally, sport was the focus.

> Why do people gamble? What kind of things do people gamble on?

All major events now have 'odds' on them happening or their outcome – you can bet on anything that does not have a guaranteed outcome. Remember that there are casino complexes now, poker on the TV, bingo halls and online betting.

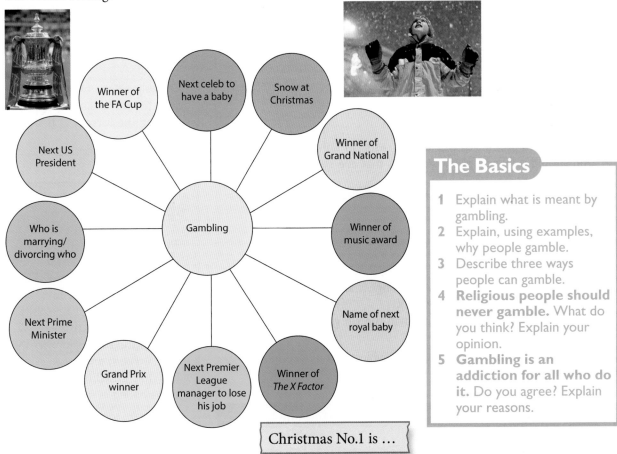

- Winner of the FA Cup
- Next celeb to have a baby
- Snow at Christmas
- Next US President
- Winner of Grand National
- Who is marrying/ divorcing who
- **Gambling**
- Winner of music award
- Next Prime Minister
- Name of next royal baby
- Grand Prix winner
- Next Premier League manager to lose his job
- Winner of *The X Factor*

Christmas No.1 is …

The Basics

1 Explain what is meant by gambling.
2 Explain, using examples, why people gamble.
3 Describe three ways people can gamble.
4 **Religious people should never gamble.** What do you think? Explain your opinion.
5 **Gambling is an addiction for all who do it.** Do you agree? Explain your reasons.

Religious attitudes to gambling

Gambling is quite a big part of this topic. General ideas about how people should acquire wealth and also about how we use wealth (using the teachings on the religious attitudes section of this chapter, pages 149–51) will help you. However, if you are able to refer to specific teachings about gambling from the religion/s you have studied, you will show a much higher level of understanding.

Look at the following beliefs and teachings.

 ## Buddhism

- Craving (tanha) associated with gambling and wealth will not bring true happiness.
- Wealth should be earned honestly (right livelihood).
- We need wealth to meet our needs but no more in case we become attached to it.

 ## Christianity

- Gambling denies the biblical work ethic that associates honest labour with deserved reward.
- A greedy person is an idolater who cannot obtain salvation. (Gambling implies greed.)
- The *love* of money is the root of all evil. (New Testament)
- Some accept fundraising by raffles and some agree the lottery is fine in moderation.

 ## Hinduism

- Uncontrolled pursuit of wealth will result in unhappiness.
- One should only accept those things that are set aside as his or her quota.
- Some do see the lottery/gambling in moderation as acceptable.

 ## Islam

- O you who believe, wine and gambling … are filthy tricks of Satan; avoid them so you may pray.
- The profit from gambling is less than the sin gained. It is haram.

Most teachings are not directly about the subject – you need to be able to apply them.

 Now you can give a top answer to a question on gambling!

Task

Using the teachings below, explain what you think the religious attitude/s would be to the following gamblers:
1 A person who once a year puts a £10 bet on the Grand National horse race
2 A person who is addicted to gambling and gambles every day, whether they have the money or not
3 A person who needs the money from gambling to pay off debts
4 A person who puts £10 on the lottery twice a week every week

 ## Judaism

- Money should be earned from working – doing G-d's work on earth.
- The motive of gambling is greed. It is not forbidden but the spiritual consequences are a worry.
- Gambling does take place as part of festivals such as Purim.
- Playing the lottery is fine in moderation.

 ## Sikhism

- Kirat-Karni – means earning one's money by honest means including labour. The Guru Granth Sahib says money should not be spent on gambling and drinking.
- Two of the five major vices – lobh (greed) and moh (worldly attachment) – lead to gambling or are fed by gambling.

Other causes of poverty

It is true to say that many of the problems that leave people in poverty are linked – many people are affected by more than one factor that leaves them in poverty.

My name is David. I've been on the streets for 'bout two years. I've no money – left home with nowt – mum don't care! It's cold. Need to get warm. I do drugs to take away my thoughts – it's good to block out the world. Nothing to look forward to – I'm on my own, it's up to me.

My name is Joe and I'm 44 … Had a heart attack last year and now can't work much. I don't get a lot in benefits because they say I am not that bad – but they don't really know how I feel. I am frightened that it could happen again if I do too much. I am too young to die. I can't afford much (no luxuries) so I really struggle.

I'm called Becky – I am 14. I live at home with my dad and his girlfriend. I have a brother and two half-sisters. Dad got made redundant and now only works part time so we haven't got much. Perhaps if he didn't smoke and drink so much I might have been able to go on the school trip! He does try I guess but I never have trendy clothes and feel ashamed when I'm with mates. I try at school coz I want a better life than this. I want stuff for my children.

I'm Jason. School was a waste of time – couldn't be bothered with all that stuff. Teachers just shout and you can't do what you want. Didn't go to many lessons – skived off with mates. Didn't do homework – stupid after being at school all day! Most days didn't get up 'til 11 – liked lying in bed better. Now I'm unemployed – claim Jobseeker's Allowance but it ain't much. Can't buy stuff I want but don't want a job either.

My name is Claire. I had to help mum when I was young so I missed a lot of school – she sent me out shopping cos she couldn't be bothered. Now I can't get a decent job with money, can't read much and don't have any confidence to do stuff.

Poverty is a complex issue, one with many causes, but the effects on those suffering from it are difficult to solve. In developing countries, poverty is usually not a matter of blame – natural disasters and weather, for example, cannot have real blame attached. In Britain, however, poverty is often associated with blame – some people think that poverty in Britain is usually caused by a person's actions or inactions. They might say 'Well if they hadn't done … ' or 'It's their own fault because … ' or 'It's their choice to be … ' and so on. Despite this blame issue we still have a responsibility as individuals and as religious people to help people in such situations.

 Now you know all about some causes of poverty

Where do people get their wealth?

Business and enterprise

Many people earn their wealth from the businesses they run. A good education has set them up well to start their own business. They have worked hard at a trade and been successful. Some people might be entrepreneurs who have designed something new and made a fortune from it. Hard work has paid off and money has been made.

Gifts and inheritance

Others might be wealthy by virtue of the family they were born into or have received money through **inheritance** (money left to them in a will on the death of someone).

They have wealth through no efforts of their own. However, the person who gave the money may have earned it through hard work.

Earnings and savings

A person may have a good job and have been paid well. They have earned their money. Perhaps they have been careful and invested money or saved it. The issue here is the job that earned them that money. Does a premiership footballer *do enough to earn* their living? Could it be argued that a nurse, for example, works much harder but earns much less and deserves more? On the surface it appears fine to earn money but does it matter *how* it is earned?

Dishonest means

These *are* other ways that people become wealthy. Many ways are illegal, for example, drug crime; others are against religions, for example, from gambling. However, none of these are ways that people *should* be making themselves wealthy. Wealth is often gained at the expense of the suffering of another.

Practice makes perfect ...

… so let's do some evaluation questions on this topic.

a It does not matter where a person's wealth comes from.

b It is better to earn money than to inherit it.

c If you give to charity it does not matter how you earned your money.

d Jobs in the caring professions should earn the most money.

Think about how to agree and disagree with the above statements. They are all asking whether it matters where money comes from or whether if you use wealth in the right way this makes up for where it comes from. The same ideas could be used for them all. You just need to be able to adapt them. Discuss the questions in pairs – jot down some ideas in bullet points. Keep it simple and remember it for the exam.

 Now you know the causes of wealth

Religious attitudes to the poor and to the use of money

For the exam you need to know what the religious views are on money and giving to the poor. The issue of money is about how people earn their money or where their wealth comes from. It also focuses on how people view and use money in their lives. Is it more important than anything else? Does the quest for money rule people's lives? Is it about greed and selfishness?

With regard to the poor in Britain, the exam will focus on religious attitudes to the different groups of people who are poor for the various reasons we looked at earlier. The general response is that, from a religious perspective, we should help anyone in need, regardless of whether it is their fault that they are in such a position. We are not here to judge. Judgement will come later, either from God or in the process of rebirth. All you have to do is to learn some teachings to support this view. It is as simple as that!

Buddhism

Buddhism believes that there is essentially nothing wrong with wealth but the issue is about how it is used.

- Riches ruin the foolish … through craving for riches, the foolish one ruins himself. (Dharmapada)
- Acquiring wealth is acceptable if, at the same time, it promotes the well-being of the community or society. (Phra Rajavaramuni)
- Unskilful thoughts founded in greed are what keep us circling in samsara, in an endless round of repetitive, habitual attachment. (Kulandanda – a leading member of the Western Buddhist Order)

Buddhism encourages right action, right thought, right intention and right livelihood. Therefore, to see poverty and ignore it would be wrong. Buddhists have a duty to help the poor.

- Dana (charity or generosity) is part of the basis of merit making that the Buddha taught.
- Karuna (compassion) is wishing others to be free from suffering.
- 'In our world today everyone is looking for personal happiness. So, I always say, if you wish to be happy and aim for self-interest, then care for others. This brings lasting happiness. This is real self-interest, enlightened self-interest.' (Dalai Lama)

Christianity

Christians believe that there is nothing wrong with wealth in itself; it is how we use that wealth which is important. We can use it for good and bad. If we have wealth, it is seen as a gift from God. Our money should come from lawful means. In the Bible there is the warning that the wrong attitude to money could lead people away from God.

- People who want to get rich fall into temptation and into foolish and harmful desires that plunge men into ruin and destruction. The love of money is the root of all evil. (New Testament)
- No one can serve two masters … You cannot serve both God and money. (Bible)
- Be on your guard against all kinds of greed: a man's life does not consist in the abundance of his possessions. (New Testament)

Christians believe that whatever the reason for a person being poor, we have a duty to use our wealth to help them. It is not our right to judge but to help.

- Go sell everything you have and give it to the poor and you will have treasure in Heaven. (New Testament)
- If anyone has material possessions and sees his brother in need, how can he love God? (New Testament)
- What good is it if a man claims to have faith but has no deeds … If a brother has no clothes or food what good is it to wish him well without caring for his physical needs? (New Testament)

ॐ Hinduism

Rich devotees are not to hoard wealth, but to operate as a steward and distribute that wealth. It is important to create wealth (artha) to provide for family and the maintenance of society. A requirement for religious living is to share wealth. There is a danger of excess wealth as it leads to overindulgence and a materialistic rather than a spiritual life.

- Money causes pain when earned, it causes pain to keep and it causes pain to lose as well as to spend. (Pancatantra)
- Happiness arises from contentment; uncontrolled pursuit of wealth will result in unhappiness. (Manu 4)
- 'Act in the world as a servant, look after everyone and act as if everything belongs to you, but know in your heart that nothing is yours – you are the guardian, the servant of God.' (Shri Ramakrishna)

Hindus believe that life is all about good deeds here and now. This not only helps the individual but it helps their own rebirth.

- Some believe that by helping those in poverty (even if it is their own fault), they can improve their own karma and rebirth.
- Hindus have the principles of daya (compassion) and dana (giving to charity).
- It is taught that 'it is the same God shining out through so many different eyes. So helping others is no different than helping ourselves.'

Islam

In Islam to be wealthy is to be given a gift from Allah. We, as humans, are caretakers of Allah's wealth. We will be judged by the use of it.

- Riches are sweet, a source of blessing to those who acquire them by the way – but those who seek it out of greed are like people who eat but are never full. (Hadith)
- To try to earn a lawful livelihood is an obligation like all other obligations in Islam – no one has eaten better food than what he can earn by the work of his own hands. (Hadith)
- It is not poverty which I fear for you, but that you might begin to desire the world as others before you desired it, and it might destroy you as it destroyed them. (Hadith)

Islam teaches that wealth comes from Allah for us to use it to benefit humanity. If we have wealth it is a test for us to see what we do with it. The Pillar of Zakah commands us to help the poor.

- He who eats and drinks while his brother goes hungry is not one of us. (Hadith)
- If the debtor is in difficulty give him time to pay – but if you let it go out of charity this is the best thing to do. (Qur'an)
- Zakah (the Third Pillar) is giving an annual payment to be used for worthy causes as well as a special zakah on Eid ul Fitr. Sadaqah is giving voluntarily to charity.

Practice makes perfect ...

... so let's look at the following questions:

1 Using beliefs and teachings, explain why religious people help the poor in Britain.

It could be that this type of question is focused on one type of poor in particular, as in question 2.

2 Using beliefs and teachings, explain why religious people should help the homeless.

It might have asked about drug addicts or those who are lazy or people who have gambled money.

3 Using beliefs and teachings, explain attitudes to the use of personal wealth.

Make sure you actually apply the teachings to the topic by connecting them to the question. Students often just include teachings in their answers without showing any understanding of them.

Judaism

Judaism believes that wealth is a gift from G-d and can be used for the self and others. The Tenakh clearly states that money can only be earned in the correct way. Materialism can lead to people sinning – if your heart is filled with the desire for money then there is no room for G-d. The Talmud does, however, see that a decent standard of living is needed for the well-being of the individual.

- Do not weary yourself trying to become rich. (Proverbs)
- He who loves silver cannot be satisfied with silver. (Ecclesiastes)
- He who has a hundred craves for two hundred. (Midrash)

Money is not desired but it is necessary. A Jew is expected to look after their home and give to the poor. Even the poorest of people can give something. The giving of tzedakah (correctness) is not seen as charity because it is not a matter of doing someone a favour: it is giving the poor what is rightfully theirs.

- 'You shall not burden your heart or shut your hand against your poor brother.' (Torah)
- It is forbidden in the Torah to charge a fellow Jew interest on money.
- The Talmud suggests that anyone who can afford it should give to the poor cheerfully, compassionately and comfortingly.

 # Sikhism

Sikhs also believe that a person who possesses riches is blessed by God by virtue that they are able to help the poor. Livelihoods should be made by honest means. Anything that is earned dishonestly is seen as the 'blood of the poor'.

- One who lives by earning through hard work, then gives some of it away to charity, knows the way to God. (Guru Granth Sahib)
- Be grateful to God for whose bounties you enjoy. (Guru Nanak)
- Those who have money have the anxiety of greed. (Adi Granth)

Sewa (service to others) is a distinctive aspect of Sikhism. Guru Nanak thought sewa was a way of teaching man humility and a sense of responsibility to all those in need. It is also an act of worshipping God. It is obligatory for all Khalsa Sikhs as a duty. At the langar, a community meal is served for any who want it – Sikh or not. In Indian gurdwaras, tens of thousands of meals a day are given free.

- The sign of a good person is that they always seek the welfare of others. (Bhai Gurdas)
- A sign of divine worship is the service of one's fellows. (Bhai Gurdas)
- A place in God's court can only be attained if we do service to others in the world. (Adi Granth)

How to revise more easily

There are a whole range of teachings in this topic but for revision purposes you don't need to know that many. Make sure you know the general teachings from the front of the book and, from pages 149–51, learn either two from one religion if you are studying one religion or one from each if you are studying two religions.

Try writing on a piece of paper two teachings on each subject for each of the topics you are studying. Put it up somewhere so you can take a look every so often. You will be surprised how quickly you know them off by heart.

 Now you know the religious teachings on attitudes to money and helping the poor

What do we do to help in Britain?

If we accept that poverty exists in Britain then, as a developed, democratic country, we should have things in place to help. In fact help comes from many areas – charities and religious organisations, the government and direct help.

Many charities in Britain work for the people of Britain. They find it hard to raise money, probably because they don't have major disasters to publicise with heart-rending pictures of suffering. At the same time there are many people who believe that if you are in Britain and poor then you only have yourself to blame and do not deserve any help.

Shelter helps millions of people every year who are struggling with bad housing and homelessness – and campaigns to prevent it happening in the first place. Shelter has been around since 1966, when it was set up by founder Bruce Kenrick in response to the massive housing crisis and inner-city slums of the 1690s. Shelter has campaigned ever since for key policy changes to help people facing homelessness, or suffering in bad housing. Shelter exists today so that no one has to fight bad housing or homelessness on their own.

Shelter has many fundraising initiatives. One annual event is Vertical Rush, which sees volunteers run up the stairs of London's Tower 42. In 2014, the event raised over £500,000.

The Salvation Army? Yes, it's those people who we see at Christmas in shopping centres playing music and with collecting tins! They actually work all year round:

- rebuilding lives – offering a hand-up to homeless people, a family tracing service, drug and alcohol rehab, anti-human-trafficking services
- offering comfort and support – food parcels, lunch clubs for older people, supporting the emergency services during major fires and incidents, visiting prisoners
- giving people the chance to belong – kids and youth clubs and music groups, for example.

As a Christian Church and registered charity, The Salvation Army also supports children, the homeless and older people who would have little or nothing at Christmas time. It runs homeless resettlement centres, care homes for older people, employment services for the long-term unemployed, and home-visiting services in local communities. All this is done by volunteers and ministers who believe in putting their Christian beliefs into action – to follow Jesus' example to help (not judge) anyone who is in need.

Gamblers Anonymous is a fellowship of men and women who share their experience, strength and hope so that they may help themselves and others to recover from a gambling problem. The only requirement for membership is a desire to stop gambling. It is estimated that more than 450,000 people have a serious gambling habit in Britain today.

 Now you know about some of the charities that work in Britain

Government help

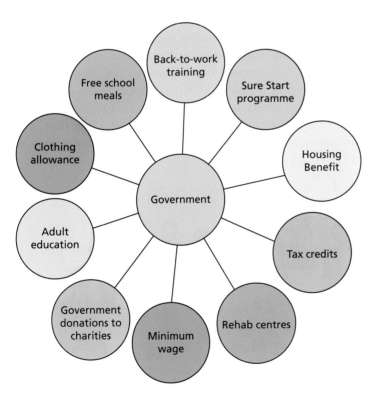

The spider diagram is looking at what governments can do for the poor, whereas the picture is looking at what decisions can be taken by those in poverty to help them improve the situation that they are in.

Task

Thinking about the options available, answer the following questions:
1 Explain where people in poverty can get help from.
2 Is it better to accept the help available or initiate recovery from poverty yourself?
3 Why might some people not claim the government help available?

The minimum wage and excessive salaries

There are two key terms that might be specifically referred to in your exam: **minimum wage** and **excessive salaries**.

The *minimum wage* is the least amount of money an employer can legally pay a worker per hour. It is set by the Government. In March 2014, it stood at £6.31 for people aged 21 and over; £5.03 for those aged 18–20; and £3.72 for under-18s.

> Why is this a good idea? Why would religious people support this?

Well, firstly it protects workers at the lowest end of the pay structure from employers trying to **exploit** them as 'slave labour', as it is commonly known. Secondly, it protects British workers from some foreign workers who are willing to work for much less. Thirdly, it protects the employers from workers challenging their pay. Religious people believe in fairness and the idea of a fair day's work for a fair day's pay. The only real downsides are that, for example, when a young worker reaches eighteen they might find an employer trying to get rid of them in order to bring in another under-eighteen so they are able to pay less. In Britain a person is an adult at the age of eighteen and could therefore have the same rights and responsibilities as a 22-year-old (a family, for example) so why should age make a difference to how much they are paid? From a business point of view, a company might not be able to employ as many people because of financial constraints.

At the other end of the pay spectrum is the issue of *excessive salaries*. These are salaries that are very high in relation to the job that is being done. Is a footballer worth £250,000 per week, plus bonuses for winning and sponsorship deals? In the city, top workers earn millions and company bosses often have exorbitant salaries and get paid bonuses whether the company is doing well or not. At the same time, workers are often given a pay rise that is below the level of inflation. This raises the question of value for money for the work done. Also there are other people doing very valuable jobs who are paid much less, such as nurses. However, others would argue that they are at the top of their respective professions, they have worked hard to get there or they have a special talent. If the country weren't willing to pay such salaries, these people might leave and go to countries that are willing to pay them.

Who should care about the poor?

Charities

Religious communities

Poor people

An MP

Families

Tax payers

Businesses

Task

Explain why the people in the pictures above have a responsibility to care for the poor.
Do you think some have more responsibility than others? Explain your opinion.
How much responsibility lies with the poor person themselves?

You've just won £26.4 million ...

Now that's serious money! A lottery win could make you very, very rich! That is why people play it – a win would make a very real difference to their lives. There are lots of arguments regarding the issue of gambling on the lottery. The fact that it is just about luck and involves no skill or hard work is a problem for some people. To others it isn't really gambling; they see it as a game, a bit of fun.

> Think about the statements below. What issues do they raise about the lottery? In pairs, write down your ideas.

The lottery makes people millionaires. I think the prizes should be less so that the money is spread out among more people.

The issue is not about gambling; it is about what you do with the money. If you help family and friends, and give to charity, then this justifies the gambling.

It is too much money to win – it gets spent on wasteful things.

I would buy a big house, flashy car, have a luxury holiday, oh and go shopping to fill my wardrobe.

It would change my life. How can you carry on as normal with so much money? New friends, begging letters, everyone wants something off you ... I just want a normal life.

The chances of winning are slim. People spend more than they can afford and this gets them into further debt.

Winning the lottery would answer all my problems.

Winning big would make anyone happy – you would be able to do whatever you want.

> Having discussed the issues, would you want to win the lottery? Why/why not?

> How would a lottery win help these people? How would they spend it, do you think? Do you think they deserve it? If only one of them could win, who do you think deserves it the most?

For religious people there are still issues with the lottery – greed, selfishness, wasting money, materialism versus spiritualism, people winning at others' expense, tickets you cannot afford, misuse of money .... But the lottery does have a positive side – giving money for good causes, helping families, giving people opportunities, giving money to places of worship, having the ability to make a real difference.

This is an interesting topic with plenty of scope for questions to be asked about it. You need to be able to think and discuss both sides of the argument – and you just did! So, if you learn the issues, you are prepared for the exam!

✓ **Now you know about the lottery**

Religious attitudes to world poverty

Having looked at the issue of rich and poor in Britain in the last section, we now move on to the topic of world poverty. Although at first glance this can be seen as being a very similar subject area, the reasons why it is happening and what it involves are totally different. So, what do we mean by poverty in the world context?

When most people talk about poverty they think about money or indeed the lack of it! However, when we are looking at world poverty it is a far more complex issue. The pictures above might give you some clues as to what is involved. The focus for this course is on the areas of the world commonly known as Less Economically Developed Countries (**LEDC**s). Many of these countries are south of the Equator, have high populations which are growing, have an issue with their climate, are prone to natural disasters, have been (or still are) ravaged by civil wars, have massive national debt and are exploited by richer nations. In such countries the issue is about survival and what people need simply to stay alive – the basic needs of life.

What do you need to know?

You will need to understand the key issues that cause poverty in LEDCs, religious attitudes to poverty and how the religions and religious believers try to help, the work of charities with long- and short-term aid, **world trade** and **global interdependence**.

Task

Find out which countries are categorised as LEDCs, and why they are categorised as such. This will be useful as you start to understand the causes of world poverty.

Key concepts

In relation to world poverty and how religion responds to it there are three concepts to know:

- *Justice* – the idea that people have a right to be treated fairly, in this case by the sharing of wealth, and by non-exploitation
- *Stewardship* – the responsibility to look after the world and everything in it, particularly those who are poorer or less fortunate than us
- *Compassion* – loving kindness – the ability that humans have to be affected by the suffering of others and want to care for and help them

The basic needs of life

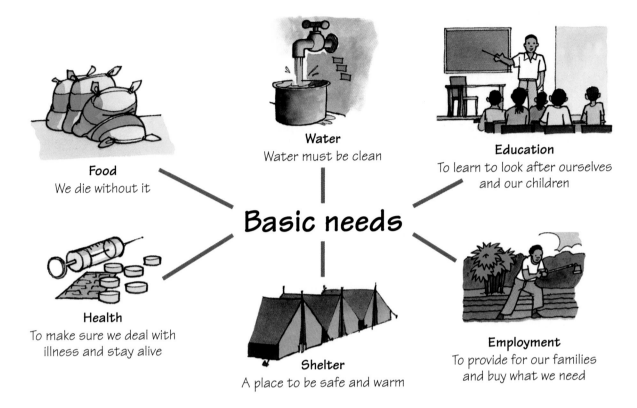

Food
We die without it

Water
Water must be clean

Education
To learn to look after ourselves
and our children

Basic needs

Health
To make sure we deal with
illness and stay alive

Shelter
A place to be safe and warm

Employment
To provide for our families
and buy what we need

Fact file

- One in eight people in the world do not have enough to eat – many survive on one simple meal a day.
- Every ten seconds a child dies of a hunger-related disease.
- 1.7 billion people do not have access to clean water – millions die every year from drinking dirty water.
- Only one child in four has access to secondary education in developing countries – many girls remain illiterate.
- Three-quarters of the people in developing countries have only limited access to doctors and medicine.
- Many homes have no running water or electricity and many people are homeless.
- Real jobs are sparse; 75 per cent of the world's poorest people have to live off what they grow.

The Basics

The following tasks can be done in groups. Each group should write one of the six basic needs of life in the middle of a large sheet of paper and then do the following.

1. Write down three different reasons why people need it or access to it.
2. Write down three ways help could be given to solve the problems caused by the lack of it.
3. Decide on a scale of 1–6 (where 1 is most important) for survival where it would come. Explain why.
4. Decide which of the six needs you would focus on if your group had unlimited money. Explain why and what you would do.
5. Report back as to the decisions you have made.

For a homework task you could research your topic for some actual statistics from developing countries to help you learn the key issues.

Now you know about the basic needs of life

157

What causes all this poverty around the world?

Climate

Many areas of the world suffering poverty are situated near the Equator – Africa, Central and South America, India, the Middle East and South and East Asia. The climate of such areas has a massive effect on people's lives. Many places are very hot and rainfall is minimal – for many months there is no rain at all and yet when it does rain, it is so hard that the land floods. Land is dusty, little grows and people go hungry because the crops fail. The lack of water, and clean water in particular, means that disease spreads.

Added to this are environmental problems – global warming and climate change. Recently in Britain and Europe we have experienced climate problems such as droughts (leading to bans on using hosepipes or washing cars) and severe floods (leaving people homeless and businesses ruined). The difference is that we have the means to cope. Imagine having no food for your family because nothing grows, nothing to sell at market, no clean water to drink because the rivers and lakes have all dried up, diseases and hunger spread, animals that you cannot feed, dry land all around, and no government help for these difficulties. In the rainy season too much water arrives too quickly – the land floods, homes are destroyed and people killed. This is a year-on-year problem.

Natural disasters

The poorest countries in the world are at risk of the worst natural disasters. These are caused by natural occurrences that we cannot control. Environmental experts say that through global warming and pollution, man is having an impact on nature itself. Recent disasters include droughts in Ethiopia, an earthquake in Haiti, storms wrecking islands in the Philippines, an earthquake in Pakistan and a tsunami in the Indian Ocean. Floods in particular are a real problem; the countries are too poor to prepare for them or deal with them alone when they happen. Usually they result in thousands of deaths. The countries rely heavily (not through choice) on aid from rich nations.

 Buddhism

- Karma – the belief that our actions will affect our rebirth
- Ahimsa – the idea that nothing should suffer
- Dana – charity or generosity, part of the basis of merit making that the Buddha taught
- Karuna – compassion (wishing others to be free from suffering)
- 'I always say, if you wish to be happy and aim for self-interest, then care for others. This brings lasting happiness. This is real self-interest, enlightened self-interest.' (Dalai Lama)

 Christianity

- Jesus told us to 'love thy neighbour'.
- 'Treat others as you wish to be treated.'
- Jesus said to a rich man 'go sell all you have and give to the poor then you will have treasures in heaven'.
- If a rich person sees his brother needs help, he should help him. If he does not then he cannot claim to love God.
- The Parable of the Sheep and Goats – it is those who have helped others that are rewarded in heaven.

Tip

You must be able to apply these teachings. It does not matter what area of poverty is stated in the question, the passages you can use (probably three) will be the same.

War

War is a major contributory factor to poverty. In many LEDCs, even if we just focus on the last 30–40 years, there have been unstable governments, infighting causing civil wars and wars between poor countries. War causes poverty in two main ways. Firstly, the money spent on weapons costs millions of dollars – money that should be spent on improving the lives of the countries' people. While many people suffer extreme poverty the governments of some of these countries are actually very rich. They just don't spend money in the right areas. Secondly, war destroys crops, homes, schools, hospitals and families. People flee their own country and become refugees, which also puts pressure on other poor countries.

Corruption

In many LEDCs one of the key issues is corruption. This is firstly at government level. Usually the government has not been democratically elected by the people of the country. It has come to power by force or civil war and it is kept in power by the support of the army. Many of these governments are brutal regimes. They take the wealth of the country and spend it on weapons, keep themselves in power through bribery and fear, and spend huge amounts on luxuries for themselves. People who oppose the governments usually disappear without trace. Examples of such corruption would be President Amin in Uganda, the North Korean leadership, and Robert Mugabe in Zimbabwe. On a local level, council officials are equally as corrupt. All this means that the people of the country are left very poor and with no means to change the system that keeps them poor.

🕉 Hinduism

- Hindus accept that suffering in the world is a result of bad actions in a previous life.
- By helping those in poverty, people can improve their own karma and rebirth.
- Daya (compassion) and dana (giving to charity) encourage help for others.
- 'It is the same God shining out through so many different eyes. So helping others is no different than helping ourselves.'
- 'Act in the world as a servant, look after everyone; you are only the guardian, the servant of God.' (Shri Ramakrishna)

☪ Islam

- He who eats and drinks while his brother goes hungry is not one of us. (Hadith)
- Allah rewards us in heaven for our good deeds.
- If the debtor is in difficulty give him time – but if you let it go out of charity this is the best thing. (Qur'an)
- Zakah (the Third Pillar) is giving an annual payment to be used for worthy causes. Sadaqah is giving voluntarily to charity.
- Muhammad (pbuh) set the example in the early Muslim community to share with each other.

The Basics

1 Give three causes of poverty.
2 Explain the attitude of one religion to those who live in poverty.
3 **War is the main cause of poverty.** Do you agree? Give reasons for your answer, showing you have thought about more than one point of view. Refer to religious arguments in your answer.

Debt

Many LEDCs have to borrow money from banks or the World Bank. This money allows them to start to develop. However, the interest that has to be paid is very high and quite often the interest payments are higher than the foreign currency the LEDCs earn from the exports they make. Hence their national debt is always increasing. In July 2005 at the meeting of the G8 (the world's richest countries) in Edinburgh, decisions were made to try to help this situation. It was stated that reductions in debt payments would only be made to countries that allowed democratic elections to take place. This was done because over the last twenty years massive amounts of money have been poured into Africa in particular, and yet much has gone into the pockets of their corrupt military leaders rather than helping the people it was aimed at. So, corruption has been a linked cause.

Unfair trade and exploitation

Small-scale farmers in developing countries grow vegetables and fruit for their own consumption and keep animals for meat, milk and eggs. Many also grow export crops such as tea, coffee, rice, fruit and cotton as their major source of cash income to sell at market or to traders. It is difficult for most of these small farmers to trade their goods on the global market, because international trade rules are weighted in favour of rich countries. They usually have to sell to middle men who buy small amounts from many farmers, and then sell them all to one company. Often, the middle men know that the farmer has to sell, and so will sell at a much lower price if it guarantees sales in the future. This allows the middle men to offer very little money, and get very good deals, making a good profit for themselves. This system keeps small farmers in poverty, as they are never able to earn enough to escape from poverty.

The other issue here is *exploitation* of workers. Often multinational companies have their products made in LEDCs. The point of this is that workers in these countries are prepared to work for really low wages because it is better than nothing. Women, and indeed children, work in sweatshops and factories many hours a day, in very hot conditions, where they have no workers' rights and are paid only pennies per day! Much of what we wear and what we eat is produced in these conditions. What do you think religions would say about this? Are we prepared to pay more so that people can earn a respectable wage or do we just buy these products without giving a thought to their origins?

Judaism

- You shall not burden your heart or shut your hand against your poor brother. (Torah)
- It is forbidden in the Torah to charge a fellow Jew interest on money.
- Amos suggests that if you skimp on a measure, boost the price, cheat the scales and so on, G-d will not forget.
- The Talmud suggests that anyone who can afford it should give to the poor cheerfully, compassionately and comfortingly.
- He who pursues righteousness and kindness will find life and honour. (Proverbs)

Sikhism

- Dhan (part of sewa) means service to humanity by giving to charity and giving time to help people in need.
- There can be no worship without performing good deeds. (Guru Granth Sahib)
- Heaven is not attained without good deeds. (Guru Granth Sahib)
- After you shall depart this life, God shall demand a reckoning of your deeds that in his ledger are recorded. (Guru Granth Sahib)
- Vand Chhakna encourages Sikhs to live generously.
- Daswandh involves giving a tenth of surplus wealth to serve people, for example, for famine or other disaster relief.

Where are the LEDCs?

These countries are mainly situated south of the Equator, in Africa, Asia and South America. However, over the last 30 years these areas of the world have seen different rates of development. There are 48 countries that are classed as less economically developed. Within this number some are the *'least developed'* where there is extreme poverty, civil war, political corruption, epidemics, low incomes and human resource weaknesses; these are economically very vulnerable places such as Somalia, Sudan, Haiti and Yemen. There are also some countries with *'emerging markets'* such as Brazil, China, South Korea and Turkey.

Task

Tough decisions

Imagine that you run an aid agency. This year you have collected just over £5 million. How would you respond to the following requests? The country where the need has been identified is important. Is it a least developed or an emerging economy? Does it make any difference to your decision? Think about how much money you have to spend and what that money could be spent on. Be realistic and prioritise!

Our village is a shanty town just outside the centre of Sao Paulo in Brazil. We have no running water, and many of our young people have died due to dirty water. Our houses (made out of what we can find) are cramped and we have no electricity. Water comes from the well in the next village ten miles away.

My country, Somalia, is torn by civil war. It is terrible. Families are being torn apart – no one is spared. Our food supplies are affected by the fighting and there are not enough people to work in the fields. Many of our young men have been forced to fight, our girls have been raped and our houses destroyed. Our hospitals are damaged – many doctors and nurses are dead. People are homeless. The UN has set up refugee camps but they are badly in need of supplies.

Our country (China) has suffered another earthquake. Of our young people, 60 per cent are displaced and have no homes. Many people have died or disappeared – probably buried! People are looking for their loved ones but are scared that the rubble will collapse. Communication links are down, there is no clean water and food is in short supply.

My country, Ethiopia, is very poor. The levels of health care and education are low. We want to advance as a nation and compete in the world. Many of my people work hard and their produce is sold to dealers in other countries. They earn very little for this because trade is not fair and they haven't the business knowledge to improve. Often these cash crops mean that people here have very little to eat.

Charities

Buddhism

Tibet Foundation

History – Tibet Foundation was established in 1985. It is a London-based and Tibetan-led charity (no.292400) that gives practical support to Tibetan communities, and operates both in and outside Tibet. It aims:

- To promote the culture, religion and way of life of people of Tibetan origin.
- To relieve poverty amongst Tibetan people.
- To support and facilitate healthcare training and amenities for Tibetan people.
- To support and encourage the education of Tibetan children.
- To preserve and support the continuity of Tibetan Buddhist culture, and create greater awareness of His Holiness the Dalai Lama's message of peace.

Recent projects – To further these aims, Tibet Foundation runs four main programmes: Tibetans in Exile, Aid to Tibet, Buddhism in Mongolia and Art and Culture.

✝ Christianity

CAFOD

History – This was set up in 1962. Historically, Catholic churches generated charity funds on one specific day of each year. They themselves decided what to do with this money. CAFOD was the organisation set up to centralise this fundraising, and be more effective and wide-ranging with it. Work which began as disaster relief and aid work now includes campaigning for a fairer world, and a vast array of educational work, including a schools magazine, as well as church magazines.

Recent project – Cafod is working with communities in Brazil to help some of the poorest and most vulnerable people. This work includes: improving living conditions, defending land rights, educational work with children living in violent shanty towns, to providing landless families with a more secure place to live, and lobbying the Government for better health care and education facilities.

ॐ Hinduism

SEWA International

History – This is a UK charity, entirely run by dedicated volunteers from all sections of the community, working towards serving humanity. It funds long-term projects for economic development. It tries to combine modern and indigenous techniques to improve living conditions in affected disaster areas of India. It focuses on education, orphanages, village amenities and employment.

Recent project – The Women's Empowerment Project runs in Odisha, India. Its major focus is to form village women's committees. This tries to give women a greater say in the decisions made in their village. It also educates women, because it is proven that for every year of education a woman has, the better her children's lives will be and the better their life chances in the future. Her education encourages theirs and gives her more ideas for what they could do and more ambition for them.

The Basics

1 Give two reasons why the work of charities is important.
2 Explain why religious people want to give to charity.
3 **Religious people should always help those who ask for it.** What do you think? Explain your opinion.
4 Charities try to help people to help themselves. Why is this important?
5 **Charities should only help people of the same religion as they represent.** Do you agree? Give reasons and explain your answer, showing you have thought about more than one point of view. Refer to religious arguments in your answer.

Islam

Islamic Relief

History – Set up in 1984, this was the first Muslim relief charity in Europe providing humanitarian aid during emergency situations, and working for the long-term development of the world's poorest nations. It aims to try to alleviate the suffering of the needy wherever they are. It works in over 30 countries in Africa, Asia and the Middle East.

Recent project – In Kenya, drought has become the norm. Islamic Relief is working with farmers to introduce new crops that can survive drought, providing new greenhouses for vegetable growing, providing vaccinations for animals against diseases brought by drought and flood, and training women and young people to set up businesses not reliant on farming. This is making a difference to lives and communities.

Charities form a major part of the world's attempt to help the less fortunate. They fundraise throughout the year so that they are in a position to help when that help is required.

We only usually hear about them when they carry out emergency relief, but as well as this they are doing long-term work throughout the year, much of which goes unnoticed.

Judaism

World Jewish Relief

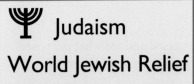

History – World Jewish Relief was founded in 1933 to rescue Jews from the horrors taking place in Nazi Germany and brought 70,000 Jewish people to safety before the start of the Second World War. After the war, work began to respond to the needs of Jewish refugees and communities all over the world, with the aim of supporting Jews in distress. Its work involves empowering local communities by teaching them to be self-sufficient. Today World Jewish Relief stands as the leading UK international agency responding to the needs of Jewish communities at risk or in crisis, outside the UK and Israel. At times of major international disaster, it leads the UK Jewish community's response to others in need all over the world.

Recent project – In Syria, the ongoing war has led to the greatest humanitarian crisis in the world today. Over nine million people have been affected – mainly women and children. World Jewish Relief, as well as meeting the most critical short-term humanitarian needs of refugees, is also working with partners to plan for long-term needs, such as psychological counselling and treatment of post-traumatic stress among women and children.

Sikhism

Khalsa Aid

History – Established in 1999, Khalsa Aid is an international non-profit aid and relief organisation founded on the Sikh principles of selfless service and universal love. It is a UK registered charity and also has volunteers in North America and Asia. Khalsa Aid has provided relief assistance to victims of disasters, wars and other tragic events around the world.

Recent project – In 2014, Khalsa Aid 'adopted' a small town in the Philippines following the typhoon which had wiped out many communities. San Dionisio was in the direct line of the typhoon, and over 90 per cent of the local community was affected. KA commissioned a group of carpenters to help build new boats, so that the community could resume their fishing which will help them rebuild their communities. KA also provided food and temporary shelter, as well as helping with the clear-up operation.

Task

Research the work of the charity of the religion/s you are studying. Do it in more depth using the internet or by contacting the charity itself. In groups, create a presentation about the charity and the kind of work it is currently doing.

Types of aid

What do we mean by aid? How is it organised and for what purposes? There are three types of aid: emergency, short-term and long-term.

What do you think is the difference? Try writing down a definition for yourself. Can you think of some examples for each one?

Emergency aid and short-term aid

Emergency aid is aid that is given in the first few days after a disaster happens. It is the immediate response to a crisis like a flood or an earthquake. Think, for example of the Asian tsunami, the Indian flood, the Burmese floods, the Chinese earthquake and the Kenyan civil war. Emergency aid provides for the crucial immediate needs: helping the living; finding the dead; providing medicine, food, clean water, tents and blankets. Often, charities join forces when things like this happen to raise money, distribute goods and help with the clean-up. Governments often promise money and aid (USA and Britain usually respond fairly quickly) but they are not in a position to get it to the disaster areas. The charities, however, are already present in countries that have a history of natural disasters. Many of these places are war torn or have unco-operative governments, and charities are often the best groups to negotiate these difficulties. This relief work, or emergency aid, will become *short-term aid* as it continues to be needed until the country is more stable.

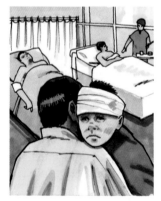

Once short-term aid has been put into action, **long-term aid** starts to rebuild the lives of the survivors. It is really important to try to get people back into some kind of normal life. This helps them recover from the death of loved ones, destroyed homes and ruined livelihoods. To focus on recovery is to heal emotional wounds.

Task

The ideas below are examples of emergency and short-term aid that have been used over recent years. For each one, explain in what situation and how it might be used:
- Sniffer dogs and specialist search teams
- RAF aircraft
- Tents and refugee camps
- Water cleaning tablets
- Dehydration kits
- Clearance teams

The Basics

1 What is meant by a) emergency aid and b) short-term aid?
2 Why are charities in a position to act so quickly when a disaster happens?
3 What is long-term aid?
4 Which is more important – short-term or long-term aid? Why?
5 **Sending food is no good because it runs out too quickly.** What do you think? Explain your answer.

Long-term aid

The key aim of long-term aid is to set up projects that will last and which the people of the country can manage. Examples of projects might be the building of schools and education programmes, hospital and medical projects and building wells for clean water in villages. The whole idea is to give people control of their own futures. This is aid over a long period of time.

 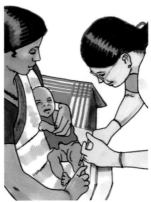  

Gandhi, the great Indian leader, once said:

Give a man a fish and he can feed himself for a day; teach him how to use a fishing rod and he can feed himself forever.

This statement really embodies the difference between the types of aid.

Fact 1

One in four people do not have access to safe water and hundreds die each day from dirty water.

There is a school located in Anuradhapura in Sri Lanka that had no electricity or running water. More families from the coastal areas arrived in town. The school could not cope with this growth. Long-term aid has provided an electric supply to the school and sufficient electricity to power a water pump to provide kitchen facilities and proper sanitation for the children and teachers.

Fact 2

AIDS is killing hundreds of thousands in Africa.

In Uganda there are whole villages without adults because of HIV/AIDS. The Children of Uganda Charity is currently involved in education and food programmes. It has set up long-term sponsorship of children, orphanages (which are available until the age of eighteen) and national medical projects to inform about AIDS. It also keeps the profile of the charity high through people like the U2 band leader, Bono.

Fact 3

One-third of people in the developing world are totally illiterate. Around 77 million children do not go to school.

Millions of school-age children will never go to school. Millions more find themselves in overcrowded classrooms with untrained and underpaid teachers and no books or equipment.

Millions drop out of primary school before they get a basic education. Save The Children has set up preschools and schools in refugee areas, providing qualified teachers and equipment.

✓ **Now you know how long-term aid works**

Sustainable development

This was defined by the UN's World Commission on Environment and Development as 'development that meets the needs of the present without compromising the ability of future generations to meet their needs'. In other words, growth and development must take place within the limits of ecological systems without major social and cultural disruption, and use technology that can be maintained locally. Ideally, the social, cultural, environmental and technological factors should be in balance.

From the environmental point of view, the local ecosystem should be able to support industries without damage from pollutants and waste. The natural resources of a country or area should be used carefully and not over-exploited and depleted. Industries should also be efficient in their use of energy.

Emerging technology – leads to unemployment

Shortage of water to drink and irrigate the land – leads to fighting for resources and destruction of land

Population growth – too many people for the land to support

■ MEDCs   Developing countries   ■ LEDCs

Problems of **sustainable development** in developing countries.

Task

There are plenty of **sustainable development** projects across the world. Research one for yourself, or in pairs or in groups. Find out what the organisation does, what its current projects are, how money is raised and how the volunteer system works. You could start with those mentioned on this page at: **www.villagevolunteers.org** and **www.rainforestalliance.org**

Village Volunteers

Village Volunteers aims to improve life in villages. It is based upon the ideas of:

- sustainable livelihood with social equality and justice
- economic growth
- health care and community development
- volunteer programmes
- women's rights.

The idea is to work in partnership with indigenous people to renew areas affected by poverty and disease, support cultural heritage and support achievement of their goals for the good of people and the environment.

Rainforest Alliance

As an independent, non-profit conservation organisation, the Rainforest Alliance works around the world to ensure that forestry, farming and tourism protect the environment and bring social and economic benefits to workers, their families and communities. Farms and forests that meet standards for sustainability earn the Rainforest Alliance Certified™ seal. These standards increase efficiency, reduce waste, minimise pesticide use and ensure that workers and their families have access to schools and medical care. The Rainforest Alliance involves businesses and consumers worldwide in the effort to bring responsibly produced goods and services to a global marketplace where the demand for sustainability is growing steadily.

Rainforest Alliance

Fairtrade

When we talk about '**fair trade**', we mean trade between people that does not exploit either side – the farmer doesn't get too little for their produce, so they can afford to live; the buyer doesn't pay too much, so they can also make a decent profit. It means both sides get a fair deal. It is a more just system of buying and selling, which implies equal respect for and from both sides.

Fairtrade is a trademark for goods that have been sold to give a fair price to the farmer. You will have seen many of them in shops, and may even have some on sale in your school shop.

The Fairtrade Mark is internationally recognised. Products carrying it are guaranteed to have met international standards. These standards ensure that those people in developing countries who produced the goods (whether farmed or made) received a better deal, including a fair price for their work and an additional sum to invest in community projects. The standard is not just about the farmer or artisan, but also about the community they come from – it is a way of improving life for many.

The Fairtrade system, in 2013, was working with 1.3 million farmers and workers across more than 70 developing countries. Three-quarters of these people are smallhold farmers, working farms not much bigger than the size needed to feed their own families. Sugar, coffee and cocoa are three of the most common Fairtrade products, and the lives and communities of farmers of these have now been transformed.

Research Task

Research Fairtrade, and find out about the range of products involved. Find out the names of some companies that are Fairtrade and where they get their goods from. Find out the impact on the farmers/workers and their communities of this system.

The Fairtrade Foundation

- There were 878 Fairtrade schools in the UK in 2012.
- 354 companies in the UK are licensed to trade Fairtrade goods.
- 89 per cent of British people trust the Fairtrade brand, and see it as an ethical option.
- In 2012, sales of Fairtrade products reached £1.5 billion in the UK – an increase of 18 per cent on 2011.
- A quarter of all Fairtrade sales in the UK are chocolate!
- Fairtrade products are now sold in 125 countries worldwide.

®

FAIRTRADE

How can religious people help those in poorer countries?

As individuals: donate money or goods; buy Fairtrade; volunteer time in charity shops, or to fundraise; organise fundraising and awareness raising events; volunteer skills in the developing country, for example, by helping in disaster relief, working as a teacher in a developing country; pray (for ideas, for help for them, etc.).

As groups: raise awareness in their religious and/or secular communities; set up organisations to help the poor in developing countries; campaign politically for Governments to help.

The Basics

1 Explain what is meant by fair trade.
2 Explain why religious people should support fair trade.
3 Explain how religious believers could help those in LEDCs.
4 **People should only buy Fairtrade goods.** What do you think? Explain your opinion.

Help, help, help, help!

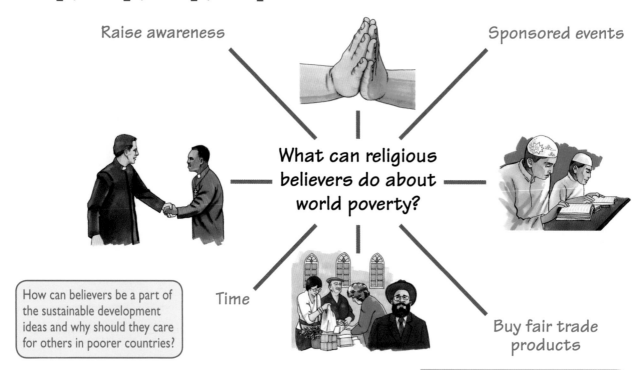

Raise awareness

Sponsored events

What can religious believers do about world poverty?

Time

Buy fair trade products

How can believers be a part of the sustainable development ideas and why should they care for others in poorer countries?

Why do we help?

So, if all the above things happen when there is a disaster, or in a more long-term way, we must ask the question why? Why is it often the case that religious people (as well as many non-religious people) respond in a positive way? The answer goes back to the very first page of this topic. People with a sense of justice, equality and compassion respond when they see the suffering of others. Apparently a study has been done that indicates that compassion is a uniquely human feeling. The animal kingdom does not have a response like this (although in a recent study of a group of African elephants and dolphins, some animal behaviour experts have noticed signs of compassion). However, if we stay with the human aspect of this, when we see images of suffering they spark in us a sense of sorrow and the desire to do something to help. When we help, we feel that we are doing something really worthwhile. This could be a simple action of donating money, or actually volunteering to give up time to help. For example, a doctor or a teacher may feel that to practise medicine or teach in a poor country is more valuable than working in a hospital or school in their own rich country. This may be because they feel that their work is more appreciated and that they are really making a difference to the lives of those who have very little. To do something for others is a great act and there is the belief among religious people that they will find reward in the use of their money – despair and suffering replaced by hope and smiles.

 Now you know something about compassion

Tip

This question regarding how religious people can help in a given situation appears on exam papers regularly. You can use a pretty standard answer irrespective of the issue referred to in the question. Firstly, whatever the problem, religious people could pray, read their holy book, organise something at their local place of worship or raise awareness about the issue. Secondly, we have to remember that religious people are ordinary people and can respond in a way that is not specifically religious – by taking part in a sponsored event, giving time, giving money, buying products. If you learn these ideas it cuts down on how much you have to learn overall. You just have to use these ideas to relate to the question set.

Task

Explain how and why religious believers help those suffering from poverty.

Morality Appendix I

Revision outline

This is a revision guide for the Religion and Morality unit. It follows the outline of topics in the specification. If you already know all of the answers when you read through it, you will probably do brilliantly!

Use the guide as a checklist of what you know, and what you have still got to get to grips with. You could even use it as a last-minute check before you go into the exam. When you have finished all your revision, you should be able to recognise each word. Each phrase should trigger a whole lot of ideas in your head – definitions, examples, explanations. When this happens, you are ready.

Topic	Words to learn	Subjects within topic – do you know …?
7 Religious Attitudes to Matters of Life (Medical Ethics)	Sanctity of life Quality of life Medical research Fertility treatment AIH/D Surrogacy Cloning Genetic engineering Embryology Stem cell therapy Designer babies Saviour siblings Transplant surgery Blood transfusion Human experimentation	• What religions believe about life • The benefits of medical research • The problems associated with medical research • Why (religious) people agree/disagree with human genetic engineering • Why (religious) people agree/disagree with embryo research • Why (religious) people agree/disagree with cloning • Why (religious) people agree/disagree with stem cell therapies • Why (religious) people agree/disagree with designer babies • Why (religious) people agree/disagree with saviour siblings • Why (religious) people agree/disagree with transplant surgery • The problems associated with xenotransplantation • Why (religious) people agree/disagree with blood transfusions • Why (religious) people want to have children • Why people need to use fertility treatment • Why (religious) people agree/disagree with IVF • Why (religious) people agree/disagree with AID/H • Why (religious) people agree/disagree with surrogacy • Whether any/all of these methods overstep the mark of 'playing God'

Topic	Words to learn	Subjects within topic – do you know …?
8 Religious Attitudes to the Elderly and Death	Sanctity of life Quality of life Senior citizenship Ageism Retirement Care home Hospice Hospital Life-support machine Death Euthanasia Active euthanasia Passive euthanasia Life after death	• Why life is sacred/special • Why quality of life is important • The problems old people face • How families can support their elderly relatives • How the state supports old people • Why we should look after the elderly in society • What the law says about euthanasia • Whether it is okay to switch off life support • Whether life support is 'playing God' – in switching off or keeping on • Whether we should have the right to choose when we die • Who should be involved in decisions about death • The difference between active and passive euthanasia • Why some people want euthanasia • Why (religious) people agree/disagree with euthanasia • How (religious) people support the dying • Beliefs about life after death in at least one religion
9 Religious Attitudes to Drug Abuse	Mind Body Sanctity of life Medicine Legal drug Illegal drug Recreational drug Taxation Classification of drugs Rehabilitation	• Religious attitudes to the mind and body • What rights and responsibilities people have regarding drug use • Why (religious) people use drugs • The different types of drugs available – including their effect on the mind and body • The effects of legal drugs • Whether taxes should be used to fund medical research and treatment for drug users, including alcohol/tobacco-related illness • The problems associated with addiction • How (religious) people and society can help addicts and their families • The effectiveness of treatment and rehabilitation programmes • Whether (religious) people and society should help addicts and their families • The law on drugs • Whether the laws relating to drugs are appropriate • Whether religious believers should look after their mind and body

Topic	Words to learn	Subjects within topic – do you know …?
10 Religious Attitudes to Crime and Punishment	Law Order Conscience Duty Responsibility Crime Punishment Crime against person Crime against property Crime against state Crime against religion Protection Retribution Deterrence Reformation Vindication Reparation Young offender Imprisonment Parole Capital punishment Tagging Probation Fines Community service Prison reform	• Religious attitudes to law and order • The concept of right and wrong • Responsibilities (religious) people have to follow the laws in a society • How conscience affects our behaviour • Why (religious) people commit crimes • What different types of crime there are, including examples of each • Why we punish people – the different aims of punishment • How punishment is matched to crime • How young offenders should be treated • How prisoners should be treated • The issues associated with life imprisonment • The issues associated with parole and early release • Why (religious) people agree/disagree with the death penalty • The alternatives to imprisonment, and how effective they are
11 Religious Attitudes to Rich and Poor in British Society	Rich Poor Money Wealth Poverty Charity Inheritance Wages Homelessness Apathy Gambling Addiction Counselling Minimum wage Excessive salary Responsibility Community Lottery	• Why people are rich in the UK • Why people are poor in the UK • The different ways in which personal wealth can be created • Religious attitudes to money • Religious attitudes to being rich • Religious attitudes to earning money • Religious attitudes to responsibility for the poor • Religious attitudes to the personal use of wealth • How (religious) people help the poor in the UK • Why (religious) people help the poor • How the state tries to help the poor in the UK • Whose actual responsibility it is to help the poor in the UK • Whether it is right to gamble • Whether it is right to gamble on the lottery • How the lottery has created wealth in the UK

Topic	Words to learn	Subjects within topic – do you know …?
12 Religious Attitudes to World Poverty	Poverty LEDC Justice Stewardship Compassion Exploitation Debt Unfair trade Natural disaster War Global interdependence World trade Charity Emergency aid Short-term aid Long-term aid Sustainable development	• Religious attitudes to injustice • Religious attitudes to poverty • What is meant by justice, stewardship and compassion in the sense of world poverty • Why some countries are poor – the factors that have brought them/keep them at that level of poverty • Some examples of LEDCs • How global interdependence and world trade help/hinder attempts to help these countries • Why (religious) people help the poor in other countries • How (religious) people help the poor in other countries • The work of organisations in these countries • Why emergency aid is needed • The difference between emergency and long-term aid • Issues caused by these types of aid • Why sustainable development is needed, and its benefits

Morality Appendix II

Mock paper

(See page 82 for information about the exam papers.)

For practice

Choose any **four** questions from these six to answer.

Each question is worth **18 marks** in total.

If you wanted to practise one topic – testing your knowledge, you could give yourself a 22-minute time-test.

1   **Religious Attitudes to Matters of Life (Medical Ethics)**

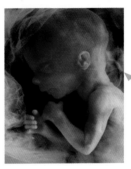

Image helps you with part 01.

(01)   What is meant by the term embryology?   *(1 mark)*

(02)   Explain why many religious believers would say that human genetic engineering is wrong.   *(3 marks)*

Stick to saying *why* it is wrong.   Give two reasons and explain one of them.

(03)   **Religious people should accept not being able to have children.** What do you think? Explain your opinion.   *(3 marks)*

You could give just one side in your response, but a two-sided answer is likely to be stronger.

(04)   Explain religious attitudes to blood transfusion. Refer to beliefs and teachings in your answer.   *(5 marks)*

You could talk about attitudes generally, or in one specific religion. Don't forget – blood transfusion is about helping people, so use your arguments about helping others.

(05)   **Organ donation should be compulsory for everyone.** Do you agree? Give reasons for your answer, showing you have thought about more than one point of view.   *(6 marks)*

Use the DREARER formula (see page 174)!

2   **Religious Attitudes to the Elderly and Death**

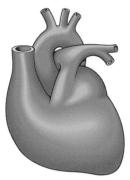

(06)   What is euthanasia?   *(1 mark)*

It is only 1 mark, so just write one sentence.

(07)   Describe religious beliefs about life after death.   *(3 marks)*

Just write about beliefs from one religion.

(08)   **Religious people should always look after the elderly.** What do you think?
Explain your answer.   *(3 marks)*

(09)   Explain religious attitudes to active euthanasia. Refer to beliefs and teachings
in your answer.   *(5 marks)*

If you answer from the perspective of two
religions, your answer will be stronger.

(10)   **Hospices are a waste of money.** Do you agree? Give reasons for your answer,
showing you have thought about more than one point of view. Refer to religious
arguments in your answer.   *(6 marks)*

This is deliberately provocative – make sure you keep a
focus and still answer from more than one point of view.
Remember DREARER (below)!

Learn the DREARER formula for good evaluative responses:

Disagree with the statement

Reasons why you disagree

Explanations of some of those reasons

Agree with the statement

Reasons why you agree

Explanations of some of those reasons

Religious argument must be in there

3   Religious Attitudes to Drug Abuse

DRUG ABUSE ON THE INCREASE

(11)   Name a Class A drug.   *(1 mark)*

Be sure to name the right kind of drug in your answer.

(12)   Give **three** reasons why some people do not take drugs.   *(3 marks)*

The key phrase is 'do not take' – get this wrong and you'll get no marks.

(13)   **Religious believers should not smoke tobacco.** What do you think?
Explain your opinion.   *(3 marks)*

Focus only on tobacco, no other drugs.
Remember that only Sikhism forbids tobacco.

(14)   Explain religious attitudes to drug abusers. Refer to beliefs and teachings
in your answer.   *(5 marks)*

This is about people who misuse
drugs – do not just write about drugs.

(15)   **Religious people should not take any kinds of drugs.** Do you agree? Give reasons
for your answer, showing you have thought about more than one point of view.
Refer to religious arguments in your answer.   *(6 marks)*

This question covers all drugs – legal, illegal, medical.
Make sure your answer does as well.

4   Religious Attitudes to Crime and Punishment

HARSH PUNISHMENTS PROVED TO REDUCE CRIME

(16) What is meant by deterrence?   *(1 mark)*

> Write a simple, one sentence definition.

(17) Explain briefly why prisons are used as a form of punishment.   *(3 marks)*

> This wants you to link prison as a punishment to the aims of punishment.

(18) **Religious people should support young offenders.** What do you think?
      Explain your opinion.   *(3 marks)*

(19) Explain religious attitudes to crime. Refer to beliefs and teachings in your answer.   *(5 marks)*

> This is a tough question, so expand your
> answer by writing about upholding what is right
> and fighting what is morally wrong.

(20) **Capital punishment is wrong.** Do you agree? Give reasons for your answer,
      showing you have thought about more than one point of view. Refer to religious
      arguments in your answer.   *(6 marks)*

> Give reasons to agree with it and to disagree with it.

5   Religious Attitudes to Rich and Poor in British Society

(21)   What is meant by the term homelessness?   *(1 mark)*

(22)   Why are some people homeless?   *(3 marks)*

Just give three reasons.

(23)   **Religious people should not gamble money.** What do you think?
         Explain your opinion.   *(3 marks)*

(24)   Explain, using beliefs and teachings, why religious people help the poor.   *(5 marks)*

This is asking you to explain *why* they help – religious motivation.

(25)   **People who earn excessive salaries should pay taxes to help the poor.** Do you agree?
         Give reasons for your answer, showing you have thought about more than one point
         of view.   *(6 marks)*

This means two sides – agree and disagree (with reasons
and explanations) and at least one religious argument.

6   Religious Attitudes to World Poverty

(26) What is meant by fair trade?   *(1 mark)*

(27) Explain how war makes some countries very poor. ←   *(3 marks)*

> Think about how money is diverted into weapons, how war affects
> people's lives so that they don't farm, buildings are damaged, etc.

(28) **All religious believers should volunteer to help the poor.** What do you think?
Explain your opinion.   → *(3 marks)*

> You can give one side or two sides on these 3-mark questions.

(29) Explain religious attitudes to the poor in LEDCs (Less Economically Developed
Countries).   *(5 marks)*

> If a technical abbreviation is used, it is usually
> written out in full in brackets to help you.

(30) **World poverty will always be an issue.** Do you agree? Give reasons for your answer,
showing you have thought about more than one point of view. ←   *(6 marks)*

> This is asking if it can be resolved – you could agree or disagree,
> but you could also consider whether it can be partially resolved.

Morality Glossary

Active euthanasia mercy killing (euthanasia) where the patient is killed before the illness kills them

AID/H Artificial Insemination by Donor/Husband (type of fertility treatment)

Akhirah ☾ belief in Judgement Day, heaven and hell

Blood transfusion medical procedure where blood is replaced within the body, either because of loss of blood through an accident, or in an operation

Capital punishment the death penalty; state execution where the prisoner is put to death for the crime(s) they have committed

Care home for the elderly home where elderly people go to live, and where they can be looked after

Classification of drugs the legal system which classifies illegal drugs into Class A, B or C

Cloning the scientific method by which animals or plants can be copied exactly to create a DNA-identical new being

Community service punishment whereby the offender has to work for between 40 and 300 hours serving the community

Compassion loving kindness; helping others with no desire for reward

Conscience sense of right and wrong, often thought of as good/bad voices in the head which guide your behaviour

Crime action which breaks the law

Death end of life; when there is no longer any brain stem activity, and organs cease to function on their own

Designer babies babies whose DNA has been modified to ensure they have specific characteristics

Deterrence punishment to make the offender or others not repeat the crime

Drug abuse misuse of drugs, often so that it has serious, negative side effects

Duty the role someone has; what they have to do

Electronic tagging punishment; anklet which tracks the movement of offender, so that they can be monitored

Embryology study of and research using embryos

Emergency aid aid which is given in emergency situations, for example, after a natural disaster

Euthanasia mercy killing; helping someone to die to ease suffering, out of compassion and with their agreement

Excessive salaries term given to salaries which most people think are too big for the job done

Experimentation scientific way of checking and proving hypotheses (in this book it is related to medical experiments on humans)

Exploitation misuse of power/money to get others to do things for little/unfair reward

Fair trade trade in which the producer gets a fair return for their work/produce

Fertility treatment medical treatment to aid fertility

Fines where the offender has to pay money as their punishment

Gambling placing of money on an uncertain outcome to win more money back

Global interdependence the idea that countries depend on other countries around the world and are themselves depended on

Homelessness the status of having nowhere to live

Hospice a place for the dying, where they can have dignity while they die

Hospital a place where people are treated for illness and accident

Human genetic engineering modification of genetic make-up (DNA) to change the features of a human

Illegal drugs drugs that are not legal, for example, heroin, cocaine

Imprisonment punishment in which an offender is locked up in jail for a period of time

Inheritance money gained from family death

IVF in vitro fertilisation; fertility treatment resulting in 'test tube babies'

Justice fairness; what is right; making up for wrongs done

Law and order justice system which helps support good behaviour in society by punishing bad behaviour

LEDC Less Economically Developed Country

Life after death idea that when we die, there is a next life, either through reincarnation, rebirth or Judgement Day (heaven/hell)

Life-support machine machine that keeps people alive when their own organs are unable to do so

Long-term aid aid that is long lasting, and designed to continue without total external support, for example, building of a medical centre

Lotto national lottery game in the UK; a form of gambling

Medical research research that is designed to lead to medical advances, and so improve medical treatment

Minimum wage the legal minimum an employer can pay to an employee

Parole punishment; where a prisoner is released from prison, and is still monitored through the parole service for a set period

Passive euthanasia mercy killing; euthanasia whereby medicines/treatment are removed so that the person will die more quickly from their illness

Poverty condition of being without money, food, shelter and other basic needs of life

Prison reform changes made to prisons to improve their potential to look after and rehabilitate offenders

Probation punishment whereby an offender is monitored for a set period of time

Protection aim of punishment, which makes sure others are safe from the offender

Punishment what is done to a person because they have committed a crime

Quality of life measure of fulfilment; how good life is

Recreational drugs drugs that are taken in social settings, e.g. alcohol

Reformation aim of punishment, which is to make someone a better person, understanding what they did was wrong and why it was

Rehabilitation procedure to support drug addicts/prisoners back into society as normal members of society, and not going back to previous behaviours

Reparation aim of punishment whereby the offender is making up for what they have done; paying back

Responsibility the thing(s) that we have to look after

Retirement ending working life

Retribution aim of punishment; to get revenge

Sanctity of life idea that life is special or sacred

Saviour sibling baby born, perhaps with modified DNA, to become a donor for a sibling and so save/improve their life

Senior citizen person over a certain age (65)

Stem cell therapy medical treatment that uses stem cells from embryos to treat conditions such as Parkinson's disease

Stewardship idea that humans have a duty to look after the world

Surrogacy where one woman becomes pregnant and carries the pregnancy to full term in order to hand the baby over when born to another woman for its upbringing

Sustainable development development that will be sustainable, i.e. keep going, and not be limited by time/money/environmental issues

Taxation a portion of the cost of items which goes to the government; also taxation on wages

Therapeutic cloning use of DNA and cells to create a replica organ for use in medical research, medical treatment and transplant surgery

Transplant surgery medical treatment to replace faulty/damaged/useless organs and hence improve life for someone

Vindication aim of punishment whereby the breaking of the law must be shown to be respected by applying a punishment to the offender

Wealth having sufficient money/possessions for a good life

World trade trade between countries in the world

Young offender person under the age of eighteen who has committed a crime

Index